The Gospel of
Numbers and Letters in Scripture
Door Steps to the Kingdom

The Gospel of
Numbers & Letters in Scripture
Door Steps to the Kingdom

By Darren R. Kelley

Books By the same author

Will the Real God Please Stand Up!
Historical Theology in Conflict

Full Half Vision
The Hidden Meaning of Birthdates

Dedication

This book is dedicated to my Dear Mother Carolyne L. Kelley who passed on 5/1/2006.

This book is also dedicated to my son Darren Kelley II and my daughters Ivey Kelley Michay Burnes.

I also would like to dedicate this work to my dearest friend, Valerie Malone for all of her support and inspiration while working in this project. Thank you for the sincere interest and wonderful ideas I needed to finish this work. Most of all, thank you for believing in this God given gift when so many turned their faces. Thank you my dearest friend.

Acknowledgments

Pastor Phyllis Burgess
I would like to thank Pastor Phyllis Burgess for all of her insight on spiritual warfare. Second, I would like to thank Pastor Burgess for her constant guidance and counseling during this project and my walk in ministry.

Pastor Etta Banks
I would thank Pastor Banks for showing me how to enter the presence of God. Thank you for being a constant spiritual anchor in my life. Also, thank you for being my personal Pastor who was available.

My Mom
Carol Kelley, thank you for all the Reality checks, insight and loving advice you have provided during this project and throughout my life. Your wisdom has helped me avoid plenty of pitfalls and traps.

My Pops
I would like to thank my Father, Lenzy Kelley for being the intelligent man that he is and for being the best Father a son could have.

My Niece
I want to thank my Niece Amber Kelley (Amfooboo) for helping me keep track of the pages during the progression of this book. I really did not know the number of written pages until you kept count of the pages (smile).

Rev Jeanne Hill
You are God's Biblical paralegal. Thank you for getting me through the number Ten.

Darren and Ivey Kelley
Besides my Mother, you two have always been my motivation and inspiration for everything

My Family
I would like to acknowledge my sister Stacie Kelley and my hero and Big Brother Lenzy Kelley, my Aunt Bootz, Aunt Peaches, Aunti Fritzel. Lastly, I want thank my Grand Ma for being an excellent Grand Mother. And our Grand Father Author Graham, thank you for the all of the family stories. Your presence is very important in my life.

Table of Contents   Page

Chapter 1…
An Introduction to Numbers and Letters   1

Chapter 2…
The use of names in the Bible   7

Chapter 3…
The Prophetic Call of a Name   14

Chapter 4…
The Hebrew Alephbet   18

Chapter 5…
Numbers 1 to 31 in the Bible   102

Chapter 6…
Categories of Prayers & Seasons   245

Chapter 7…
The History of Languages   250

Chapter 8…
Bible Name Definitions   260

Reference
The Hebrew Alepbet   325
The Greek Number System   326
The Hebrew Number System   327
The Hebrew Months   328

COPY RIGHT © 2007 Darren R. Kelley. All Rights Reserved.

No part of this book may be reproduced, stored in a retrieval system, or transmitted by any means without the written permission of the author.

First published by HoneyGraham Publishing

ISBN:
978-0-6151-7892-9

Cover Designed by Darren R. Kelley

Printed in the United States of America

PREFACE

The Prophetic Call.

Mathematics is the basis of life. Numbers and letters represent mathematics. We cannot live without mathematics. The more we understand, the more we know about our lives, our earth, the universe and finally, God. Letters represent the various flavors of each number. Numbers are infinite and dynamic. For example, the number 1 exists in the form of 10 (1+0=1) 19(1+9=10=1+0=0) and 28 (2+8 = 10, 1 = 0 = 1). Each number represents a character. For instance, the number seven in Hebrew represents the letters "o and "z". In Greek, the number seven represents the letters "g, p and y". Therefore, the life of each number merges with the character of each letter to produce a unique definition. The letter "g" comes from the Hebrew "Gimeel" which is symbolized by the camel. The letter "p" comes from the Hebrew "Pe" which means to confer power and uses the mouth as its symbol.

      The purpose of this book is to introduce the concept of the "Prophetic call" which is to simply understand the meaning of your name and the numbers of your name. Also, to understand any number associated with who you are. Numbers were used by the Magi to locate Jesus. How the Magi located Jesus is another topic but whatever they used as a tool depended on mathematics. If math was used to find Jesus, can we use math to find you? In order to understand the name, one must know the numbers or mathematics associated with the letters used to form names in question. We have entered a time where knowing the definition will not suffice but know we must know the nature and character of the letters which are used to define the name. Some names are positive and some names are negative. The idea is to understand your name and change it if necessary in order to walk into your Prophetic call. The Prophetic Call represents your name and your numbers. Though we are in Christ, we are under the influence of our names because each number, letter and word possesses power. This power calls us into action. Often, the lack of knowledge can lead to destructive and stagnating behavior. This book will help you understand the prophetic power of every letter and number in your life. May this work be a blessing to you? Understanding your Prophetic Call will help you in your walk as a Disciple of Christ.

Chapter 1
Introduction

The Bible teaches that God is a spirit (John 4:24) and we must worship him in spirit and truth. There is one certain truth concerning God, he reveals himself in the scriptures through patterns and cycles. Specifically, God uses numbers and letters to express his intentions and to sign his mighty creations. For example, the number seven means to be *full, satisfied* and *it's enough*. Through the number seven, revealed that his creation was full and it's enough. God was satisfied with his work. Each time the number seven is encountered the scriptures, something "is enough". What can we learn from numbers and letters? Each number and letter is a precept of the Kingdom of Heaven. Each number and letter in the scriptures is a door step to the mysteries of Heaven and the knowledge of God the Father. Most of all, numbers and letters serve as metrics for those serious about the pursuit of sanctification and righteousness. What does this mean? Numbers not only teach us how to qualify and quantify areas in the educational, scientific and world of commerce. Numbers and letters can be used to help us qualify and quantify our behavior. As children we often received report cards in the form of a number or a letter (A, B, C 100, and 50) to describe our academic performance as students. Likewise, the Bible presents its own performance standard by way of numbers and letters. How is this possible? All one has to do is look at what is taking place when a number or letter is used.

Numbers and letters are also signs. What is a sign? A sign always points to something greater than itself. A red light is a sign warning you about the moving traffic beyond the red light. This is why we should not worship the sun, moon and star because they only serve as signs. Astrology can be dangerous because many people become dependant on the fruit produced from this area of study. Also many have lost faith in the true and living God as a result of eating this forbidden fruit. Almighty God is a Spirit; therefore, the Father uses sign, symbols, patterns and cycles that we can follow. As humans, we do not have direct access to time and space; this is why we use arithmetic in the form of numbers and letters to guide our daily affairs. What a wonderful idea!

The Bible teaches that "no man knoweth the time or day". We should be mindful of prediction about our personal lives and events. There are so many people interested in end-day prophecy, why? My view is simple "good children at home in the absence of their parents have no reason to worry about when they return". As Disciples of Christ, we should yearn for the desire to live a sanctified life. The desire for righteousness is something we should want for ourselves as well as pleasing Almighty God the Father.

The Bible provides a simple way for us to understand who we are by way of numbers and letters. There is a practical use of numbers and letters in the Bible which has nothing to do with the world of the occult or New Age doctrine. The first use of numbers in the scripture is to aide us in keeping rhythm with the hand and spirit of Almighty God. As you will soon find out, each number and letter has its own personality and reveals the character and movement of Almighty God. These numbers are not just about us, the numbers are about Almighty God. The second use of numbers and letters is to improve the efficiency of our prayer life by understanding the power of the very words we speak. For example, the letter "P" is the first letter of the word "Prayer" but what is the definition of the letter "P"?. Moreover, what happens when this letter is vocally invoked with the proper intentions? In this book, you will learn how to apply prayers and numbers to add power and effectiveness to your prayer routine.

In the book of Ecclesiastes, Solomon states there is a time for all things (**Ecclesiastes 3**). According to the scriptures, there is a time to eat, sleep, pray and kill. Jesus also taught us to watch as well as pray. In other words, Jesus taught that while we are praying on one issue, we should keep an eye another. Numbers teach the critical art of timing. However, timing is useless; if one does hear the voice of the Father, obey the voice of the Father and finish "thus saith the Lord". Such is the case with Moses when he completed the tabernacle in Exodus 40:33. Timing is critical because of the many decisions we must make in life. In addition, we must be mindful of God's timing. We must ensure our actions are lined up for His will for our lives. Remember, God had his hand on Jeremiah before he became a prophet for the nations (Jeremiah 1:1-3).

I am convinced that my mission in life is to write this book. The Almighty One through the power of the Holy Spirit guided my thoughts and hands for this assignment. Full Half Vision was the first version of this book. Full Half Vision covered the numbers 1 through 31; however, the personalities of people were the basis of the book. The ability to use the scriptures for numbers 1 through 31 was a blessing. I had to go based on experience and 16 years of secular study. There was no doubt that I was able to help people by knowing their name and birth date but I felt something was missing. The last six years of my studies became biblical in nature. In other words, I removed the secular books purchased from the bookstores. I strictly studied numbers based on the scriptures. At first, I did not see a conflict in the definitions. Later, I noticed the biblical definitions had more depth than 99% of the books I read and purchased from bookstores in the occult section. I stopped reading those books in the bookstores because they lacked depth. The biblical definitions had more depth and the scriptures forced me to study the Bible to understand each number. I thought after completing Full Half Vision, I would sell FHV to any and everybody. I shared my work with many Pastors and Ministers. They wanted this book to have a strong Biblical presence. I was ready to sell Full Half Vision (FHV). Many of my friends and family patiently waited to buy this book. This book contained many references from the Bible.

Most people, who know me, did not know I was struggling in my spirit to release FHV. The closer it came time to move into production, I became scared and nervous. There was nothing stopping me, so I thought. FHV not only covered numbers 1 through 31 personally but it included the meaning of the entire Hebrew Alphabet as listed in Psalm 119. One day, all of what I thought changed while walking to work. I heard a voice of the Father speak to me, it was about 6:45am. The Lord said the following "take the chapter on the numbers and remove every comment that refers to describing people. Only discuss the meaning of numbers based on the scriptures". I began to think, "humm", that is an interesting thought. I listened to the voice of the Lord. It was a journey and it was a blessing as well. Despite having 17 years of experience, I realized that I did not know these numbers as well as I thought because of the instructions to remove "people" out of the equation. I knew each number from 1 to 31 personally but I did not know the numbers 1 to 31 biblically. Oddly, I found out there were a few people that knew them as well. Even the great E.W. Bullinger (1865) skipped the number 18. The Bible does not much information on this number. Sadly, it was through death that learned about this number. Though seldom used, there is a purpose for this awesome number. I realized that it was my 17 years of secular experience that needed reshaping. The power of the Holy Spirit allowed me the insight to bring the public understanding of numbers and letters back to the scriptures where they belong. I have gained a unique view about the personal and Biblical use of numbers. I noticed many of the secular books on numerology found in bookstores take God the Father out of the equation and empower the individual. The Holy Ghost wanted me to help people learn about numbers and letters as applied to understanding inheriting the Kingdom of Heaven within ourselves. I was taught by the Holy Ghost that we should study the pursuit of the Father's presence and there we will find everything we need to know about ourselves. In other words, God the Father will filter what we need to know at the right time. Numerology attempts to replace God and that is not ideal for anyone serious about Discipleship in Christ Jesus.

  The use of numbers in the Bible keep God in the equation and empower the individual through faith, fasting, prayer, sacrifice and offerings. Many secular books on numerology may mention God or even a few scriptures but individual encouragement to "lean to your own understanding" is present. The issue of empowering the individual is not a matter of accuracy but the issue comes down to faith. Sure, the secular information can be accurate but it can be misleading. Just like the great prophet Jeremiah who was called by the Lord before his birth (Jeremiah 1:1-3). Imagine if Jeremiah took his future into his own hands and leaned to his own understanding. Would God steer him back on path or replace him? Also, would Jeremiah pay a price for deviating from God's will? Who knows, but this is what can happen to us if we buy into the so called accurate knowledge of numerology and astrology. Let me go a little further, numerology can be predictive if you go high into the various techniques used by skilled craftspeople. We can fall into a trap where we are stealing information or knowing about ourselves before we need to know.

This is the same as a child who finds his or her Christmas gifts in a closet and knows what to expect on Christmas day. Whether the child realizes what has occurred, the child robbed him or herself of a pleasurable experience. Besides, such an act can also steal from the pleasure the parents receive when watching their child open their gifts for the first time. The entire Christmas experience is an exercise in faith and this includes the child and the parents. The parents hide the gifts hoping the child will be patient and waiting for Christmas day. Thus, the child has faith the parents will bring home the desired gifts. Christmas is all about faith in our selves, our family and in Christ. So it is with the numbers. We must be careful not to steal information and exercise faith in knowing our God will guide and direct our paths. Numerology can be fun except when it used as a way for prediction and a replacement for faith in Christ Jesus. I need to be very clear on this next point. There is a difference between personal prediction and Biblical prophecy. The Bible is rich in prophetic code. I recall talking to a friend after thinking how I was going search for Biblical code and clues. I became so overwhelmed because there is so much code embedded in the scriptures. The idea of what I had to do to uncover this information was just mind-boggling.

The use and study of numbers is interesting and exciting but I caution you to be wise about whatever you are able to discover. I have a problem with using numerology to find out what is going to happen next week. I do not have a problem learning to define my name and my birth date. The birth date is important. If the birthday is important then why is it celebrated? Please do not tell me you celebrate your birthday just because the same month and day has reoccurred? Many say, I am happy to be alive? Oh really, how subjective. Why are you happy to be alive? We should be happy to be living everyday we wake up from sleep. In theory, nobody has a birthday. A true birthday includes the day, month and year. The month may repeat and the day may repeat but the year will never repeat.

In reality, the actual date does not repeat at all. The birth date is critical because it tells me about the environment I entered: wind speed, wind direction, dew point, tempature, barometer, longitude, and latitude. This information may not appear important but the conditions in which one is born should always be taken in account. Weather conditions determine the success and growth of crops. In the Bible, the Magi knew all the conditions surrounding the birth of Jesus. We are all strategically born into this world. Suppose Herod, Jesus, Mary and Joesph were in an ice-covered Europe? Mary and Joseph would have had a hard time getting away from Herod. Jesus was born in the right time, season, conditions and place. Everyone should want to know everything we can about ourselves. Our lives are built on mathematics. The time has come to apply mathematics to self. How can we use math to improve the quality and quanitity of our lives? The birth name and birth date are the keys to applying mathematics to self.

The birth date sets the counter for every day of life. Each age represents a degree. There are 360 degrees in a circle. Your current age represents the degree in which you are currently positioned. I am in the 43rd degree of my life because I am 43 years of age. This means I will be challengned to finish specific tasks and elevate my spiritual walk. The number 43 will prophetically call me to master the art of setting limits.

I do not have a problem with learning the meaning of the individual letters and numbers which make up my name. Understanding the meaning of numbers and letters is the purpose of this book. I did not use any tricks or treats (secular formulas) because the scope of this work is purely academic and Biblical. The Holy Ghost will show you everything necessary concerning your next step in this field of study. God is real and we can learn to follow the hand of the Lord through the numbers. The definitions of the letters and numbers will help you have a better understanding of yourself and the scriptures. As Disciples of Christ, we are challenged to manifest the constructive side of every number and letter. Secular numerology impresses the individual to study his or her own numbers and letters which only takes the Kingdom of Heaven out of the equation. Every number and letter should be used as a tool for Kingdom living.

Chapter 2
The Usage Of Names In The Bible

In this American culture, when one chooses a name for a child, the meaning of that name typically has no significance to the parent. During the days of the Bible, the meaning of a name was very important and played a key role in the development of one's character. The Bible informs the reader about the definition of many names mentioned in the scriptures. Individuals such as Adam, Cain, Seth, Noah, Abraham, Isaac, Jacob (and his 12 sons), Perez, Peleg and Jesus all have the meaning of their names given in the Bible. Each of their names reveals the individual story of why or how they were born.

DESCRIBING CHARACTER
1 Samuel 25:25 we find a perfect example on how a name describes the character of a person:
Let not my Lord, I pray thee, regard this man Belial, even Nabal: for as his name is, so is he; Nabal is his name, and folly is with him".

BIBLICAL NAME CHANGE
Jesus performs a name change in John 1:42 by changing Simons to name to Cephas.
And he brought him to Jesus. And when Jesus beheld him, he said, Thou art Simon, the son of Jona: thou shall be called Cephas, which is by interpretation, 'A stone'.
Jesus knew that for Simon to do his work, he could not have the name Simon for his name did not have the strength and fortitude needed to be a disciple. However, the name Cephas gave Simon the qualities he needed to be a disciple, and what qualities did he need? He needed the hard and tough qualities of a Stone. So, we as followers of Christ have a clue regarding the qualities we need to be disciples for the Body of Christ.

THE COMING OF JESUS
In Matthew 1: 21, we read about the coming of Jesus. The name "Jesus" defines his mission.
And she shall bring forth a son, and thou shall call his name Jesus: for he shall save his people from their sins.

BAD NAMES
Many people are unaware they have a negative name.
In 1 Samuel 21 we read:
And she named the child Ichabod, saying, the glory has departed from Israel: because the ark of God was taken, and because of her father-in-law and her husband.
In the movie "Headless Horsemen", Johnny Depp played Ichabod Crane the main character who fought against the headless horseman.

NAMES IN THE BOOK OF REVELATION
Revelation's is one of my favorite books in the Bible because it is full of code and hidden messages. There are several themes that are consistent throughout Revelation, which includes the Devil and the Four Beast. Let us turn to Revelation 15:2. The subtitle for this book is "Preparation of the seven vials. Seven means "enough" and the letter "V" is the plural of the letter "F": Loaf/Loaves, Leaf/Leaves, Life/Lives. Therefore, we can also read this subtitle as the "seven files". The word "preparation" implies a quantity which is seven, seven vials or seven files (computers) which is enough (seven). This is an example of prophetic material in the book of Revelation. We read in chapter 15 which means the devil or personal passions. The number 15 reduces to a number 6 (1+5=6) the number of incompletion.

In Revelation 15:2 we read the following:

And I saw as it were a sea of glass mingled with fire: and them that had gotten the victory over the beast, and over his image, and over his mark, and over the number of his name, stand on the sea of glass, having the harps of God.

There are several key points in this passage of scripture:
Victory over the beast came in three ways.
1: Victory over the image of the beast: (Behavior)
2: Victory over the mark of the beast: (Bondage)
3: Victory over the number of his name: (Influence)

Victory over the **Image** refers to how the beast was able to control the behavior of the masses: TV, Cable, Internet, and Media. Most of us act based on what we see with our eyes. How does one control behavior? Behavior can be controlled through Bondage which is the **Mark.** For example, the slave master branded a seal on a slave to proof of ownership for the slave. The current tax laws can qualify as an institution of bondage. The current social security program can also qualify as a form of bondage. Tracking and watching people will be possible because of names and numbers. Identification is the primary purpose for creating and using a name. The name will also inform the government where we live and how we live. Names can lead to freedom or bondage. Every name is associated with a number. The discount cards used at many super markets can be stored in a database which can be queried to track the habits of any of person or groups of people.

REVELATION 2:17
The Message to the Church at Pergamos

He that have an ear, let him hear what the Spirit saith unto the churches: ***To him that overcometh will I give to eat of the hidden manna, and will give him a white stone, and in the stone a new name written, which no man knoweth saving he that receiveth it.*** Hallelujah, Amen.

We read what happened in Rev 15: 2 when the beast was overcome (image, mark, name number). Though written for the church of Pergamos, the benefits apply to today's church. Jesus said, "I have overcome the world". He did it, he did it first, and he did it as a man. This means we can do it too. He did his part and now we must do our part. This is nothing but a spiritual version of "follow the leader" or "Simon says". This is not a game. Look at what we get when we overcome. ***To him that overcometh will I give to eat of the hidden manna, and will give him a white stone, and in the stone a new name written, which no man knoweth saving he that receiveth it.***

Here is my favorite part: ***and in the stone a new name written, which no man knoweth saving he that receiveth it.*** Now that's what I'm talking about. A new name, whoever gets this name, must surely have earned it. I want a new name. A name nobody can calculate or figure out. This new name will reflect my newness in the spirit. When we understand who we are, then we are halfway ready to battle self- and the world. Who are you and what does your name mean? What does each letter in your name mean? Walking around rebuking the Devil and quoting scriptures will not be enough.

REVELATIONS 13:16-18

16 And he causeth all, both small and great, rich and poor, free and bond, to receive a mark, or in their right hand, or in their foreheads.
17 And that no man might buy or sell, save he that had the mark, or the name of the beast, or the number of his name.
18 Here is wisdom. Let him that hath understanding count the number of the beast: for it is the number of a man: and his number is six hundred threescore and six.

In verse 16 we read that all people big and small, rich and poor will have the mark of the beast. Also, we read that nobody will be able to make a transaction without the mark. Verse 16-18 can be as simple as using Ivory soap or any Proctor & Gamble household product.

If you recall in the middle 1980's, a Proctor & Gamble official admitted on the Oprah Winfrey Show that their company (Proctor & Gamble) financially supported the Church of Satan. They even left a phone number for people to call and ask questions. I remember the show as it aired while I was in College. I even called the number. They may have changed the logo. Proctor and Gamble had a picture of a half-moon with 13 stars. Is it possible that if you used their soap, dishwashing liquid that we may already have the mar of the beast?

About the mark of the beast and being able to buy and sell products, the internet, credit cards, and computers all come to mind. All of this is leading to a cashless society. This has already begun with technologies such as EDI (Electronic Data Interchange), Ecommerce, Imaging, XML, and BPML. The idea is to create a cashless society then justify the use of small wafer sized implants that will serve as a credit cards and national ID's. All of this will occur in the name of Homeland Security and Terrorism. EDI has been around since the sixties. Many businesses are no longer using paper for purchase orders, invoices, and forecasts. Mail slows down the business process between the customer and vendor. EDI improves the business process between the customer and vendor because the transactions occur electronically. Each industry has its own set of transactions. The transactions start from 100 to 998. EDI conforms to several standards: ANSI X-12 and EDIFACT just to name a few.

The computer is the main culprit concerning the creation of a cashless society. Life as we know it cannot exist without computers. Concerning the beast and computers, one must think of IBM. Even though IBM is not the PC giant it was in the 80's, they were the guys to beat. What I find interesting about IBM is that if you write down every letter preceding each letter in the name IBM one will get HAL. (HI AB LM). HAL was the name of the supercomputer in the movie 2000 Space Odyssey. This computer was so advanced that it became its own life force.

The astronauts tried to pull its plug to shut it down but the computer would not allow that to happen. It is an old but good movie. The Church of Satan was charted in 1966 in the State of California. Guess who was the Governor? The Governor was none other than Ronald Reagan. The founder of the Church of Satan was Anton Sanzador Lavey.

MORE ON ANTON LAVEY

Anton Lavey was an interesting man; I suggest that every Christian read about this man. He wrote a Book called the "Satanic Bible". You can read about him on the internet. I believe his daughter may have replaced him, but I could be wrong. He received a call by a famous novelist named Roman Polanski who was creating a film called "Rosemary's Baby". You should remember this movie and Roman Polanski. He dated Sharon Tate who lost her life during the Charles Mason murders. She also had a small role in Rosemary's Baby.

Though not listed on the credits, Lavey helped Polanski with directing the movie (all the satanic scary stuff). There was real stuff in that movie. For instance, in the movie, Rosemary (Mia Farrow) was watching the Pope on his way to Yankee Stadium but he stopped on 72nd street at the Dakota Inn. The movie was showing the Pope on real T.V. The Dakota Inn was used to film many of the Vincent Price horror movies. John Lennon lived there as well. What I find shocking is what is behind the Dakotas, the largest Parapsychology Institute in this country and probably the world.

What is Parapsychology? Watch Ghost Busters, Freddy Kruger and any Jason film, then you have it in a nutshell. Parapsychology deals with human psychic abilities, ESP, clairvoyance, dream control, and soul travel. So why would the Pope stop on this street?

As you see, the Book of Revelation reveals more than you think. It is a book of today. We read in Rev 13:18: ***Here is wisdom. Let him that hath understanding count the number of the beast: for it is the number of a man: and his number is six hundred threescore and six.*** We should know about Ronald Reagan's numbers and the 666 "thing", that is old news. We now know about Anton Lavey, IBM, HAL, and Proctor & Gamble and the Church of Satan. All of this is in our current Bible and the numbers give it all away. To be fair to the former President, he did not get a fair shake on the "666" incident. But he was still Governor of California when he chartered the first church of Satan. There are plenty of people whose names could have the same numbers. In fact, Ronald = (4), Wilson=(7), Reagan=(8)=19/1. I used the Hebrew System for the calculations. His name number does not total 666 in any system. Now, if each name had a numerical value of 6, and he was born in the sixth month, day, and year, then I would have another position. Anyway, a "six" year only occurs once every nine years. So tracking the antichrist is not as easy as many may think, but this makes for good bible study. However, there are people that work on these formulas and track people as they come and go in the media. On last point about California. Everybody talks about California and earth-quakes. Many say California will slide into the Pacific Ocean because of the San Andreas Fault. Oops there goes those letters F & V, Vault & Fault. Does anybody out there hear me! *Calif* relates to the word *Kalif* which means *pit or vault* (ouch)! The root word *fornia* comes from the word *fornication*. Am I making sense yet? Based on the numbers, I would say all of that California Earthquake stuff is credible.

Chapter 3
The Prophetic Power Of A Name

Numbers reflect vibrations and letters are variations of those vibrations. We see this in the notes of the musical scale. Everything in the universe moves and is constantly vibrating, which life is measurable. Each number and vibration contains its own distinctive law. We do not see the law, but we know it exist. We do not see the law of cause and effect, but we know it exist. Science has proven that every physical manifestation has its own wavelength; a measurable frequency of electromagnetic energy. The energy and frequency of each number represents a letter which is form of energy. I will prove this point shortly.

According to the 1st law of Thermodynamics, energy cannot be created nor destroyed. When you pro-create a name, the owner takes on the energy of that name. Each number has its own qualities and its own opposites. If not careful, one can select an opposing or negative name. Revelation 15:2 says "count the number of the beast for it is the number of a man", an opposer of God's will. For example, the letter "A" represents the number one which is active and outgoing. The opposite of one is inactivity and laziness. Some names are just negative and contain other words that reveal the inner nature of the name such as Hitler. When we dig further, we see other words such as hit, lie, let, and tie. These words surely describe his actions as a leader. The letter H represents captivity for a chain of (H's) resembles a fence or gate used for containment (HHHHHHHHHHH).

One must be careful when selecting a name for a child. They may take on the qualities of that name whether it is good or bad. I talked with a man from India. He told me that in his part of India, they consider the positions of the planets (the 3 magi) and the birth dates of the parents (House of their fathers in Exodus), then the child is named. In America, we often have the child's name before the birth date and on what basis? Jesus was named on the eigth day after his birth according to Luke 2:21. The day of circumcision was performed on the eight day.

Typically, many choose names based on how it sounds or feels and what the other parents may or may not like. Surely this is not the sign of an evolved and educated society. In many cultures, naming the child could take months. Why? The name is believed to determine one's character and destiny.

In American culture, we name our children after inanimate objects, animals and nature: Sandy, Wendy, Cliff, Annette (a net), Crystal, Ruby, Robin, Phillip (fill up), Rochelle (roach shell). Concerning last names: Wolfe, Lyon, Byrd, Street, Hill, Brown, Ledge, Rock, Stump, Beetle, Black, Green, White, Berry, Hall, Waters, Little, Grant and the list goes on. Does this mean everyone will take on these qualities if they have one of these names? Well, not exactly. It depends on other reasons such as the birth date and the placement, sequence of one's numbers and letters in the birth name and birth date.

Regarding the name Lyon, you hear the hidden word lie. Those bearing this name will be subject to lying. Does that mean that all people with that last name will lie? No, but they need to be mindful of the positions they place themselves in and watch their character because the prophetic power of the name will dictate character.

Let us look at another name: Robin. This name bears the mark of a thief or one who takes. The sub word or hidden word is not invisible, it sticks out, and you have to look hard to see it. The sub word is <u>rob</u> which is to steal or take. Do you remember Robin hood, what did he do? He stole from the rich and gave to the poor. The word door, <u>nob</u> and <u>bin</u> are sub words of the name Robin Hood

Does this mean that all "Robin's steal? No, but they need to be mindful of taking from other people. It could be anything, but it will surely be something that will not belong to them, and this includes anything from stealing to adultery.

The name Robin also leaves the owner open to being self-centered, self-absorbing, and consuming. For these are the innate qualities of a thief. Remember, this name has the mark of a justified thief; therefore, at that moment of stealing they may feel justified in what they are doing or what they have done.

You may look in a name book and the book may say the name means this or that or sugar or spice. But, those type books are not in sync with the numerical values or the hidden qualities of the name in question. Let us go further. Look at the word Negro, this is a bad thing, a bad word, and we should not use it for any reason. Notice the words Negro and Necro: G and C being the focal point. The letter C did not exist in Hebrew, but it came from the Hebrew G (Gimel), which means camel. The Greeks changed Gimel to Gamma and used it as a consonant. The Romans then borrowed Gamma and used it as K and G. Later the Romans created C, the 3rd letter of the English alphabet, which still means camel. In my view, some group of wise people knew they could stifle the so-called black race just off the name 'Negro', which is related to 'Necro', which means dead or void. The behavior of Black folk in America speaks for itself.

WHAT IS IN A NAME

The following is an excerpt from MSN Learning & Research on 7/3/2003...Article by Martha Brokenbrough.

If you've ever picked up a book about names, you probably flipped to the page containing yours to find out what it meant. I did this many years ago and learned that I was "a lady." The next thing I did was to look up the meaning of my middle name, Elizabeth. "Consecrated to God," the book said. After looking up the word consecrated, I came to realize that if I really lived up to my name, I would be a nun. (Every child's dream!) And that's not even considering my odd ball last name, which few people can pronounce correctly, and fewer people—plus a town in England—share. But here I am, all grown up. I did not become a nun, although I did dress as one once for Halloween.

So what's the point of names meaning anything, if you don't actually become what they mean? What's the point of having a name in the first place? For that matter, why *do we have three names—and sometimes more? The last two questions are pretty easy.*

Your name sets you apart from other people. This is why we have last names, for example. According to Leonard Ashley, author of What's in a Name?, *the tradition of last names started with the Romans, who used family names to create more specific identities. (Jewish people have had their version of family names since ancient times, too. David Ben Isaac means "David the son of Isaac.")*

The practice caught on in England during the Middle Ages, when people needed to set themselves apart from all the other Johns and Marys running around. People carried this further during the 16th century in England; Ashley says, by taking middle names—a custom that caught on in the United States, as well. What names mean is a harder question. Let's pick on my name some more.

The original meaning of the name Martha was "lady." But nowadays people think Martha is an overweight, old-fashioned blond. She also is strong, solid, loud, and, fortunately for me, likeable. I learned this from The Baby Name Survey Book, by Bruce Lansky and Barry Sinrod. These authors surveyed 100,000 people for their opinions about all sorts of first names. Except for the overweight and blond parts (both of which can be fixed), I am everything people think Martha should be. I'm even likeable ... *or so my dog would have me believe. Did I become these things because my name is Martha? And would my life have been different if I had been given a different name? I suppose I'll never know, unless I become one of the people who gets a new identity through the United States Marshals Service's Witness Security Program. But since I am not planning to get involved with the mob, my only other alternative is to change my name. Let's say I'd rather people thought of me as "a rich, successful business woman, most likely a player on Wall Street-drop-dead gorgeous and a city girl to the core." In that case, I would change my name to Madison, because that's what Lansky and Sinrod say people think about women with that name.*

It's pretty clear that names have power—and lots of it. But did you know a name actually can hurt you? Maybe not like sticks and stones do, but still, names can bruise in other ways.

Studies done in the early 1900s showed that unusual names could produce maladjusted children and adults. A 1948 study, meanwhile, indicated that your name could make you more likely to get into—or flunk out of—Harvard University. Also, a 1974 study showed that rare names (a.k.a. unusual ones) were accompanied by guilt pangs, meekness, and low self-esteem. It all depends on your definition of unusual, and that certainly has changed since the 1970s.

Another scholar found in 1983 that an off beat name could prevent you from graduating with honors from school—if you were a woman. Men didn't seem to have that problem, for some reason. Another very interesting study had a group of elementary school teachers grade papers by students who were only identified by their first names. The students who got high marks were named Karen, Lisa, David, and Michael—all common and popular names. But Elmer, Adele, Bertha, and Hubert fared poorly.

So what if your name is Elmer? Does that mean you're stuck hunting wabbits? Of course not. You can always go by your middle name. Or, you can dazzle people by citing Plato's 2,500-year-old dialogue Cratylus. (By the way, did you know that Plato's real name wasn't Plato? It was Aristocles. But he was called Plato, which means "The Broad," because of either his planet-like forehead or his stout shoulders.) Cratylus asks a simple question: Shouldn't people have names that fit them? The dialogue puts Cratylus against Hermogenes, whose name means "Son of Hermes." Cratylus wanted to know why Hermogenes, an unlucky, penniless guy, was named after Hermes, the god of good luck, wealth, and clever negotiations? Hermogenes didn't care that he wasn't living up to his name. Names are arbitrary, he argued. So if you have a name that people question, you can just say you're with Hermogenes, not Cratylus, and then you can get on with your day. Meanwhile, your antagonists will be left scratching their heads wondering who Hermogenes and Cratylus are.

The final option, of course, is for you to make a name for yourself. This choice basically means to do something so great that the name Elmer is thereafter stuck in our collective consciousness as the name of a hero. Stuck firmly, as though with glue. Elmer's Glue, perhaps. But that is another topic altogether, isn't it?

Names dictate character and behavior. The time has come for the Christian community to understand the role and importance of names. There are plenty of books on the market that discuss the meaning of names. In addition, I would also consider the numerical values in the name as well. For example, I would not use the name
Annette for a child born on 5/5/1954 because the letters N and E have a value of five. This will only expand the birth month (5) and the birthday (5). The person can be slowed down with the addition of a seven letter (G, P, Y, or O, Z) or apply structure with a four-letter (D, M, V).

This is a brief example of what takes place when properly choosing a name. A society which "pulls" names out of the air to name their children will produce a nation with character out of the air. Most of us suffer because we do not know who we are. You may be in Christ, but who are you in Christ? What is the Christ containing and protecting? If you notice, the first two letters of the word Christ are "CH" which means *defense*. Many of us accept Christ Jesus then dump it all on Jesus by not taking ownership for our actions which connects to our names. It is very important that we understand the meaning of our names.

Chapter 4

THE HISTORY OF THE HEBREW ALPHABET

To understand the use and value of each letter, the reader must understand the history of each letter. In addition, the reader must be familiar with the numerical values for each letter. The author strongly suggests the reader completes chapter 7.

Attention

Each letter of the Hebrew alphabet is a precept of the Kingdom of Heaven and the Kingdom of God. Each letter is designed to further our awareness of the Father, through the Son who is Christ Jesus. The proper application and interpolation of letters and numbers takes years of study and practice. Most of all, one must be lead through prayer and through guidance of the Holy Spirit. This is truth! The study and application of each letter and number will help us in becoming effective Travelers in Christ. Each Hebrew reprents an English letter but not in the sequence of the English alphabet. Each chapter starts with an English letter, the defintion, a charge of the letter and what to avoid. Following the first page of each letter the next page will contain a history of that letter and the verse where that letter is mentioned in the Book of Psalm. The entire Hebrew alphabet is listed in Psalm 119.

THE OXHEAD

The charge of Aleph: Silence, Focus, Hard work, production. Avoid laziness and being stubborn.

HEBREW LETTER –ALEPH (ah-lef)
SYMBOL: OXHEAD
ENGLISH VERSION: A
ORIGINAL PHOENICIAN: Alpu: (Ox, Cow, Teacher, Master)
GREEK VERSION: ALPHA
ROMAN VERSION: A

BIBLICAL VERSE: PSALM 119 1-8
The Lords judgments are righteous
1: Blessed are the undefiled in the way, who walk in the law of the LORD.
2: Blessed are they that keep his testimonies, and that seek him with the whole heart.
3: They also do no iniquity: they walk in his ways.
4: Thou hast commanded us to keep thy precepts diligently.
5: O that my ways were directed to keep thy statutes!
6: Then shall I not be ashamed, when I have respect unto all thy commandments.
7: I will praise thee with uprightness of heart, when I shall have learned thy righteous judgments.
8: I will keep thy statutes: O forsake me not utterly.

HISTORY
Aleph or Aluph is a masculine word which means chieftain or leader. The Symbol of Aleph is the Ox which is sacrificed for the production of work. Therefore, Alpeh is a living and breathing sacrifice. Aleph is also known as "The one who pioneers out-front".

As a prefix, Aleph means to separate, depart as seen in the words absorb, avert, abstain, abstract. As a suffix, the masculine is turned into feminine: El Nino-El Nina, EL and La. This is a letter of leadership, innovation, action and activity. Aleph is the first letter of the Hebrew alphabet and is silent in sound. Aleph has a value of 1 in the Bible PSALM 119 1-8. To pronounce Aleph, the speaker must create the sound by using a well hidden, distant region found in back of the throat for correct pronunciation. The pronunciation of Aleph requires faith because the sound is never heard when spoken. The sense of hearing is removed from the equation of detection. Faith is based on the absence of what can be detected by the five senses.

Aleph is hidden and so is the Holy Ghost who is a Spirit. Aleph was the breath of life which made Adam a living soul. Like Aleph, The Holy Ghost is not seen or heard but the work of the Holy Ghost is visible and felt. Aleph teaches us the sacredness of silence. This allows us to focus and work as the Ox who plows through the fields of life. The Ox is strong and is not distracted. The Ox works in the hot sun and is fearless. Therefore, Aleph reminds us of the power of silence, faith, focus and work. In Exodus 40:36, the presence of the Lord was symbolized by the presence of the cloud. The cloud covered the tent but it was the unseen glory of the Lord that filled the tabernacle. Aleph represents faith because it is not seen with the eyes but felt in the sprit. In John 14:17 (KJV) we read *"Even the Spirit of truth; whom the world cannot receive, because it seeth him not, neither knoweth him: but ye know him; for he dwelleth with you, and shall be in you"*.

(A) Questions:

How is Aleph working in your life?
Are you working on anything which will produce life and not death?
Have you mastered the art of silence?
Do you understand the difference between silent and sneaky?
Do you have a work ethic?

B

The House or Enclosure

The charge of Beth: Diplomacy, Communication, Covenants and Peace. Avoid: Fickleness, Indecision and Weakness.

Bet
(B/V)

B

HEBREW LETTER: BETH (BAYTH)
SYMBOL: HOUSE
ENGLISH VERSION: B
ORIGINAL PHOENICIAN: BEYTU (House)
GREEK VERSION: BETA
ROMAN VERSION: B

BIBLICAL VERSE: PSALM 119: 9-16
Thy word have I hid in mine heart
9: Wherewithal shall a young man cleanse his way? By taking heed there to according to thy word.
10: With my whole heart have I sought thee: O let me not wander from thy commandments.
11: Thy word have I hid in mine heart, that I might not sin against thee.
12: Blessed art thou, O LORD: teach me thy statutes.
13: With my lips have I declared all the judgments of thy mouth.
14: I have rejoiced in the way of thy testimonies, as much as in all riches.
15: I will meditate in thy precepts, and have respect unto thy ways.
16: I will delight myself in thy statutes: I will not forget thy word.

HISTORY
Beth means *house of, house, dwelling place*. Beth is the second letter of the Hebrew alphabet and is a feminine letter where Aleph is masculine. In the Bible, PSALM 119: 9-16, Beth has a value of 2. Beth reflects humanity and social reformation. In English, Beth is a female name. Beth means to *house*, this is a letter of union and reformation.

Beth is a prefix and suffix in Hebrew. In addition, notice the "housing nature" of Beth in words like Bethlehem which is the *house of bread*; Balbeth which is *the house of the Sun*. Bethel, which is the *house of God or house of EL*. You will also notice the word "EL" (singular) which is Elohim or God in the plural. As well as meaning *house*, the mouth and womb is another symbol for Beth. The womb is where the fetus resides prior to birth. Words are housed in the mouth before they are pronounced. So we are to think about what we say before we speak. This means we can speak life-or-death.

Beth is a letter of housing and union, it is also a letter of secrecy and this is because of its enclosed geometrical design. Therefore, Beth can be sneaky and BETRAY. The geometrical design of Beth also provides great memory, which can be bad if used for the wrong reasons. Let us dig further into this letter. I once engaged in a discussion with Pastor Phyllis Burgess from Baltimore, Maryland. She said "Son, God is now". She went on to say that we must operate like everything is now and not tomorrow. She said "miracles are things that already are". Pastor Burgess also said "everything we need to succeed in this life can be manifested in the physical through having "Now Faith".

The letter B has a value of two in both the Hebrew and Greek numbering systems. The number two is known as a number of preparation, communication, reformation, relationships, unions and diplomacy. The number two expresses itself through the letter B or Beth. Therefore, the letter B is designed to prepare us for being at one point and going to another. Beth is like pit stop (temporary place). In a pit stop, the race car is repaired, cleaned, fine tuned and then it put back on the track to contend with the other cars. Therefore, the letter B or Beth contains the preparation attribute of the number two. Concerning the letter B or Beth, notice the words buffer, baby, blessing and belief. A "buffer" is cushion zone or temporary place of storage. A "baby" represents a temporary time in the stage of human development.

A "blessing" is a positive and quick change of circumstances. Blessings do not last long, they are temporary. However, the effects of a blessing can be long-term. A "belief" is a temporary place of thought which exists outside the learning process of thinking, knowing and understanding. For example, one plus one equals two. Initially, you think about this simple equation and afterwards you know that one plus one equals two. You may not understand it; however; the longer you think about what you know, the better you understand that one plus one equals two. Is there a need to believe $1 + 1 = 2$? There is no need for belief when one comes into knowledge. A belief provides a shortness of time until one completely understands what is perceived to be known. I know my name is Darren therefore I have no need to believe my name is Darren. The belief of my name is behind me and I cannot be convert away from what I know. We cannot be converted away from Christ Jesus once we know him. Many have walked away from the faith because of not being firmly rooted in the knowledge of Christ. We must "Know the ledge" between belief and knowledge or one may fall off the cliff of ignorance. Beth is used to *house* and *provide* union. A union consists of two or more parties. Beth is a symbol for our flesh as well. We are to uphold the temple of our flesh to welcome the presence of The Holy Ghost. Beth teaches us be mindful of what we house into our body, spirit and soul.

(B) Questions:
What is in your Beth?
What are you housing in your temple?
What are you preparing in your temple?
Have you embraced diplomacy to advance nonviolence?
Have you embraced communication to advocate peace?
Have you embraced the ?

C

The Camel or Carrier

The charge of Gimeel: Compassion, Creativity, Mercy, Coverage, Completion and Focus. Avoid being Scattered, Procrastanation and Gossip.

Gimel
(G)

HEBREW LETTER: GIMEL. GAMAL, GEMEEL
SYMBOL: CAMEL/THROAT
ENGLISH VERSION: C
ORIGINAL PHOENICIAN: Gimu (Camel)
GREEK VERSION: GAMMA
ROMAN VERSION: C

BIBLICAL VERSE: PSALM 119:17-24
Thy testimonies, Are. My delight
17: Deal bountifully with thy servant, that I may live, and keep thy word.
18: Open thou mine eyes, that I may behold wondrous things out of thy law.
19: I am a stranger in the earth: hide not thy commandments from me.
20: My soul breaketh for the longing that it hath unto thy judgments at all times.
21: Thou hast rebuked the proud that are cursed, which do err from thy commandments.
22: Remove from me reproach and contempt; for I have kept thy testimonies.
23: Princes also did sit and speak against me: but thy servant did meditate in thy statutes.
24: Thy testimonies also are my delight and my counselors.

HISTORY

The letter C comes from the Hebrew Gimel (gemeel). The camel represents the symbol for this letter. The Roman letter C came from the Hebrew letter G. The letter C has a value of 3 in the Bible: PSALM 119:17-24. The letter C represents scattered energy and symbolizes the hallow part of the hand. This letter reflects the act of covering, containing, molding and shaping. The containing nature of the letter C is revealed in words such as can, church, cave, container, cup, keg, camera and Christ.

G is a letter of coverage, transport and represents the throat, which is used to transport food from the mouth to the stomach. Also, a Camel is used to carry or transport its owner from place to another. Words such as guard, god, gate, guts, ground, get, and glove are used to reveal the covering and carrying nature of the letter G. Most importantly, G has significant spiritual tendencies. The camel crosses the hot burning sands of the desert. Notice G (OD), C(hrist) and the sacrifice of Christ. The throat is a delicate member of the alimentary canal via salivation. As well, salvation is a delicate part of the life-and-death.

The letter C did not exist in Hebrew, but it came from the Hebrew G (gimeel), which means camel. The Greeks changed Gimeel to Gamma and used it as a consonant (G). The Romans then borrowed Gamma and used it as a C for both C & G sounds. Later the Romans created C with a K sound (3rd century B.C), the 3rd letter of the English alphabet, which still means camel. In addition, the Romans created a horizontal bar line for the letter G. The problem with C and G is the numerical value. In the Hebrew numbering system, C and G have a numerical value of 3. Even in the Indian Vedic system, C and G have a value of 3. The Romans assigned a numerical value of 7 to the newly created G in the 3rd century B.C. What is more disturbing is that it even makes sense. I always liked G as a 7 but this could never be the case in the Phoenician and Hebrew script. In the Pythagorean system G, P and Y have a numerical value of seven. Of course, I have a problem accepting P as a 7 and only on a good day with a good argument could I accept Y as seven because I know it was a 10 in

Hebrew (Yod). The camel is a mysterious animal. The Hebrew language is rich in color, depth. The camel is the symbol for the letter G/C. Studying the life of the camel reveals the character of the letter Gimel which gave birth to the letters G and C. What can we learn about camels that we can apply to our lives as Disciples of Christ? Camels are even-toed ungulates in the genus *Camelus*. Evolution has bred them to survive in the harshest of environments, and while they do not have the same turn of speed as the fast running the horse, they can maintain a fast pace for a greater distance. The name *camel* comes to English via the Greek κάμηλος *(kámēlos)* and from the Hebrew *gamal* or Arabic *Jamal*. The dromedary, one-humped or Arabian camel has a single hump. The Bactrian camel has two humps. Camels have broad, flat, leathery pads with two toes on each foot. When the camel places its foot on the ground the pads spread, preventing the foot from sinking into the sand. When walking, the camel moves both feet on one side of its body, then both feet on the other. What an inspiring creation and how fitting the letter C/G represents this awesome creature. A camel can go 5-7 days with little or no food and water, and can lose a quarter of its body weight without impairing its normal functions. A working camel traveling across an area where food is scarce can easily survive on thorny scrub, bones, seeds, dried leaves. Concerning a marriage, there is wisdom in studying the camel's foot. While walking on sand, the two pads of the camel's foot spread on impact preventing the foot from sinking into the hot burning sands of the desert. Think about Adam and Eve. The left pad does not think it rules the right pad. Both pads work together for a common goal. One of those goals is to not sink into the burning sands of life.

(C) Questions:
Are you in Christ?
Why is the letter C a letter of coverage and containment?
How can the toes of the camel be compared to a marriage?
Are you showing care and concern by covering the weaknesses of another?

D

The Door or Womb

The charge of Daleth: Structure, Rule, Foundation, Plans, Kindness, Softness and Preparation. Avoid Hardness, Being Rigid, Unstructured.

Dalet
(D)

HEBREW LETTER: DALETH
SYMBOL: DOOR or WOMB
ENGLISH VERSION: D
ORIGINAL PHOENICIAN: Daltu (Door, a poor man, lift up, elevation)
GREEK VERSION: DELTA
ROMAN VERSION: D

BIBLICAL VERSE: PSALM 119: 25-32
Make me to understand they way
25: My soul cleaveth unto the dust: quicken thou me according to thy word.
26: I have declared my ways, and thou heardest me: teach me thy statutes.
27: Make me to understand the way of thy precepts: so shall I talk of thy wondrous works.
28: My soul melteth for heaviness: strengthen thou me according unto thy word.
29: Remove from me the way of lying: and grant me thy law graciously.
30: I have chosen the way of truth: thy judgments have I laid before me.
31: I have stuck unto thy testimonies: O LORD, put me not to shame.
32: I will run the way of thy commandments, when thou shalt enlarge my heart.

HISTORY
The letter D stemmed from the Hebrew word *Daleth* which means *door*. This letter suggests separation or division.

It also indicates the past tense such as died, passed, and cooked. As a prefix 'De' is used to show separation or a decrease. Daleth is the fourth letter of the Hebrew alphabet, which means door or womb. D is a letter of transition. When one dies or enters death, the first letter D implies the existence of another (d)imension, nobody lies in a grave or a common grave (Jehovah's Witness). Energy cannot be created or destroyed (1st law of thermodynamics) and the spirit is always moving unless destroyed by Almighty God the Father. The womb can also serve as a door because the newborn must cross the doors of the womb to enter this world. In the Bible, the story of Jacob's ladder represents Daleth where the Angels of God descended and ascended on a la(dd)er. The Greek Tetragrammaton 'YHVH' contains four letters, four being a number of rule and structure. The number "four" symbolizes rules and order. Woman and Man must pass door to door until sin and passion are under control. We must continuously die to the flesh by entering the sacred (other) door of transition, which is fueled by our choices. The letter D also corresponds to the fourth commandment (rule), "Remember the Sabbath, to keep it holy." Adherence to personal rule and structure will free us from bondage of the flesh

    The Greeks borrowed Daleth and changed it to Delta. The geometrical design of Daleth is open because the Hebrews saw Daleth as going in and going out. Unlike the Greeks, who saw Delta as shutting items in or shutting items out; they used the closed triangle. The Greek Delta took on the form of the original Phoenician Daleth. Keep in mind the Hebrew script came from the Phoenician script. One can say the Hebrews deviated from the geometrical design of the Phoenician Daleth. The Greek Delta also had a "th" sound as in "they". When the Romans adopted the letter D, they rounded off the left tip of the triangle and turned it to the right to form the Roman and English letter D. In the Bible, the letter D has a numerical value of 4 (PSALM 119: 25-32).

The letter D teaches us there is another side of existence when we transition from this life. The Hebrew alephbet (alphabet) is a religion in its own right. The letter D describes the precept of death itself. This natural life as we perceive it is far from the last stop. Where you go after death is another story and discussion. If you want order and structure in your life, study the letter D: do, don't, dig, dare, dump, demonstrate, die, dupe, dip. Look deep into how this letter drives the meaning of every word starting with this letter.

(D) Questions:

Is your life governed by any rules or structure?
Are you prepared for the other side of Daleth?
Have you given Daleth back to the world in the form of donations, duty, dedications and devotion?
What is on the other side of your Daleth?

H, E

The Window

The charge of Hey: Vision, Responsibility, Procreation, Holiness and Containment. Be weary of illusion and deception. See life for as it is. Be careful of how you use your eyes.

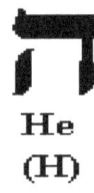

He
(H)

HE

HEBREW LETTER: HE
SYMBOL: WINDOW
ENGLISH VERSION: E
ORIGINAL PHOENICIAN: Heyu (to be broken, to take seed, to behold, revelation)
GREEK VERSION: EPSILON
ROMAN VERSION: E

BIBLICAL VERSE: PSALM 119: 33-40
Give me understanding
33: Teach me, O LORD, the way of thy statutes; and I shall keep it unto the end.
34: Give me understanding, and I shall keep thy law; yea, I shall observe it with my whole heart.
35: Make me to go in the path of thy commandments; for therein do I delight.
36: Incline my heart unto thy testimonies, and not to covetousness.
37: Turn away mine eyes from beholding vanity; and quicken thou me in thy way.
38: Stablish thy word unto thy servant, who is devoted to thy fear.
39: Turn away my reproach which I fear: for thy judgments are good.
40: Behold, I have longed after thy precepts: quicken me in thy righteousness.

HISTORY (H & E)
Hey is related to Semetic HEH which means *here is, lo, behold*. H is the messenger of intellect and strength. I am reminded of the popular terminology "Hey You" which is used to call someone's attention. The letter Hey *has a value of 5 in the Bible:* PSALM 119: 33-40.

The symbol of H is the window. A window allows one to see the world, enable vision, mobility, mental and emotional travel. This letter indicates constriction and words that confine: hell, bell, tell. As a prefix, E means to be outside of or near: exit, entrance, emit (belief). He is the fifth letter of the Hebrew alphabet, which uses the window as its symbol. Unlike the door, which is used for transition, the window is used for vision. The window will help one decide if the door should be used. This letter represents perception of self, the Father and the Kingdom of Heaven. The letter H also resembles a ladder and when linked, H resembles a fence: HHHHHHHHHHHHHHHHH.

In the Bible, the names of Abram and Sarai are changed and H played a major role in both name changes. God changed Abram's name to Abraham. H was the fifth letter and it is the fifth letter in the Hebrew alphabet. Even with Sarai, the fifth letter of her name (i) changed to (h), why? Abraham was the Father of many nations and the name Abram & Sarai could not bring the blessing of Abraham's seed. The letter H is symbolic of seeing the future and blessings of Abraham's seed. Many people today are unknowingly unable to accomplish their goals due to the use of the wrong name.

The letter H also corresponds to the 5th Commandment: "thou shall not steal". Remember the fence or field of the H-HHHHHHHHHHHHHHHHHHHH. Thou shall not take from thy neighbors' side of the fence or your neighbors' field. H is a letter of vision (Height), protection (Help) and confinement (Hell, Heaven).

Lastly, we see the feminine attributes in the Tetragrammaton YHVH (Yod-He-Vau-He). In Hebrew, Yod is masculine, He is feminine and Vau is masculine and feminine. 62.5% of YHVH is feminine (He, Vau, He) where 37.5% is masculine (Yod and Vau). The male and female have separate yet equal positions. The name Elohim, the fourth letter H (he), is the cornerstone letter. God is the English translation of Elohim.

Not only is the fourth letter (h) feminine, the first four letters *Eloh* are feminine and the last two letters (im) are masculine. What can we learn from this letter? The letter *He* teaches us about relationships and equality. Through the advent of Christ, man and woman are on equal footing where each member submits to each other to express unity and the will of Lord on earth as it is in Heaven. How significant is equality in a relationship and the future of humanity? Abraham and Sarah both received the letter "H" in the fifth position of their new names. H has a numerical value of Five which is a number of grace, change and chance. Equality in the home leads to equality in the market.

(H,E) Questions:

1. What type of future do you see through the window of your life?
2. Do you embrace gender equality?
3. Does your name prophetically call you into your destiny?
4. Like Abram, do you require a name change?

V,F,U,W

The Nail or Peg

The charge of Vau: Self Control, Sacrifice, and Peace, Initiation. Avoid Lust, Vengence, Selfishness and Belligerence.

Vav
(V)

V & F —U,W

HEBREW LETTER: VAU/WAW
SYMBOL: PEG OR NAIL
ENGLISH VERSION: U,V,W,F
ORIGINAL PHOENICIAN: Wawwu (Hook, Peg, Mace, Club)
GREEK VERSION: DiGAMMA
ROMAN VERSION: V

BIBLICAL VERSE: PSALM 119: 41-48
I trust in thy word
41: Let thy mercies come also unto me, O LORD, even thy salvation, according to thy word.
42: So shall I have wherewith to answer him that reproacheth me: for I trust in thy word.
43: And take not the word of truth utterly out of my mouth; for I have hoped in thy judgments.
44: So shall I keep thy law continually for ever and ever.
45: And I will walk at liberty: for I seek thy precepts.
46: I will speak of thy testimonies also before kings, and will not be ashamed.
47: And I will delight myself in thy commandments, which I have loved.
48: My hands also will I lift up unto thy commandments, which I have loved; and I will meditate in thy statutes.

HISTORY:
Vau-V
There is a connection between the letters F and V. They have the same Semetic definition, which means nail. A nail is hard and designed for driving and penetration. We see the nature of the nail by noting the following words: victory, vice, vampire, void, virus, and dive.

The sharp tip of the arrow of this letter allows exploration and investigation: invade, invaginate. The letter V represents virulent events and behavior. V is the sixth letter of the Hebrew alphabet and has a value of 6 in the Bible: PSALM 119: 41-48. The Greeks developed two Phoenician letters Wau: U (Upsilon) and F (Digamma). The Romans borrowed the DiGamma (which resembled today's English (f)) from the Etruscans and made it into the Roman/English F as a consonant. The Romans also used the Upsilon as a V which represented U, V and W in sound.

V is a letter of passion. V has a numerical value of six which represents the planet of love (V)enus. V also represents the Vagina and the geometrical design of the female reproductive system which resembles the letter V. Look at the description "sexual victim", the (v)ictim is the object of (v)iolent (v)irulent behavior sex/six. In the Hebrew Tetragrammaton (Yod-He-Vau-He), Vau, the third (3-creative letter) is both masculine and feminine and the act of passionate sexual intercourse will initiate pro-creativity. The letter *V* symbolizes passion and the senses. Notice that Eve had a problem with her passions. Eve had her eyes on the Tree of Good and Bad.

The peg or nail is the symbol of the letter V. Notice the phallic shape of the peg and nail. Pegs and nails connect objects, they hold items together and this could be for good or evil. We must be for God or Satan; there can be no in-between for the letter *V (Matt 3:16)*.

The letter F is a Roman letter created around 200 BC. The hard and soft sounds of V and F have two distinguishing sounds. F and V are interchangeable in English by using plural and singular tenses: loaf, loaves, leaf, leaves. F is also a letter of connection or joining: fetch, fit, and feel. F is also diminishing: flop, fly, fade, frozen. The letter F can also be festive: flirt, fun, friend, feast, fond and flashy. Observe the definitions of names starting with the letter "F": fidel-faithful, Forbes-prosperous, Felicity-happiness, Fred-peaceful.

U

HISTORY
Vau-U
SYMBOL: NAIL
ENGLISH VERSION: U
GREEK VERSION: UPSILON
ROMAN VERSION: V
BIBLICAL VERSE: PSALM 119: 41-48

HISTORY:
The Semetic letter U means nail.
This is a letter of connection and joining. U is also a letter of reception and blessings and it represents birth, gifts and being new. There are two sides to the letter U. The first side is used to express pessimistic or negative emotions: undertaker, user, underworld, ugly, upset, ulcer and uppity. The letter U also expresses oneness and togetherness: union, unity, understanding and united. The book of Zechariah has a chapter which expresses the essence of the letter U in the form of the word "Union". Zechariah 11:7-8 7 *So I pastured the flock marked for slaughter, particularly the oppressed of the flock. Then I took two staffs and called one Favor and the other Union, and I pastured the flock. 8 In one month I got rid of the three shepherds. The flock detested me, and I grew weary of them.*

Zechariah 11:14.(NIV) Then I broke my second staff called <u>Union</u>, breaking the brotherhood between Judah and Israel
Zechariah has been called to assist with the restoration of Judah. He has been chosen to Shepherd God's flock, which has been sold, into slaughter by wicked shepherds (Ze 11:5). Breaking Favor symbolizes a broken covenant. The breaking of union, symbolizes breaking the brotherhood of Judah and Israel. The breaking of union represents the false shepherds who have neglected the Lord's sheep. The letter U challenges those in leadership to be mindful of not being a good shepherd. Jesus was known as the Good Shepherd because he did not

screw his sheep!

THE ENGLISH VERSION W

BIBLICAL VERSE: PSALM 119: 41-48

HISTORY
The letter W also comes from the Semetic Vau which means nail. This letter primarily means to reflect, think or question: what, where, who, why, wonder, when, and women. Historically the letter W referred to items that would bend and twist: weave, wrong, whirl and wobble. This letter can be unpredictable in nature; this can be seen by looking at the up and down geographical topology of the letter. The letter W is a popular first name letter: William, Walt, Walter, Willie, Wanda and Wilma. This letter relates to people: witty, wealthy, wise ands wonderful. W has a negative association to events when not directly linked to people: war, woe, wicked, weapon, warning, wrong.

(U,V,W, F) Questions: What can we learn from these letters?
1. Do you have control over your passions?
2. Do you have a passion for upward thinking?
3. Are you one with yourself and your maker?
4. Have you applied the idea of unity to family, loved ones and most of all, your community?

Z

Sword and Arrow

The charge of Zayin: Focus, Aim, Upright Character. Avoid Distraction and Confusion.

Zayin
(Z)

Z

HEBREW LETTER: ZAIN/ZAYIN
SYMBOL: WEAPON, SWORD, ARROW.
ENGLISH VERSION: Z
ORIGINAL PHOENICIAN: Zain (Sword, Weapon, Species, Gender, To Sustain)
GREEK VERSION: ZETA
ROMAN VERSION: Z

BIBLICAL VERSE: PSALM 119: 49-56
Thy statutes have been my songs
119:49 Remember the word unto thy servant, upon which thou hast caused me to hope.
119:50 This is my comfort in my affliction: for thy word hath quickened me.
119:51 The proud have had me greatly in derision: yet have I not declined from thy law.
119:52 I remembered thy judgments of old, O LORD; and have comforted myself.
119:53 Horror hath taken hold upon me because of the wicked that forsake thy law.
119:54 Thy statutes have been my songs in the house of my pilgrimage.
119:55 I have remembered thy name, O LORD, in the night, and have kept thy law.
119:56 This I had, because I kept thy precepts.

HISTORY
The letter Z comes from the Hebrew Zayin which means arrow. In the Bible, Zayin has a value of 7: PSALM 119: 49-56. Force and power represents the letter Zain. The arrow represents primary potential and the possibility of destruction or construction.

The nature of Z is manifested in the duality of force and power. The letter "A" is the first letter of alphabet, the letter Z is the last letter of alphabet. The letter "A" is a leading letter, which must standout and lead the way for the other letters b-y. The letter Z takes up the rear fighting to ensure nothing attacks from the rear. Aleph is the head and Zain is the tail.

Zain, also a consonant, is the seventh letter of the Hebrew alphabet. The symbol for Zain is the sword, weapon, arrow and the scepter. Zain represents precise aim for conquest. Zain represents the tongue. The words that proceed out of the mouth are symbolic of arrows. The sharp tip of the arrow allows for cutting. But there are two sides to this letter. Z contains two sevens, one upright and other upside down. Z can be upright, focused, healing, faithful, and analytical. This letter also can be upside down and do the opposite: wound, ignore and lose focus due to excessive worry. Regarding speech, we read in proverbs 12:18 "There are those whose speech is like the piercing of a sword: but the tongue of the wise heals. Notice the numerical value of the scripture when reduced (12:18= 3:9=12/3), three being the number thought and expression. Twelve is the number of discipline and 18 is the number of warning and awareness. The legal age of an adult is 18. (see chapter on number 18).

Z has a numerical value of 7 in the Hebrew system and has a value of 8 in the Pythagorean system. The Pythagorean system framed the numerical values of the English language. The Greeks borrowed Zain and named it Zeta (Life). It was the Romans who borrowed the Phoenician glyph and made it the 26th letter of the alphabet. Therefore, H, Q, Z have a value of eight, where O, Z have a value of 7 in the Hebrew system. The letter Z produces energetic words such as zest, zip, zoom, zippidy -doo-dah, zany, and zealous. Names such as Zoe (life), Ziv (very bright), and Zelia, (eager) reveal the energetic qualities of this letter.

(Z) Questions to consider:
1. Are you fighting for justice or injustice?
2. What types of arrows proceed out of your mouth?
3. What is the aim of your life?

Field or Fence

The charge of Cheth: Timing, Family, Protection, Coverage And Vision. Avoid Tyrannical And Controlling Behavior.

Chet
(Ch)

CH

HEBREW LETTER: CHETH/HETH
SYMBOL: FIELD/FENCE
HEBREW VERSION: CH
ENGLISH VERSION: CH (Sound)
ORIGINAL PHOENICIAN: Khatu (Fence, Field, Life)
GREEK VERSION: ETA

BIBLICAL VERSE: PSALM 119: 57-64
The earth, O Lord, is full of thy mercy
57: Thou art my portion, O LORD: I have said that I would keep thy words.
58: I intreated thy favour with my whole heart: be merciful unto me according to thy word.
59: I thought on my ways, and turned my feet unto thy testimonies.
60: I made haste, and delayed not to keep thy commandments.
61: The bands of the wicked have robbed me: but I have not forgotten thy law.
62: At midnight I will rise to give thanks unto thee because of thy righteous judgments.
63: I am a companion of all them that fear thee, and of them that keep thy precepts.
64: The earth, O LORD, is full of thy mercy: teach me thy statutes.

HISTORY:
The Hebrew letter "Cheth" correlates to the letter H which means fence. In fact, if you connect several H's together, you will notice the image of a fence. The fence allows the mind and body to be productive with out external distraction.

In the Bible, PSALM 119: 57-64, this letter has a value of 8 which represents humanity and reformation. The letter H reflects the following: focus, narrowing, enclosure, impact, grasp, contact and limitation. Words that reveal the nature of this letter includes hamper, hesitate, hang, heed, handle, hell, heaven and hit. Cheth or Heth is closely related to He, the difference comes in sound. If the sound is CH, then it has a value of 8. If the sound is HEH as in head, then the value is 5. Cheth is known as the cultivated field. The Phoenician glyph for Cheth resembles a ladder or a window. The Greek symbol also resembles a window and the letter H.

Notice what occurs when you connect a several H's together, one will see the image of a fence which keeps some things in and some things out: HHHHHHHHHHHHHHHHHHHHHHHHHHHHHHH. The letter (he) is feminine in Hebrew. Regarding cultivation, we see many words that come into play: Church (cultivate the people), children (need cultivation), Choir (cultivate sound). Choir (cultivates work), Chump (cultivates weakness), and Champion (cultivates victory). Notice the word Church has the (CH) in the beginning and in the end of word. This symbolizes the cultivation of civilization required by the church (supreme and divine cultivation). Cheth requires intuition for higher living on Earth. Even so, those in the church are expected to display higher living in the church which uses the world as its fence.

As Disciples of Christ, we all need cultivation. This is why we accept Christ Jesus as Lord and Savior. In Christ, we are covered and contained (C). The letter 'H' shows our future through salvation. The "CH" in Christ directly suggests we are in a field, a protected field. This field has power in the natural and in the Spirit. Consider John 20:31 *But these are written that you may believe that Jesus is the **Christ**, the Son of God, and that by believing you may have life in his name.*

2 Corinthians 12:2
I know a man in **Christ** who fourteen years ago was caught up to the third heaven. Whether it was in the body or out of the body I do not know—God knows.

2 Corinthians 12:9
But he said to me, "My grace is sufficient for you, for my power is made perfect in weakness." Therefore I will boast all the more gladly about my weaknesses, so that **Christ**'s power may rest on me.

(CH) Questions:

1. Are you helping your Church to defend and protect?
2. Are you fenced in by your passions?
3. Placing your man made religion aside for a moment, are you in Christ?

T

GOODNESS

Charges of Teth: Constructive choices, Compassion, Truth, Justice. Avoid Being Uncompassionate, Materialistic And Belligerent.

Tet
(T)

T

HEBREW LETTER: TETH/TET(No. 9)
SYMBOL: Wheel
ENGLISH VERSION: T
ORIGINAL PHOENICIAN: t, x
GREEK VERSION: Tau
ROMAN VERSION: T

BIBLICAL VERSE: PSALM 119: 65-72
Teach me good judgments
65: Thou hast dealt well with thy servant, O LORD, according unto thy word.
66: Teach me good judgment and knowledge: for I have believed thy commandments.
67: Before I was afflicted I went astray: but now have I kept thy word.
68: Thou art good, and doest good; teach me thy statutes.
69: The proud have forged a lie against me: but I will keep thy precepts with my whole heart.
70: Their heart is as fat as grease; but I delight in thy law.
71: It is good for me that I have been afflicted; that I might learn thy statutes.
72: The law of thy mouth is better unto me than thousands of gold and silver.

HISTORY:
Teth transliterates to the English T. Teth is the ninth letter of the Hebrew alphabet. The symbol for Tet is the wheel and has a numerical value of nine. Tet is found in the Hebrew word *Tov* or *Towb* which means *good; well*. Tov appears in Genesis 1:4 "A*nd God saw the light, and it was good. And God divided the light from the darkness.*

The word tov (good) first appears in Genesis 1:4 and last appears in Malachi 2:17. *Ye have wearied the Lord with your words. Yet ye say, Every one that does evil is good in the sight of the Lord.* The symbol of Tet is the wheel that is a closed looping object. The idea is that a wheel will always move in the direction it is pushed or pulled. In Genesis 1:4, God saw the light was good, meaning it was created correctly, the first time. The light is doing what it is supposed to do. The light was so good; God separated the light from the darkness. Goodness leads to sanctification. Tet means good and if we are good, our deeds will head in one direction, like a wheel, and not go back and forth (depending on who is pushing or pulling). In Malachi, the prophet is saying the people have not divided their goodness from evil but they are justifying their actions with words. God become weary about their prayers because of their actions. The people of God did not separate the light in their lives from the darkness in their lives which is a lack of true repentance or change. To drive this point home, John the Baptist is introduced in the next chapter, Matthew, the first Book of the New Testament. What John's key message in the book of Matthew? The key word for John was REPENT. The wheel always moves in the direction it is pushed or pulled. In other words, we will continuously do what we push or pull ourselves to do. Tet teaches us to head in one direction, preferably the light. One cannot pray one thing and purposely live another. Darkness is the absence of light and so it should be in our personal lives. Darkness should be absent from our lives because of walking the light of self and Christ. The wheels of our lives should be pulled or pushed towards the light, continuously like the wheel. Embracing Tet is the very act engaging in repentance.

The letter Tet is known to save or slay. This letter can bring down the many or raise the many: troops, tyrant, tears (sadness, joy) and try. T should build rather than destroy. T can also be a peacemaker "time-out". T is a letter of influence (trust). Tet calls every person into goodness of behavior and goodness in skill set.

(T) Questions:
1. Is the wheel in your life heading towards darkness or light?
2. Do you build or destroy (condemn) people with your words?
3. Are you good at your skill-set, if you checked your work, would it be good?

Y, J

Charges of Yod, (J): Stillness, Patience, Trust. Avoid Being Selfish, Stubborn And Lazy.

Yod
(Y)

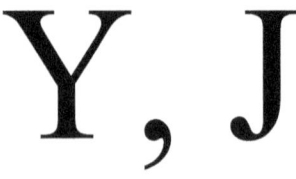

Y, J

HEBREW LETTER: YOD
SYMBOL: HAND
ENGLISH VERSION: J
ORIGINAL PHOENICIAN: Yadu (Arm with hand, Open, To Thrust)
GREEK VERSION: IOTA
ROMAN VERSION: J

BIBLICAL VERSE: PSALM 119: 73-80
Let the proud be ashamed
73: Thy hands have made me and fashioned me: give me understanding that I may learn thy commandments.
74: They that fear thee will be glad when they see me; because I have hoped in thy word.
75: I know, O LORD, that thy judgments are right, and that thou in faithfulness hast afflicted me.
76: Let, I pray thee, thy merciful kindness be for my comfort, according to thy word unto thy servant.
77: Let thy tender mercies come unto me, that I may live: for thy law is my delight.
78: Let the proud be ashamed; for they dealt perversely with me without a cause: but I will meditate in thy precepts.
79: Let those that fear thee turn unto me, and those that have known thy testimonies.
80: Let my heart be sound in thy statutes; that I be not ashamed.

HISTORY:
The letter J is closely related to the letter I, one basic difference is that J is a consonant and I is a vowel. Yod has a value of 1 in the Bible: PSALM 119: 73-80. Yod comes in several flavors: Y, J and I. For our purposes, I will cover the letter Y and J. The Hebrew letter Yod means *hand*. Yod is the smallest letter in the Hebrew Alphabet.

This letter first appears in Genesis 3:22 *"And the LORD God said, "The man has now become like one of us, knowing good and evil. He must not be allowed to reach out his **hand** and take also from the tree of life and eat, and live forever."* The charge of Yod centers on the use of the hand which is a result of what one thinks. In Genesis 3:22, Adam chose to use his hand to partake of the Tree of Good and Bad. Adam made a choice and he was denied the option of eating from the Tree of Life. Adam chose to disobey God's command to not eat of the Tree of Good and Bad (Torah). In Genesis 4:11, let us review how Cain chose to use his hands *"Now you are under a curse and driven from the ground, which opened its mouth to receive your brother's blood from your hand"*. God did not respect Cain's offering because he did a fast, sloppy job by just picking up fruit off the ground.

Some say God rejected Cain's offering because the ground was cursed (Adam) but the firstlings offered by Abel benefited from this same soil, so this cannot be the reason for God's lack of respect for Cain's offering. The problem with Cain's offering centered around his attitude. Abel put his best into bringing the best. Abel brought the 'choicest' of the firstlings. Cain did the opposite. He picked up whatever he could find on the ground. Cain's entire outlook was dark. In a sense, Cain was not a cheerful giver, he had an attitude problem which pored over into everything he did and this included God's offering. God told him "if you do right, there is uplift". At this point, God is giving Cain an opportunity to think positively. God also says "if you do not do right, sin sits at the door, its urge is toward you, yet you can master the urges of sin". God has presented Cain with enough encouragement and instruction to correct his attitude about the offering and life in general. So what does Cain do? His bad attitude causes him to use his hands to kill his brother when all he had to do was change the state of thought processes on the next offering. In other words, all Cain had to do was think with light and think in the light and not harbor dark thoughts. We must be careful to not harbor dark thoughts or it will affect our offering as well. This is why many people have a negative outlook on what they offer God, particularly in the form of money. These types of people have dark thoughts and dark reasons on why they should not cheerfully pay tithes and offering.

They have all kinds of reasons on why not to pay tithes as though we must pay tithes. Tithing is a choice not a commandment. And that is the "give away"; nobody has to do anything if one chooses not to do anything at all. The Bible talks about the cheerful giver 2 cor 9:7. The Bible also talks about reaping what one sows (Matt 25:24, 1 Cor 9:11). There is nothing in the Bible which states "You must pay tithes", it's all about following Abel's lead by willingly offering one's best. God is looking at out our hearts, not the theology or thoughts of man.

Back to Cain, he had options, how do we know he had options? First, God gave him an option. Second, the letter Y has two prongs, a fork in the road. Yod represents choices and decisions that are manifested by the action of the hand. The works of your hand reveals the real you. The last time we see Yod at work is in Malachi 7:13 *"Another thing you do: You flood the LORD's altar with tears. You weep and wail because he no longer pays attention to your offerings or accepts them with pleasure from your hands.* Malachi is clearly telling the people of God that obedience is better than fasting. And no matter how much they cry and yell at the altar, God is not paying any attention to their offering because of the works of their hands. Adam was disobedient in the first occurrence of Yod in Genesis 3:22. The Israelites were disobedient in the last occurrence of Yod in Malachi 4:22. This letter is charging us to be wise concerning the works of our hand. We must be mindful of the consequences of our choices.

The Roman's changed the Hebrew 'Yod' to the letter "J". If you study many words that begin with the letter "J" you will notice the following attributes: compression, jumpy, jolting and bouncing, jig, jabber, javelin, jostle, junk, and jigsaw. The letter J also denotes the act of catching by its hooked shaped.

As Jesus was a fisher of men, he catches us by the hook of his name. Think of a person who has gone fishing. A calm fish can have the hook pulled out of its mouth with little damage. However, a wild uncontrollable fish will only make the catch more difficult by to much movement because of fear and the need to survive. If the fish fights too hard, the hook will cause damage to the fish and even the fisher. So it is with being caught by the hook of Jesus the Christ.

As he pulls us out of the water (people) on earth, we struggle and we cause ourselves unnecessary pain and affliction by not being like a calm fish. Christ Jesus will not fry us in a pan which is fueled by fire; but he will purge us of sin by going through the fire with us. Thus, purifying us like gold with fire. Jesus, the Son of God, is the steady hand which will guide us and carry us. Jesus will also catch us if we are willing to be caught. Once we "Accept" Christ, we become like fish in the water asking to be kindly hooked with a little pinch. We experience a little pain in birth, life and death and so it is with accepting Christ. We experience a little pain because of being torn from the cares of this world.

(Y, J) Questions:
1. Do you harbor dark thoughts about yourself and other people?
2. What do the works of your hand reveal about you in the areas of church, home, the community, the family and parenting?
3. What type of attitude do you have towards tithes and offering?
4. If the works of your follow you, what is following you, blessings or stagnation?

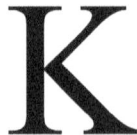

The Palm or Grasping Hand

The Charge Of Kaph: Overcoming, Clear Intentions, Self Control, Humility, Care, Concern And Kindness. Avoid Being Irresponsible And Careless.

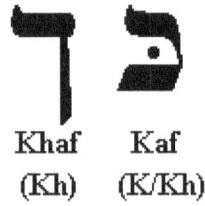

Khaf   Kaf
(Kh)   (K/Kh)

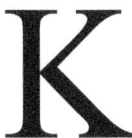

HEBREW LETTER: KAPH/CAPH/KAP
SYMBOL: PALM OF HAND
ENGLISH VERSION: K
ORIGINAL PHOENICIAN: Kappu (Palm of hand, Sole of foot, Clouds, Power to suppress)
GREEK VERSION: KAPPA
ROMAN VERSION: K

BIBLICAL VERSE: PSALM 119: 81-88
All my commandments are faithful
81: My soul fainteth for thy salvation: but I hope in thy word.
82: Mine eyes fail for thy word, saying, When wilt thou comfort me?
83: For I am become like a bottle in the smoke; yet do I not forget thy statutes.
84: How many are the days of thy servant? When wilt thou execute judgment on them that persecute me?
85: The proud have digged pits for me, which are not after thy law.
86: All thy commandments are faithful: they persecute me wrongfully; help thou me.
87: They had almost consumed me upon earth; but I forsook not thy precepts.
88: Quicken me after thy loving kindness; so shall I keep the testimony of thy mouth.

HISTORY:
This letter is closely related to the letter C. This is a letter of compression, molding, union and compaction. Observe the following words: King, Kiss, Kick, Cock, Click and Call. Kaph is the 11th letter of the Hebrew alphabet, which has two sounds K or Ch. The number 11 did not exist in Hebrew so Koph was given a value of 20. Koph has a value of 20 in the Bible PSALM 119: 81-88.

The Phoenician K was borrowed by the Greeks and then the Romans. This letter represents the following: holding, molding, caring, shaping and controlling nature of the "K" and has a value of 2 in the Pythagorean system and Hebrew system. The palm of the hand can be used to bring comfort in the form of a gentle rub or pain in the form of a smack. The use of the Palm of the Hand first appears in Leviticus 4:15 and Leviticus 4:24. Both of these verses address the act of consecration.

Leviticus 4:15 (KJV)
And the elders of the congregation shall lay their hands upon the head of the bullock before the Lord: and the bullock shall be killed before the Lord.

Leviticus 4:24 (KJV)
And he shall lay his hand upon the head of the goat, and kill it in the place where they kill the burnt offering before the Lord: it is a sin offering.

Just as we have two hands, the use of the Kaf is expressed in two forms: consecration and destruction. There is the fall of Dagon in 1 Sam 5:3. Also, there is the death of Jezebel in 2 Kings 9:35. Kaf teaches that our hands can be used to build our lives or be used to bring death to our lives. Ironically, the Yod (hand) and Kaf (Palm of the Hand or Sole of the Foot) are in close proximity. In Romans we read about the feet being used for destruction: *Romans 3:15 (KJV) Their feet are swift to shed blood.* This Holy letter reminds us that we have two feet and two hands and two arms. This means we have two choices; will we use our members for life or death?

(K) Questions:

1. Are the palms of your hands used for good purposes?
2. Are your hands used to produce good fruit?
3. Are you too controlling over your friends, family and loved ones?

L

THE OXGOAD: Learn and Teach

The Charge Of Lamed: To Teach, To Learn And Create. Pay Attention To Rules. Avoid Ignorance And Being Reckless.

Lamed
(L)

HEBREW LETTER: LAMED
SYMBOL: OX-GOAD, TO TEACH, URGE
ENGLISH VERSION: L
ORIGINAL PHOENICIAN:
GREEK VERSION: LAMBDA
ROMAN VERSION: L

BIBLICAL VERSE: PSALM 119: 89-96
Thy faithfulness is unto all generations
89: For ever, O LORD, thy word is settled in heaven.
90: Thy faithfulness is unto all generations: thou hast established the earth, and it abideth.
91: They continue this day according to thine ordinances: for all are thy servants.
92: Unless thy law had been my delights, I should then have perished in mine affliction.
93: I will never forget thy precepts: for with them thou hast quickened me.
94: I am thine, save me; for I have sought thy precepts.
95: The wicked have waited for me to destroy me: but I will consider thy testimonies.
96: I have seen an end of all perfection: but thy commandment is exceeding broad.

HISTORY
This letter is related to the Hebrew Lamed (ox-goad). Lamed means to *learn and teach*. This is why we go to the library. Lamed is known as the extending hand and vaulting into heaven. On the horizontal

plane we see words such as low, lie, let, and leak. Vertically, we see words such as laugh, lilt, lord, lofty, elate, elope and elevate. An example of L's extension would include: land, lane, and line, lanky, lateral and long.

The symbol of Lamed is the Ox Goad which is a long stick or rod used by the Shepherd to guide the sheep. Lamed is the twelfth letter of the Hebrew alphabet. Lamed is known as the sacrifice, this is because of the relationship with the number 12(the victim). In the Bible, Lamed has a numerical value of 30: PSALM 119: 89-96. Lamed is also known as the *outstretched arm of God*. In the book of Exodus 6:6 we read "I am Lord and I will save you with an outstretched arm". In a bent position, our arms are shaped like the letter L. If extended, our arms are shaped like a lower case 'l'. If we add the number of the chapter and the verse: chapter 6 and verse 6, we get 12, which correspond to the twelfth letter in the alphabet. Also, in Exodus, the first letter of the word Lord is (L)amed. The ox-goad not only guides but it is loving, logical, legal and likable. Because of Lamed's outstretching nature, the owner must live up to the L by learning what is being extended by the outstretched arm of God. God teaches us through precepts, meditation and the Holy Ghost. God the Father is our ultimate teacher. Lamed requires effort in the form of love, compassion and sincere guidance.

L is a letter of creation and is the tallest letter in the entire alphabet because Lamed must reach high in order to learn what comes from the Father above. This letter is actually standing in attention to learn the law of the Lord. We must also stand with attention to receive from the Lord. Lamed is expected to accomplish the highest of objectives through thought, movement and creation. The highest rules of land are established by the (L)aw and (L)egality. In the beginning was the Word (law) but the word became flesh when God outstretched his arm and brought forth salvation through Christ Jesus. Christ, who is our Shepherd, guides the sheep along the pastures or the world. The letter 'L' inserted in the fourth position of the (word) to show itself in the (world). God the Father, through his Son, will guide us through the Pastures of the world with his outstretched arm. What does the good Shepherd use to guide us, the Shepherd uses L or Lamed.

The symbol of L is the ox goad which is the stick used by the shepherd to guide the sheep. Love is the best word to describe the full manifestation of Lamed. Who is Christ? He is (L)ove and he is our (L)eader.

(L) Questions:
1. Have you embraced the outstretched arm of God to create or produce anything for the Kingdom of God on earth?
2. Are you led by the outstretched arm of God?
3. Who is the shepherd of your life and who is leading you?

WATER & MERCY

The Charge of M: Reflection, Mercy, Compassion , Planning. Accountability, Knowing Self. Avoid Cruelty, Sloppiness, Ignorance.

Mem   Mem
(M)   (M)

M

HEBREW LETTER: MEM
SYMBOL: WATER, WOMB
ENGLISH VERSION: M
GREEK VERSION: MU
ROMAN VERSION: M

BIBLICAL VERSE: PSALM 119: 97-104
How love I thy law
97: O how love I thy law! it is my meditation all the day.
98: Thou through thy commandments hast made me wiser than mine enemies: for they are ever with me.
99: I have more understanding than all my teachers: for thy testimonies are my meditation.
100: I understand more than the ancients, because I keep thy precepts.
101: I have refrained my feet from every evil way, that I might keep thy word.
102: I have not departed from thy judgments: for thou hast taught me.
103: How sweet are thy words unto my taste! yea, sweeter than honey to my mouth!
104: Through thy precepts I understand: therefore I hate every false way.

HISTORY:

The letter M is related to the Hebrew Mem (water) which also means mercy. M has a value of 40 in the Bible (PSALM 119: 97-104) If you connect several M's together you notice the hieroglyphic form of waves, which represents the flow of motherhood, life and energy.
Notice the word Mother starts with the letter M. The fetus comes out of the dark womb filled with fluid (water). M is also a letter of reflection. This is evident in seeing a reflection in a (M)irror or Water. Serotonin, a hormone, secretes during the day and is responsible for sustaining memory in the brain.

Melatonin (fluid) sedates the nervous system during the evening. M is the 13th letter of the English alphabet which reduces to the number (4) (1+3=4) which is a planning number. M is a letter of practicality, planning and movement: mark, master, muster, make, method, move and master.

Mercy is like water because it is never ending. Water always moves in one direction and so it is with mercy. Unlike people, mercy never changes. There is so much we can learn from the letter Mem. This letter is associated with mercy and water. 'M' is an upside down 'W'. If water sustains life and Mem means *mercy and water*, then we should sustain mercy for our sisters and brothers. Mercy should be the first thought to enter our mind when we rise in the morning and before going to sleep at night. How important is mercy, if we go to the New Testament, we read about peace: *Romans 14:19 (KJV) let us therefore follow after the things which make for peace and things wherewith one may edify another.* Regarding Mercy, the New Testament offers the following as well: *Galatians 5:22-26 (KJV) But the fruit of the Spirit is love, joy, peace, longsuffering, gentleness, goodness, faith, [23] Meekness, temperance: against such there is no law. [24] And they that are Christ's have crucified the flesh with the affections and lusts. [25] If we live in the Spirit, let us also walk in the Spirit. [26] Let us not be desirous of vain glory, provoking one another, envying one another.*

(M) Questions:
1. Are full of mercy for your brothers and sisters?
2. Are you flowing with compassion?
3. Mem is a letter of foundation; does your life have a foundation which can withstand the basic winds of life? (Providing for your family, keeping a roof over your head, taking care of your children, planning for the future, not living day to day).

FISH

The Charge of N: Awareness, Mobility, Freedom, Optimism. Kindness, Constant Awareness. Avoid Fear, Negativity and Evasion.

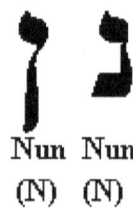

Nun Nun
(N) (N)

HEBREW LETTER: NUN
SYMBOL: FISH, SNAKE
ENGLISH VERSION: N
ORIGINAL PHOENICIAN: NUN
GREEK VERSION: NU
ROMAN VERSION: N

BIBLICAL VERSE: PSALM 119: 105-112
Thy word is a lamp...and a light
105: Thy word is a lamp unto my feet, and a light unto my path.
106: I have sworn, and I will perform it, that I will keep thy righteous judgments.
107: I am afflicted very much: quicken me, O LORD, according unto thy word.
108: Accept, I beseech thee, the freewill offerings of my mouth, O LORD, and teach me thy judgments.
109: My soul is continually in my hand: yet do I not forget thy law.
110: The wicked have laid a snare for me: yet I erred not from thy precepts.
111: Thy testimonies have I taken as a heritage for ever: for they are the rejoicing of my heart.
112: I have inclined mine heart to perform thy statutes always, even unto the end.

HISTORY:
The letter N is related to the Hebrew Nun, which means fish, growth and fertility. N is the 14th letter of the English & Hebrew alphabet and has a numerical value of 50 which means to *move* (PSALM 119: 105-112). Notice the nature of a fish is based on movement and vision.

Movement and vision determines how well and long the fish survives in the sea. The early Christians used the fish to symbolize the Messiah (resurrection). The letter N is hidden inside the letter M. Nun has many evasive, elusive, evading, and absent qualities. This is why a fish swallowed Jonah. God was showing that Jonah could not hide in a huge sea in a ship searching to bring in fish. Also, Jonah could not hide inside a big fish that has not been caught or harpooned by a big ship in the huge sea. The letter N gives birth to a host of negative or hidden words: naked (porn), not, night (full moon and crime), un, never, never, nasty, null, naughty, nick at night.

The fish and the letter Nun symbolizes how Jonah refused to do what the Lord wanted him to at Nineveh. Jonah negated the command of God. *Jonah 1:1-2 (KJV) Now the word of the Lord came unto Jonah the son of Amittai, saying, [2] Arise, go to Nineveh, that great city, and cry against it; for their wickedness is come up before me.* Notice, Nineveh starts with the letter N. In other words, this place was evading and negative in the eyes of the Lord. What part of the Americas is the United States located north or south? Between the Koreas, which is more troublesome, North Korea or South Korea?

(N) Questions:
1. Are you using your vision to be a fruitful member of your family, Church, place of employment and community?
2. Are you in Jonah mode, negating what God has for you to do?
3. Are you hiding on anyone's ship or under someone's finance's and resources?
4. Are you causing the ship of loved one or family member to sink?

The Gospel of Numbers and Letters in Scripture

SUPPORT, PROP

The Charge of Samech: Clarity, Support, Independence, Charity. Avoid dependence, Deception, Greed.

Samech
(S)

S

HEBREW LETTER: Samekh
SYMBOL: SERPENT, TENT, PEG, TO SUPPORT
ENGLISH VERSION: S
ORIGINAL PHOENICIAN: Samekh
GREEK VERSION: SIGMA
ROMAN VERSION: S

BIBLICAL VERSE: PSALM 119: 113-120
I hate vain thoughts
113: I hate vain thoughts: but thy law do I love.
114: Thou art my hiding place and my shield: I hope in thy word.
115: Depart from me, ye evildoers: for I will keep the commandments of my God.
116: Uphold me according unto thy word, that I may live: and let me not be ashamed of my hope.
117: Hold thou me up, and I shall be safe: and I will have respect unto thy statutes continually.
118: Thou hast trodden down all them that err from thy statutes: for their deceit is falsehood.
119: Thou puttest away all the wicked of the earth like dross: therefore I love thy testimonies.
120: My flesh trembleth for fear of thee; and I am afraid of thy judgments.

HISTORY:
Samekh is the 15th letter of the Hebrew alphabet. Samekh has numerical value of 60: PSALM 119: 113-120 and has one sound: S.

Samekh is associated with the number 60 which is also related to 666, the number of the beast. The number 15 reduces to a six (1+5). The X or xmach has been related to Samekh. Samekh (S) is associated with (X) and we get other words such as sex and six. Sex or procreation supports life. Too much sex is xes (excess). S is a letter of (S)upport and it also means "to be supported". In addition, we see the supportive nature of this letter in words such as save, salvation and second (I second that motion). Jesus (S)uffered on the cross and his action supported the idea of (S)alvation. It was the Serpent who was a deceptive form of support and service to Eve. The first Samekh is encountered in Genesis 2:18 with the creation of Eve. She was created to be Adam's counter part not a subservient woman waiting for her man to return home. *Genesis 2:18 (KJV) And the Lord God said, It is not good that the man should be alone; I will make him a help meet for him.* The word *Help Meet* comes from the *Hebrew "Heb. 'ezer ke-negdo: i.e., which means "a help as his counterpart" = a help suitable to him), a wife.* The word *rib* comes from the Hebrew Ha-ZeLA but when rearranged, Rib spells Le-EZaH which means advisor. All women come fully equipped with the ability to be supportive and advising: grand mothers, mothers, sisters, aunts. How fast and well the man takes advantage of this blessing (good ribs) is another story. However, every woman should review the condition of their ribs: good or evil. This is the same challenge Eve faced in the Garden. Samekh reminds to be good stewards of our passions. Procreation is supports the continuation of the Human race. However, unbridled sex is excessive and leads to war, famine and disease.

    The lesson for the male and female is learning how to allow our differences to work as a true compliment and not a detriment. Man and woman will succeed when we truly support each other. Subscribing to any theology which places a man over woman is a recipe for social disaster. All curses administered in the Garden were nullified with the advent of Christ Jesus. Jesus and Paul were very supportive to the women in their lives. It is the role of the woman to oppose the thoughts of a man when his thoughts are dark and destructive. How she opposes the thoughts of her man is another story and a matter style I suggest embracing the nine fruits of the spirit in Galatians.

The rib represents advice. This is another form of support if the man is secure enough to embrace advice from a good rib. There is hope for humanity, when men and women learn to leave a good taste in mouth of the other while giving a word of knowledge or wisdom

(S) Questions:
1. What principles do you support?
2. Do you understanding the supportive power in keeping a secret.
3. Do you see the letter S and the nature of this letter around you on a daily basis?
4. For the men, if your woman has good ribs, do you receive her support ?
5. For the women, do you have good ribs and do you have tack history of giving good advice ?

HEBREW LETTER: SAMECH
ENGLISH VERSION: X
GREEK VERSION: XI
ROMAN VERSION: X
BIBLICAL VERSE: PSALM 119: 113-120

HISTORY
This is a mysterious yet simple letter. X is known as the *unknown*. X is an unknown variable in algebra. The letter is known as being useless in sound with words such as xeno and axe. It is known to give position and connection "X marks the spot". The letter X can connect existence and nonexistence. For example: wife and ex-wife, inclusion and exclusion. The letter X has a numerical value of six (6) in the Chaldean numbering system and value of 5 in the Hebrew system. Around 1700 B.C., this letter was used to represent the consonant "S". After 900 B.C., the Greeks borrowed S from the Phoenicians and altered its form, changed its name to Xi and made the sign stand for the consonant X. This letter has a numerical value of 6 in the Pythagorean system and a value of 5 in the Hebrew system.

Questions:
1. Have you solved any unknown equations in your personal life?
2. Now that you may know who you are, do you know who you are

THE EYE

The Charge Of O: Observation, Calculation, Enlightenment. Avoid Ignorance And Sins Of The Lower Nature.

HEBREW LETTER: AYIN
SYMBOL: EYE, SOURCE
ENGLISH VERSION: O
ORIGINAL PHOENICIAN: AYIN
GREEK VERSION: OMEGA/OMICRON
ROMAN VERSION: O

BIBLICAL VERSE: PSALM 119: 121-128
I am thy servant
121: I have done judgment and justice: leave me not to mine oppressors.
122: Be surety for thy servant for good: let not the proud oppress me.
123: Mine eyes fail for thy salvation, and for the word of thy righteousness.
124: Deal with thy servant according unto thy mercy, and teach me thy statutes.
125: I am thy servant; give me understanding, that I may know thy testimonies.
126: It is time for thee, LORD, to work: for they have made void thy law.
127: Therefore I love thy commandments above gold; yea, above fine gold.
128: Therefore I esteem all thy precepts concerning all things to be right; and I hate every false way.

HISTORY:
The letter O is a letter of patience and makes an excellent first letter and 2nd second letter of a first name. Some say the letter O comes from the Semetic Ayin or Eye. In the Bible, Ayin has a value of 70 (PSALM 119: 121-128). Others say it come from the Semetic

Vau-nail. Personally, I like to use it as Ayin or Eye because of words such as observe, outreach, outsource, opinion, oscillate. When used properly as first the name, it will provide patience and observation to the owner: Ophelia, Oprah, Oscar. Ayin is the 16th letter of the Hebrew alphabet and it means "Eye". It is associated with anger. Ayin is shaped like an eye and this symbol was known as the "All seeing eye" by the early church. The word "church" comes from the Anglican root *circ* or *cyrc* which means circular. The designs of the first church were circular to represent the all seeing eye of God. In addition, we often hear about the old Church circuits in the south where the preacher would visit various churches along a circuit by means of horse and buggy. This is how the concept of church districts and conferences came into being.

O is a powerful letter. It gives the owner excellent vision or a good eye to see the ways of the masses. If you miss something you may be considered a F<u>OO</u>L. *Look* that is *Kool*. The two O's in the word FOOL indicate we have two eyes to observe the ways of self-and other than self. O has a value of 6 in the Pythagorean system and a value of 7 in the Hebrew system. The letter O is letter of emotion, excitement and surprise. This can be seen in words such as ooh, ouch, oops, ow, orgy, oh-god, outburst, outrage, oust, order. Even a Monkey knows about the letter O when they make Monkey sounds "oo-oo-oo-oo". Notice the O is the first letter of the word Orgasm and Oscillate.

(O) Questions:
1. Are you blind to ways of your lower nature?
2. Can you discern the presence of the spirit world?
3. Are your eyes spiritually open or closed?

P

THE MOUTH

The Charge Of P: Speaking Truth, Good Speech, When To Be Silent, Praising God Out Loud, Avoiding Excessive Talking. Refrain From Gossip And Foolish Discussion.

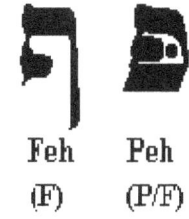

Feh   Peh
(F)   (P/F)

P

HEBREW LETTER: PHE/PE
SYMBOL: MOUTH, SPEECH, PRESENT
ENGLISH VERSION: P
ORIGINAL PHEONICIAN: PE
GREEK VERSION: PI
ROMAN VERSION: P

BIBLICAL VERSE: PSALM 119: 129-136
The entrance of thy words giveth light
129: Thy testimonies are wonderful: therefore doth my soul keep them.
130: The entrance of thy words giveth light; it giveth understanding unto the simple.
131: I opened my mouth, and panted: for I longed for thy commandments.
132: Look thou upon me, and be merciful unto me, as thou usest to do unto those that love thy name.
133: Order my steps in thy word: and let not any iniquity have dominion over me.
134: Deliver me from the oppression of man: so will I keep thy precepts.
135: Make thy face to shine upon thy servant; and teach me thy statutes.
136: Rivers of waters run down mine eyes, because they keep not thy law.

HISTORY:
The letter P is related to the Hebrew Pe, meaning mouth. This is a letter of speech and has a double meaning: power and servitude. This letter represents speaking and talking. Notice the words pastor, preacher, punch, people, peace, presence, and pick. This letter symbolizes enlightenment. P is an excellent first name letter, but often needs taming. P can also be fatherly or authoritative: paternal pope, pontiff, priest, president, prince, principle and provider.

Phe is the 17th letter of the Hebrew alphabet. P is known as "one who confers power". In the Bible, Saul's name was changed to Paul. As Paul, he did not persecute the followers of Christ. He was an enemy of the Church as Saul. As Saul, he did not (S)upport the early church; however, he persecuted Christians. P has a soft and hard sound: Pe (pen) and Phe (Phenomena). For this reason, the use of "P" can be for good or bad. The letter gives host to many words representing authority: police, pope, power, pastor, preacher. How the power of "P" is used will always be judge by the eyes of history. God needed Paul to use his power for building the Church and not the destruction of the church. God changed his name from Saul (S)amekh) to Paul. Surely Paul conferred power to the Christians of that day and the same can be said of Peter and the Popes. Peter is considered the Father of Catholicism but as a follower of Christ, he demonstrated his two sided nature when denied Jesus. Peter also-ran out on Jesus before Jesus went to the cross. History clearly proves the two-sided nature of many of the Popes throughout history.

The Greeks adopted Pe from the Phoenicians and changed it to Pi and they reversed the glyph as well which looked like the number 7. It was the Romans who enclosed the top circle and changed Pi to P then it became the 16th letter of the English alphabet. P has a value of 80 in the Bible, which means this is letter social reformation and social authority. P is an excellent first name letter because it makes the owner strong. If not tempered, the owner can be too strong and become a tyrant.

(P) Questions:
1. Are you a mouthpiece for The Kingdom?
2. Do you demonstrate soft and hard speech by speaking curses and blessings?
3. To the Church leaders, are abusive of your powers?

TZ

FISH HOOK

The Charge of Tzaddai: To strive for righteousness, Demonstrate acts of kindness in our homes and communities, Charity, Social Tithing, See the good in yourself and others. Avoid being Merciless, Uncompassionate, Mean, Greedy, Self Serving.

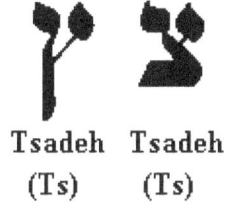

Tsadeh   Tsadeh
(Ts)   (Ts)

TZADDI

HEBREW LETTER: TZADDAI
SYMBOL: HOOK OR SCYTHE
ENGLISH VERSION: J or Y
ORIGINAL PHOENICIAN: Tzaddi
GREEK VERSION: NA
ROMAN VERSION: NA

BIBLICAL VERSE: PSALM 119: 137-144
Thy word is very pure
137: Righteous art thou, O LORD, and upright are thy judgments.
138: Thy testimonies that thou hast commanded are righteous and very faithful.
139: My zeal hath consumed me, because mine enemies have forgotten thy words.
140: Thy word is very pure: therefore thy servant loveth it.
141: I am small and despised: yet do not I forget thy precepts.
142: Thy righteousness is an everlasting righteousness, and thy law is the truth.
143: Trouble and anguish have taken hold on me: yet thy commandments are my delights.
144: The righteousness of thy testimonies is everlasting: give me understanding, and I shall live.

HISTORY:
Tzaddi is the 18th letter of the Hebrew alphabet. The meaning of Tzaddi is often described by the fishhook symbol of the letter "J" although Tzaddi is representing the Greek Iota and Roman and English letter "I". The letters Y, I and J were used interchangeably at time in history.

Therefore, many writers use the letter J to describe the meaning of Tzaddi. For this work, I describe Tzaddi through Yod. Tzaddi in my view has a closer relation to Yod than J because the letter J is a young letter created about 500 years ago.

The letter J does not have the historical depth to contain the meaning of Tzaddi. Yod is known as the hand, which is used to handle the fishhook of letter "J". One attribute of Tzaddi is to handle and manage. Tzaddi symbolizes salvation or damnation. Tzaddi is related to the Hebrew root for *righteous, just and honest*. In fact, Tzaddi is righteousness. Take notice on how often the word righteous is used for Tzaddi in PSALM 119: 137-144. We see the same idea being expressed in proverbs 10:25 "When the storm has swept by, the wicked are gone, but the righteous stand firm forever". Tzaddi teaches us to produce righteousness in our lives and in our communities. Also, concerning righteousness, Jesus says in Matt 7:12 *"So in everything, do to others what you would have them do to you, for this sums up the Law and the Prophets"*.

(TZ) Questions
1. Can you consistently demonstrate Tzaddi in your personal life?
2. Do you understand the relationship between righteousness and the principles of non-violence?
3. Have you demonstrated the meaning of Tzaddi in your community.

The Charge of QOPH: To obtain physical Wholeness, To obtain spiritual Holiness, To walk in wisdom and intelligence, To demonstrate spiritual intelligence. Lastly, to praise our God with ceaseless prayers! Avoid wickedness, Foolishness, Folly and Pride.

Qof
(Q)

HEBREW LETTER: KOPH/QOPH/KUF
SYMBOL: BACK OF THE HEAD, MONKEY
ENGLISH VERSION: Q
ORIGINAL PHOENICIAN: QOPH
GREEK VERSION: QOPPA
ROMAN VERSION: Q

BIBLICAL VERSE: PSALM 119: 145-152
Thy commandments are truth
145: I cried with my whole heart; hear me, O LORD: I will keep thy statutes.
146: I cried unto thee; save me, and I shall keep thy testimonies.
147: I prevented the dawning of the morning, and cried: I hoped in thy word.
148: Mine eyes prevent the night watches, that I might meditate in thy word.
149: Hear my voice according unto thy lovingkindness: O LORD, quicken me according to thy judgment.
150: They draw nigh that follow after mischief: they are far from thy law.
151: Thou art near, O LORD; and all thy commandments are truth.
152: Concerning thy testimonies, I have known of old that thou hast founded them for ever.

HISTORY:
The letter Q is related to the Hebrew Quoph (the back of the head). This is symbolic of the pineal gland and pituitary glands found in the back of the head. This is why Q is associated with growth and holiness. In addition, Q is associated with the Monkey.

The Monkey is considered to be intelligent in many cultures. As a result, many people eat Monkey brains to inherit its intelligence. 2 Chronicles 9:21 mention wise Solomon as having apes and baboons as part of his ship inventory. *"The king had a fleet of trading ships manned by Hiram's men. Once every three years it returned, carrying gold, silver and ivory, and apes and baboons".* The Hebrews borrowed the Quoph from the Phoenicians but the Hebrew sound was voiceless. This letter was pronounced with the back of the tongue touching the soft palate of the mouth. The Greeks changed Quoph to Quoppo/Koppa but they kept one of the original Phoenician symbols (the lollipop), which had a (K) sound. The sound of Quoph did not have a place in the Greek Script because they had K from Kappa. Therefore, it was not included in the script. The Romans then placed the line outside the circle then they curved the line to the right to arrive at the English Q.

Q is a letter of balance and reflection, inner vision, self-development, identification and resolution. Notice the word *Question* which leads to a resolution. The cue ball (q sound) is the ball used to coordinate a game of Pool (eight ball). A (q)uest leads to resolution and identification. A (q)uery retrieves specific information. A (q)uote is a specific reference to information. This is the nature of Q, which has a value of 100 in the Bible. Q is also a letter of Holiness because it is related to the Hebrew *Kedushah*, which means *holiness.* We also see another Hebrew word Kiddish, which means, "to make holy". The letter Q represents cycles, intelligence and spiritual awareness. Q teaches us to remain balanced in the physical and spiritual realm. In other words, we can achieve wholeness in the physical by being whole and not in part like a fraction. Also, we can become *Holy* in the spirit by constantly moving into higher cycles of wisdom in the Knowledge of self, other than self and the knowledge of God. As the heavenly Father revealed to me years ago, true spirituality is not solely based on action but awareness. A person is spiritual when they become aware and conscience of demonic and angelic activity.

(Q) Questions:
1. Do you have spiritual intelligence
2. Are you on the road to spiritual holiness?

THE HEAD

The Charge Of Resh: Discernment, Reformation, Refraining From Finger-Pointing, Avoid Being Judgmental, Maintain Personal Strength. Avoid Vanity, Embrace The Spirit Of Humility.

Resh
(R)

R

HEBREW LETTER: RESCH
SYMBOL: HEAD, CHIEF, BEGINNING, POOR MAN
THE ENGLISH VERSION: R
ORIGINAL PHOENICIAN: RESCH
GREEK VERSION: RHO
ROMAN VERSION: R

BIBLICAL VERSE: PSALM 119: 153-160
Great are thy Tender Mercies
153: Consider mine affliction, and deliver me: for I do not forget thy law.
154: Plead my cause, and deliver me: quicken me according to thy word.
155: Salvation is far from the wicked: for they seek not thy statutes.
156: Great are thy tender mercies, O LORD: quicken me according to thy judgments.
157: Many are my persecutors and mine enemies; yet do I not decline from thy testimonies.
158: I beheld the transgressors, and was grieved; because they kept not thy word.
159: Consider how I love thy precepts: quicken me, O LORD, according to thy loving-kindness.
160: Thy word is true from the beginning: and every one of thy righteous judgments endureth forever

HISTORY:

The letter R is related to the Hebrew Resh (head). This letter describes moving from a central point to another. R is also a diplomatic letter as expected by having a numerical value of 200 according to the Bible (PSALM 119: 153-160). R is a popular letter used in many American names. R is a letter of repetition (Repeat). The brain operates based on repetition. Thoughts are repetitious. Thoughts produce words and words produce action. Moreover, dark repetitious thought leads to dark words and dark action. Holy (other) repetitious thoughts lead to holy words and Holy actions.

Resh, (pronounced Rayesh) is the 20th letter of the Hebrew alphabet and it means head. R is symbolic of the pineal gland. It has a round shape with two cords, which connect to the brain. The letter has many negative associations such as Rude, Robber, Rebel, Ruffian, Rough, Rat, Red (blood and war), Rust (decay).

When positive, R is a letter of discernment. R has tremendous (r)eaching and reformative abilities. The brilliant strengths and weaknesses can cause this letter to head down the w(r)ong (R)oad. How does one manage the R? Study the number two. Resh shares the same root as the Hebrew rosh, which means beginning, new and head. The Jewish Holiday Rosh Hashanah means "head of the year". In English, R is letter passion and arousal: rage, rape, ravage, rub, ride, race, ripe, rose and romance. Resh is also associated with physical and spiritual poverty. In Proverbs 28:19, we read *"He who works his land will have abundant food, but the one who chases fantasies will have his fill of poverty"*. The book of proverbs addresses the management of thoughts and actions, which is wisdom. Resh is a thinking letter. Proverbs 28:19 address those who chase fantasies, which start in the head. Poverty is one of the key definitions for this sacred letter. Our thought life will either bring us richness or poverty. This letter challenges us to be aware of the position and condition of our thought life. Do we harbor vain thoughts and desires, which lead to physical, emotional, mental and spiritual poverty? Or, do we harbor rich thoughts that lead to a life abundance?

What else can we learn from the letter R? This letter teaches us how to avoid the depths of the lower self and destructive repetitive behavior. Resh teaches us how to manage the repetitious process of our thoughts, which nobody can do for us but our selves. Have you ever met a person who thinks suspiciously and negatively of people or situations in their lives or their loved ones. Most people are up to "no good "in their eyes. Be weary of such people because it means they have something in their character which needs deliverance. This letter shows the power of repentance. Repent means change. The prefix "Re" places an emphasis on repentance by suggesting that one should always continue repeat the process of changing and to never give up. Either we can rebel or receive restoration and reach new heights in higher man. Look at the reversed prefix in the word 'higher', 'er' or 're' in reverse.

We must become accountable for our thought life. Accountability is beginning of freedom from bondage, irresponsibility, addiction and a life filled with stagnation. I encourage you to account for how you think and behave and there real freedom will be found. Think about what you think about. Are you a giver or a taker? Do scheme, plot and destroy or do you exhort, edify and comfort? By our thought life, we can either ascend to the heights of heaven or descend into poverty. The height of heaven in this case refers to traveling high in the mind into the spirit realm to bask in the presence of God.

(R) Questions:
1. Have you ever basked in the presence of God
2. Do you use your intelligence for good or evil?
3. Are you rich in the body and poor in the spirit?
4. Are your passions rooted in the things of this world?

S

THE TOOTH

The Charge Of Schin: Joy, Change, Peace, Satisfaction. To Avoid Anger, Lust, Jealousy And Fleshly Greed.

Shin
(Sh/S)

S

HEBREW LETTER: SCHIN
SYMBOL: TOOTH, SERPENT'S FANG TO TEACH
ENGLISH VERSION: S (SCHIN/SIN)
ORIGINAL PHOENICIAN: SCHIN
GREEK VERSION: SIGMA
ROMAN VERSION: S

BIBLICAL VERSE: PSALM 119: 161-168
Great peace have they which love thy law
161: Princes have persecuted me without a cause: but my heart standeth in awe of thy word.
162: I rejoice at thy word, as one that findeth great spoil.
163: I hate and abhor lying: but thy law do I love.
164: Seven times a day do I praise thee because of thy righteous judgments.
165: Great peace have they which love thy law: and nothing shall offend them.
166: LORD, I have hoped for thy salvation, and done thy commandments.
167: My soul hath kept thy testimonies; and I love them exceedingly.
168: I have kept thy precepts and thy testimonies: for all my ways are before thee.

HISTORY:

The letter S is related to the Semetic *Shin, which* means *tooth*. The tooth is used to consume food for nourishment. Schin means enough or to be satisfied. Schin also means *peace* (Shalom), change and fire. Schin teaches us to be satisfied and to avoid being Schin has numerical value of 300 in the Bible (PSALM 119: 161-168).

ungrateful or unsatisfied. This letter is the 19th letter of the English alphabet. Next to the number twenty three (23), Nineteen (19) is one of the most fortunate numbers in the number system.

The S resembles a portion of the number 8 therefore sharing the controlling nature of the eight. The serpent tried to control Eve to consume the fruit in the Garden by way of the question. The letter S is a letter of preparation, consumption, digestion, nutrition and growth. This letter is known for its transmuting abilities. The letter S is used for plurals: girls, cats, dogs.

The letter S is also used for possession and plurality: my glove's, cars, and hats. The letter S is also shaped like a snake or serpent, in this case the change is seen when the snake sheds its old skin. Schin has two sounds: S and SH. Schin gave birth to several powerful names of God and other words which include Shalom, Shaddai, Shabott and Shekinah. Schin is a powerful letter.

What can we learn from schin? This letter teaches us to be careful of what we consume and what we suggest other people to consume. For example, drug dealers assist drug users with the consumption of drugs. Supply and demand can be deadly outside the will of God. The works of our hands shall surely follow us.

(S) Questions:
1. Are you self centered and consuming in any areas of your personal life?
2. Have you helped anyone consume a dangerous lifestyle or substance?
3. Are there areas of greed in your life: food, money, things, and sex?
4. What are currently sinking your teeth into?

T

THE CROSS

The Charge Of Tau: Completion, Decision, Steadiness, Fortitude. Repair Broken Relations. Avoid Pessimism, Refrain From Being Cold And Sharp.

Tav
(T)

T

HEBREW LETTER: Tau or Tav
SYMBOL: CROSS
ENGLISH VERSION: T
ORIGINAL PHOENICIAN: TETH
GREEK VERSION: TAU
ROMAN VERSION: T

BIBLICAL VERSE: PSALM 119: 169-176
I have longed for thy salvation
169: Let my cry come near before thee, O LORD: give me understanding according to thy word.
170: Let my supplication come before thee: deliver me according to thy word.
171: My lips shall utter praise, when thou hast taught me thy statutes.
172: My tongue shall speak of thy word: for all thy commandments are righteousness.
173: Let thine hand help me; for I have chosen thy precepts.
174: I have longed for thy salvation, O LORD; and thy law is my delight.
175: Let my soul live, and it shall praise thee; and let thy judgments help me.
176: I have gone astray like a lost sheep; seek thy servant; for I do not forget thy commandments.

HISTORY:
The letter T is related to the Semetic TAU which means mark, sign or impression. Teth has a numerical value of 400 in the Bible (PSALM 119: 169-176). Tau, the 22nd letter of the Hebrew alphabet, means the *sign of the cross* The nature of this letter is visible in the letter C and the symbol of the cross. The cross represents right and wrong, good and bad, up and down. The Cross symbolizes position or coordinates. Christ was positioned to die for the sins of the world. The letter T is known to save or slay, such was the case when Jesus was on the cross.

Yes, Jesus loves us but do not forget, love was not his primary motivation. Jesus wanted out; he did not want to go through the crucifixion. What drove Jesus to finish his calling? Obedience to the will of the Father was his main motivation. Jesus did not say anything about love while in the Garden talking to the Father. *Mark 14:33-36 (KJV) And he taketh with him Peter and James and John, and began to be sore amazed, and to be very heavy; [34] And saith unto them, My soul is exceeding sorrowful unto death: tarry ye here, and watch. [35] And he went forward a little, and fell on the ground, and prayed that, if it were possible, the hour might pass from him. [36] And he said, Abba, Father, all things are possible unto thee; take away this cup from me: nevertheless not what I will, but what thou wilt.*

So what is the point? Obedience is a position and love is a thought or a feeling for many. What Jesus did on the cross had nothing to do with how he felt about you or me or even himself. Jesus said "take this cup away". His position was to do the will of the Father which does not require our thoughts or feelings. Tau reminds us to be mindful our position in life and our position regarding obedience to the voice of God. Seeking the presence, and voice of the Father has it benefits. The desire to seek the presence of the Father is personal. Sometimes, we must to do things for ourselves. I meet so many people whose relationship with the Father is based on a man made religion or faith. We must desire to serve the Lord in spirit and truth and not the creed of religion. Our position and coordinates (Tau) in life must head in a direction that will invoke the presence of God the Father in our lives. Genesis 26:4-5 (KJV) *And I will make thy seed to multiply as the stars of heaven, and will give unto thy seed all these countries; and in thy seed shall all the nations of the earth be blessed; [5] Because that Abraham obeyed my voice, and kept my charge, my commandments, my statutes, and my laws.* This means the letter T is dualistic in nature. Jesus could have chosen to run out of the Garden. That would have been the best time to back out. Once he got on that cross, he would have had to violate the laws of this natural world to get off. Jesus took a position of obedience and went through the crucifixion.

The letter T represents change. I am so happy Christ Jesus did not change his mind in the Garden of Gethsemane. Concerning the letter "T", notice the word "twin". Who is the evil twin? Also recall the stereotype of the terrible two's for the age of children. In this case, two implies good or evil (positive and negative) will result if there are two objects or events: Cain and Abel, Adam and Eve, Sampson and Delilah, David and Goliath, King Kong and Godzilla, Man and Woman, Dog and Cat, Cat and Mouse, Hell and Heaven, Death and Life and sadly the Twin Towers. Teth and Tau refer to the English T. Teth, the ninth letter of the Hebrew alphabet and means roof or serpent.

(T) Questions:
1. Are you good, evil or both?
2. Are there any relationships in your life that you can repair?
3. What impression do you leave in the minds of those in your family and community?

Chapter 6:

THE MEANING OF SINGLE AND DOUBLE-DIGIT NUMBERS IN SCRIPTURE

As Disciples of Christ, we are challenged to manifest the constructive side of every number and letter. Also, we need to remember the negative and destructive side of each. Remembering the meaning of each side of every number will help us to maintain a level of accountability for our actions. Secular numerology impresses the individual to study his or her own numbers and letters which only takes the Kingdom of Heaven and God out of the equation. Numbers are used for prediction. Numbers are used for accountability and what I call "Christain-Metrics". Meaning, we can maximze our use of the Scriptures by measuring our thoughts, words and deeds. There is only so much a person can blame on the Devil. The time has come for us to know who we are and know our capabilities, both good and bad. Our birth date cannot change and neither can its meaning. The meaning of the birthdate is paramount in understand when and why we are called to this Earth. Like Jeremiah, we are called for a purpose. Lastly, the Holy Spirit has impressed upon me to tell the people of God to be weary of prediction because many have been unlawfully stealing and releasing information into the Earth. Many of the people cal themselves psychics and prophets and we must be faithful that we will hear from the Father concerning our affairs.

1

UNITY – LEADERSHIP – PIONEER-INDEPENDENCE

IN REVERSE

DIVISION – FOLLOWER – STAGNATE - DEPEDENT

The number one comes in four flavors which are 1, 10, 19 and 28.

This is known as the one line or one family.

1 is a single digit number which cannot be reduced.

10 is a compound number which can be reduced by adding 1 + 0 which equals 1.

19 is a compound number which can be reduced by adding 1 + 9 which equals 10. When reduced again, 10 reduces to 1.

28 is a compound number which can be reduced by adding 2 + 8 which equals 10. When reduced again, 10 reduces to 1.

THE NUMBER ONE (1)

SCRIPTURE:
1:1 In the beginning God created the heaven and the earth.
1:2 And the earth was without form, and void; and darkness was upon the face of the deep. And the Spirit of God moved upon the face of the waters.
1:3 And God said, Let there be light: and there was light.
1:4 And God saw the light, that it was good: and God divided the light from the darkness.
1:5 And God called the light Day, and the darkness he called Night. And the evening and the morning were the first day.

Biblical Keywords:
Beginning, Created, Moved, Let there be, Called.

DESCRIPTION
The number one represents independence, unity, primacy and beginnings. One excludes difference because it is composed of itself and no other numbers. One is a number independence and leadership. There is power is oneness. We worship and serve one God and with one God there is one set of instructions. With one God, there is one faith. Two Gods produce two faiths and two instructions and this leads to a difference, which represents the number two. The power of one leads to holiness (wholeness). There is wisdom in oneness and this wisdom exists through the number one. The righteous and wise know the benefit of speaking one-way, acting one-way, walking one-way. Consider the direction of water flowing down a stream; it flows one-way, all the time. Water does not alternate its position. The direction of moving water is set and does not change. The wind blows in one direction. I never heard of an east west wind. There are many gods in pagan culture: rain god, river god, and grain god. Therefore there were many sacrifices to many deities. If there was a problem in the land, the people had to figure out which god was angry so they could offer the appropriate sacrifice.

Through the one and true living God, we have one God, one instruction and one Son who was sacrificed (Christ Jesus). The practice of sacrificing animals in the Bible is a pagan leftover revised by the coming of Christ Jesus. Discipleship in Christ is centered on oneness. Jesus said "The Father and I are one". Meaning, we are on the same page with the same agenda. In other words, Jesus is in full compliance with the will of the Father.

BIBLICAL EXAMPLES

EXAMPLE 1
The oneness of our God teaches us there is wisdom and understanding in oneness of thought, word and deed. We read in the Book of James 4:8 *Come near to God and he will come near to you. Wash your hands, you sinners, and purify your hearts, you double-minded.* We are reminded of not being double minded in Mathew 3:16 "no man can serve two masters". The New Testament highlights the wisdom of serving one God opposed to serving many.

EXAMPLE 2
EPH 4:4-6
There is one body and one spirit. One Lord, one faith, one baptism, one God and father of all, who is above all and through all and in all.
This passage reveals the power and effectiveness of having one God because there is efficiency in oneness. The God of Israel was one, not r three; there was no confusion. With many gods, come many spirits and many faiths and instructions. We serve one God and we have one faith and one Holy Ghost. In oneness, we remove spiritual confusion. Jesus called on the one Father. Jesus never called on "God", he called on the Father.

EXAMPLE 3
Isa 43:10-11 *Ye are my witnesses, saith the LORD, and my servant whom I have chosen: that ye may know and believe me, and understand that I am he: before me there was no God formed, neither shall there be after me.11 I, even I, am the LORD; and beside me there is no savior.*

Almighty God is confirming and affirming his oneness, and that he is the first, and there is none like him, neither will there be. Almighty God has no equals.

EXAMPLE 4
Genesis 6:13-16 (New International Version)
13 So God said to Noah, "I am going to put an end to all people, for the earth is filled with violence because of them. I am surely going to destroy both them and the earth. 14 So make yourself an ark of cypress wood; make rooms in it and coat it with pitch inside and out. 15 This is how you are to build it: The ark is to be 450 feet long, 75 feet wide and 45 feet high. 16 Make a roof for it and finish the ark to within 18 inches of the top. Put a door in the side of the ark and make lower, middle and upper decks.

This passage provides an excellent example and benefit of having one God because he received one instruction. Imagine if Noah was worshipping two Gods? As the Holy Spirit revealed to me, "With many gods, come many instructions". To worship one God means to follow and submit to the authority of one God. The number one teaches us how to lead and follow to become proficient leaders and followers.

2

DUALITY - PREPARATION - DECISION

IN REVERSE

SINGULARITY- DISORDER- FICKLE

The number two comes in four flavors which are 2, 11, 20 and 29.

This is known as the two line or two family.

2 is a single digit number which cannot be reduced.

11 is a compound number which can be reduced by adding 1 + 1 which equals 2.

20 is a compound number which can be reduced by adding 2 + 0 which equals 2.

29 is a compound number which can be reduced by adding 2 + 9 which equals 11. When reduced again, 11 reduces to 2.

THE NUMBER TWO (2)

SCRIPTURE:
GENESIS
1:6 And God said, Let there be a firmament in the midst of the waters, and let it divide the waters from the waters.
1:7 And God made the firmament, and divided the waters which were under the firmament from the waters which were above the firmament: and it was so.
1:8 And God called the firmament Heaven. And the evening and the morning were the second day.

BIBLICAL KEYWORDS: Firmament, Midst, Waters, Divide, From.

DESCRIPTION
The number two is a feminine number of duality, difference and division which can be good or evil. So it is with woman and man concerning Christ. Jesus is the second figure of the Godhead who brings light into the world. Two represents preparation, reformation and difference: light and dark, up and down, good and bad, left and right. In this passage, we look for key words like *division* and *midst* on the second day of creation. In fact, this is the only time this dual concept is expressed during the 7 days of creation. The second of any number, event or person can be good or evil because it represents difference. Consider the Evil Twin. Two can also represent fickleness due to difference by going back and forth on an issue.

Biblical Examples:

EXAMPLE 1
Mark 14:13
14:13 And he sendeth forth two of his disciples, and saith unto them, Go ye into the city, and there shall meet you a man bearing a pitcher of water: follow him.
This passage represents preparation. Mark sent two disciples to the city to look for a man carrying a jar of water so they would know the place to prepare for the Passover meal.

EXAMPLE 2
Gen 19:1
19:1 And there came two angels to Sodom at even; and Lot sat in the gate of Sodom: and Lot seeing them rose up to meet them; and he bowed himself with his face toward the ground;
Two Angels came to Sodom to warn Lot and his Wife. The two Angels are symbolic of Gods difference with the sin of Sodom. This number is also symbolic of the reformation about to take place in Sodom.

EXAMPLE 3
Exodus 27:7
And the staves shall be put into the rings, and the staves shall be upon the two sides of the altar, to bear it.
Two staves were placed on both sides of the altar to bear its weight. Likewise, a man and women bear the weight of a marriage to bring about change (altar and alter), they bear the weight of a community and a nation (reformation). A successful and healthy marriage produces a successful and healthy nation. Why, because two can make the difference.

EXAMPLE 4
Luke 17:35
17:32 Remember Lot's wife.
17:33 whosoever shall seek to save his life shall lose it; and whosoever shall lose his life shall preserve it.
17:34 I tell you, in that night there shall be two men in one bed; the one shall be taken, and the other shall be left.
17:35 Two women shall be grinding together; the one shall be taken, and the other left.
Two shall be in the field, the one shall be taken and the other left. The implication is that something good will happen for one and something bad will happen to the other, the one left behind. Lot's Wife was being fickle and indecisive by going back and forth concerning the life-style she was leaving behind. As a result of her fickleness she was turned into salt. Likewise, we must choose (two) to hear and obey for the voice of the Father or turn to salt.

In other words, we will not be sensitive to desire a taste for the presence of the Lord. Our taste will remain earth bound or "on the ground". If we want the Father, we must go after him and just like the cloud that covered the tent in Ex 40:36, then the glory of the Lord will fill our tabernacles as well. Lot and his wife were running from Sodom. We must do the opposite and run to the Lord because we have a taste for the flavor of his presence.

EXAMPLE 5
Gen 25:23-25

25:23 And the LORD said unto her, Two nations are in thy womb, and two manner of people shall be separated from thy bowels; and the one people shall be stronger than the other people; and the elder shall serve the younger.

Esau, the first-born, sold his birthright that he despised to the second born child Jacob. In this passage, two is symbolic of difference, decision and reformation. The number two reminds us that decisions can make the difference between operating as the head or the tail in any relationship. Our decisions will determine if we live a life of abundance and strength or serve from a position of weakness.

3

PROCESSES - CREATION - RULES

IN REVERSE

RECKLESSNESS - WASTE - LAWLESSNESS

The number three comes in four flavors which are 3, 12, 21 and 30.

This is known as the three line or three family.

3 is a single digit number which cannot be reduced.

12 is a compound number which can be reduced by adding 1 + 2 which equals 3.

21 is a compound number which can be reduced by adding 2 + 1 which equals 3.

30 is a compound number which can be reduced by adding 3 + 0 which equals 3.

THE NUMBER THREE (3)

SCRIPTURE:
GENESIS
1:9 And God said, Let the waters under the heaven be gathered together unto one place, and let the dry land appear: and it was so.
1:10 And God called the dry land Earth; and the gathering together of the waters called he Seas: and God saw that it was good.
1:11 And God said, Let the earth bring forth grass, the herb yielding seed, and the fruit tree yielding fruit after his kind, whose seed is in itself, upon the earth: and it was so.
1:12 And the earth brought forth grass, and herb yielding seed after his kind, and the tree yielding fruit, whose seed was in itself, after his kind: and God saw that it was good.
1:13 And the evening and the morning were the third day.

Biblical Keywords: Waters, Gathered, Together, Let, Appear, Dry Land, Bring Forth, Yielding, Fruit.

DESCRIPTION:
Three is an awesome number; it can be found everywhere in God's creation. The word "trinity" is not mentioned in the Bible but the power of three cannot be denied. This dynamic number defends the concept of the Holy Trinity. I have come to know the essence of the Father and the Son through this number. I have come into the knowledge of spiritual processes, if that makes sense. The number three is all about processes and the government of processes. The understanding of numbers in general and the number three will carry you to the doorway of the spirit realm in Christ Jesus. The Christian Trinity represents a process, not an absolute number. Because of logic, theology and religion, many people may never understand the trinity. Like the atom, this number requires years of study to completely under its function and place in our world. To understand the number three, one will need to study astronomy, mathematics, physics and most all, nature. Three is a number of manifestation, processes, creation and divine completeness.

We see another triune creation used to define a solid: length, width, and depth. The strength of a rope is not determined by second strand, or the fourth strand, but the third strand. King Solomon states in Ecclesiastes 4:12: "A three-ply cord is not easily severed." Three is the symbol for a cube (x^3). Three is used to define the creation of time: past, present and future. Human capability is defined by thought, word and deed. Three is a number of creativity and talent. Three is the supreme number for thought.

The number 3hree:
- Humanity may be God's greatest creation which was made in 3 parts: body, soul, spirit "I pray God your whole Spirit and Soul and Body be preserved..." 1 Thessalonians 5:23
- Atoms consist of three constituents: protons, neutrons, and electrons.
- There are 3 types of molecular bonds: Covalent, Ionic, and Polar.
- There are 3 substances metabolized for energy needs: Carbohydrates, Fats and Proteins
- White light is composed of three additive primary hues: red, green, and blue.
- There are three basic planes: Above- Surfaced- Beneath
- There are three basic Earth divisions: Core- Mantle- Crust.
- 3 layers of skin, the largest organ of the body: epidermis, dermis and hypodermis.
- Three parts to the ear: outer, middle and inner.
- The three phases of matter: solid, liquid and gas.
- 3 main arteries of the heart: circumflex, anterior interventricular, right coronary.
- There are three possible points of view for writing: 1st, 2nd, and 3rd, or me, you, and other.
- There are many three letter acronyms or abbreviations: NBA, NFL, AFC, NFC, CBS, NBC, ABC, FOX, UPS, your ABC's.

- The earth has a big number 3 stamped on it by being the third planet from the sun.
- God created the animals and they live in 3 areas: land, water and air.
- Water is made up of 3 parts (two parts hydrogen, one part oxygen)
- Air primarily consists of 3 parts: 78% nitrogen, 21% oxygen and 93% argon.
- The Bible consists of 66 books (3 x 22).
- The OT has 39 books (3 x 13).
- The NT has 27 books (3 x 9).
- There are 31,173 versus in the Bible (3 x 10,391)
- There are 23,214 versus in the OT (3 x 7738).
- There are 7959 versus in the NT (3 x 2653).
- There were 333 prophecies concerning the coming of Jesus Christ into the world.
- Jesus Christ was crucified at the age of 33
- The ministry of Jesus lasted 3 years.
- He spent nine (3 x 3) hours on the cross, with 3 of those hours in darkness.
- He was buried for 3 days and 3 nights, and resurrected on the 3rd day.
- In fact, the word three is mentioned in the Bible 543 (3 x 181) times!
- There are three branches of Government: Judicial, executive and legislative.

BIBLICAL EXAMPLES:

EXAMPLE 1
Psalms 23:4:
4: Yea, though I walk through the valley of the shadow of death, I will fear no evil: for thou art with me; thy rod and thy staff they comfort me.
The Staff is a crooked stick that is called an *ox-goad* (represents the "L") that is used by Shepherd to guide the sheep. The letter "L" comes from the Hebrew *Lamed, which* has a value of three. Faith is a process where the sheep allow the shepherd to his job. The sheep only have to concern themselves with eating, sleeping and walking. The good Shepherd will guide and protect his sheep.

EXAMPLE 2:
Leviticus, the 3rd book of the Bible, God is calling his people for real divine worship. The first letter of the word Leviticus (L) has a numerical value of three. "L" is known as the Outstretched Hand. In scripture, Almighty God is stretching out his hand to his people.
Jesus rose on the 3rd day, which is the resurrection or the creative fulfillment of a divine operation. (Salvation for humanity).

EXAMPLE 3:
Jesus suffered on the cross for 3 hours (6th hour - 9th hour). This represents divine completeness of God. The Trinity symbolizes the will of the Father for salvation to enter the world that humanity would have eternal life through Christ Jesus who suffered on the cross.

EXAMPLE 4:
We see the lawless nature of three in Exodus 5 when Moses wanted Pharaoh to let his people go. Moses wanted his to journey into the desert for 3 days and have a feast for God or face pestilence or the sword. The use of three in this chapter is symbolic of Pharaoh's heart not to respect or revere the God of the Israelites. Pharaoh had no fear for God.

Therefore, he did not respect God's command for his people. Pharaoh said "who is the Lord that I should obey his voice". The key word is "obey". The number three is all about rules and how to follow laws because three is a scattered, lawless number when destructive, like Pharaoh. The Holy Trinity is all about following rules. For example, as Disciples of Christ, we go through the Son to get to the Father. This simple rule knocks so many people out of the program. Why is this rule so important? It prevents polytheistic or pagan worship. Many people today still have Jesus and Father confused. In the Old Testament, we see the cloud, and the glory of the Lord and the use of animals for sacrifices. In the New Testament, we have the Father, the Son and Holy Ghost. The Father is preparing us to truly understand the power in unity and oneness through established rules and order. Therefore, we go through the Son to get to the Father.

In Exodus 15:22, Moses brought his people out of the desert Mariah after 3 days but the people were not allowed to drink the bitter water. After the people complained to Moses, he went to God who showed them a tree which fell into the water and made the water sweet. The tree had not choice but to obey. If the tree complied to God's instruction, what was pharaohs problem? Also, we see God creating, and performing a miracle on the 3rd day. Why did this happen, God performed a miracle because Moses followed the rules. The number three represents rules, processes and regulations.

4

FOUNDATION – METHODS – STRUCTURE - DEVOTION

IN REVERSE

RESTRICTION – PLODDING – REPRESSION - DULLNESS

In the Bible, four comes in four flavors which are 4, 13, 22 and 31.

This is known as the four line or four family.

4 is a single digit number which cannot be reduced.

13 is a compound number which can be reduced by adding 1 + 3 which equals 4.

22 is a compound number which can be reduced by adding 2 + 2 which equals 4.

31 is a compound number which can be reduced by adding 3 + 1 which equals 4.

THE NUMBER FOUR (4)

SCRIPTURE:
GENESIS
1:14 And God said, Let there be lights in the firmament of the heaven to divide the day from the night; and let them be for signs, and for seasons, and for days, and years:
1:15 And let them be for lights in the firmament of the heaven to give light upon the earth: and it was so.
1:16 And God made two great lights; the greater light to rule the day, and the lesser light to rule the night: he made the stars also.
1:17 And God set them in the firmament of the heaven to give light upon the earth,
1:18 And to rule over the day and over the night, and to divide the light from the darkness: and God saw that it was good.
1:19 And the evening and the morning were the fourth day

Biblical Keywords: Signs, Mark, Days, Years, Govern, Give, And Separate.

Description: The Biblical keywords indicate that "Four" plans and organizes all that has been created by thought. As the old saying goes "on four squares the city stands". Four is an earthly number, a material number pertaining to structure, planning and methods. Four represents material completeness where 3 represents divine completeness. The four elements are organized as earth, water, air, and fire. When one desires structure or organization, one thinks of four. When making a decision, one thinks of four. Consider a drink of alcohol. Despite influence and desire, what are the only choices?

1. Drink the alcohol
2. Do not drink the alcohol
3. Drink water or something else
4. Do not drink anything at all

This model works well when one needs direction on any subject.
When this number is considered during the planning phase, it forces the owner to think critically and not with emotions. Four is also a number methods, plans and foundation.

BIBLICAL EXAMPLES:

EXAMPLE 1
Genesis 15:16
16: But in the fourth generation they shall come hither again: for the iniquity of the Amorites is not yet full.
The number four in this scripture suggests a plan or foundation is in motion. We see the number four hundred in verse 13 (1 + 3 = 4 foundation) where Abram's seed would be in a strange land. This number symbolizes a change in foundation which is mentioned in verse 14 (1 + 4 = 5 grace) where Abram's seed will come out with great substance.

EXAMPLE 2
1 Kings 6:37
37: In the fourth year was the foundation of the house of the LORD laid, in the month Zif:
The key word for this scripture is "foundation" which describes the nature of the number four.

EXAMPLE 3
2 Kings 25:3
1: And it came to pass in the ninth year of his reign, in the tenth month, in the tenth day of the month, that Nebuchadnezzar king of Babylon came, he, and all his host, against Jerusalem, and pitched against it; and they built forts against it round about.
2: And the city was besieged unto the eleventh year of King Zedekiah.
3: And on the ninth day of the fourth month the famine prevailed in the city, and there was no bread for the people of the land.

4: And the city was broken up, and all the men of war fled by night by the way of the gate between two walls, which is by the King's garden: (now the Chaldees). The number four represents the lack organization and foundation. There was no bread for the people of the land during the fourth Hebrew month of Tammuz. The fourth month symbolizes the loss of structure and plans because the famine prevailed. Study the fourth month Tammuz in the Bible and take notice of what occurs regarding foundation.

5

ORGANIZE PEOPLE - CHANGE - FAVOR - MOVEMENT

<u>IN REVERSE</u>

MERCILESSNESS - STAGNATION - SOBOTAGE

In the Bible, five comes in four flavors which are 5, 14, and 23.

This is known as the five line or five family.

5 is a single digit number which cannot be reduced.

14 is a compound number which can be reduced by adding 1 + 4 which equals 5.

23 is a compound number which can be reduced by adding 2 + 3 which equals 5.

THE NUMBER FIVE (5)

SCRIPTURE:
GENESIS
1:20 And God said, Let the waters bring forth abundantly the moving creature that hath life, and fowl that may fly above the earth in the open firmament of heaven.
1:21 And God created great whales, and every living creature that *moveth*, which the waters brought forth abundantly, after their kind, and every winged fowl after his kind: and God saw that it was good.
1:22 And God blessed them, saying, Be fruitful, and multiply, and fill the waters in the seas, and let fowl multiply in the earth.
1:23 And the evening and the morning were the fifth day.

BIBLICAL KEYWORDS:
Fill, Forth, Moving Creature, Fly Above, Moveth, Fruitful, Multiply.

DESCRIPTION
Five is a number of change, morals, movements, grace, events and activity. Grace can be seen by what took place on the fifth day, everything that was created was given an opportunity to "BE" or exist. Five is a number of opportunity, chance and favor. The number five is stamped all over the word grace. There are five letters in the word grace. In Hebrew, the word grace totals 5: $g3 + r2 + a1 + c3 + e5 = 14$, $1+4 = 5$. If one thinks about it, grace is change if one is in an unfortunate position in life. Grace can come from any where but it means so much when grace is shown by the Father because it proves who is in charge. The scriptures are clear on the nature of this number because movement, change and chance are all associated with grace. The human hand has five fingers on each hand. Hands are used to move, change and provide opportunities. Humans also have five senses: touch, smell, taste, hearing, and sight. The human foot has five toes on each foot. Feet are designed to move the body from one position to another, which is change. Whenever, I see the number 5, I am looking for change and movement.

In Hebrew, the name Satan has a value of 5 and he is famous for taking humanity through change. In other words, grace is not the only side to this number. God's grace is constructive. Satan's grace is destructive.

Four represents the organization of things (material /earth/matter/mother). Five represents the organization of people. Five represents the organization of humanity for the purpose opportunity, chance, change and favor. We see five in action when God changed Abram's name to Abraham by adding the letter (H) as the fifth letter of Abram (M). What was the favor, opportunity, chance or change? God blessed his seed; that was his chance and change. By the way, the letter (M) has a numerical value of four in the Chaldean and Hebrew number systems. Therefore, in the name, we see the nature and character of a name being enhanced to bring about change for a people. We see God changing Abram's name to Abraham because the man using that name (Abram) could not bring about or reflect what God wanted to do with his seed. God found favor with Abram but the change came through Abraham. What about you and me? What is the meaning of your name?

We talked about five being a number of events, movements and activity. On the 5th day that Almighty God created the birds that *fly* and everything that *creepth* on the earth. The emphasis on movement is made clear by using *fish* for moving in the sea and *birds* flying in the air and *animals* moving on land. We see CREATION on land, air, and sea (3 creation), which has an environment to thrive in (4 structure), and they can MOVE about freely because of the opportunity or chance provided by Almighty God the Father (5 change, grace).

About God's grace, humans are undeserving of God's grace because we are ungrateful and destructive with our choices, but salvation is available through the Christ, the 13th disciple or Master disciple of the Father, 1 + 3 = 4 (foundation). Salvation is God's material plan for eternal life (through Jesus the Christ), which is displayed by the number five (5), the number of grace. The presence of grace counteracts the self-sabotaging and destructive nature by woman and man.

Five demonstrates that women and men need grace because we often work against ourselves. As a result, by faith, God the Father will provide an opportunity by way of grace. If you notice, there is a five-day grace period to pay bills before one receives a late notice. Grace is such a good thing; it also represents joy because we feel joy after God the Father shines his grace upon us.

BIBLICAL EXAMPLES:

EXAMPLE 1
Leviticus 23: 6-8
We see God's grace in action in the book of Leviticus 23: 6-8 where the death angel would pass over each doorpost that was covered with blood.
Passover was on 14th day of the Month Nisan. $1 + 4 = 5$.
Chapter 23 equals Five: $2+3 = 5$. The verse 6-8 equals Five: $6+8 = 14/5$

EXAMPLE 2
Psalm 5:11-12 (The fifth chapter)
5:11 But let all those that put their trust in thee rejoice: let them ever shout for joy, because thou defendest them: let them also that love thy name be joyful in thee.
5:12 For thou, LORD, wilt bless the righteous; with <u>favour</u> wilt thou compass him as with a shield.
Grace is operating with the number Five in this passage. Notice the key s words: rejoice and favor.

EXAMPLE 3
THE WOMEN AT THE WELL
John 4:18
16: Jesus saith unto her, Go, call thy husband, and come hither.
17: The woman answered and said, I have no husband. Jesus said unto her, Thou hast well said, I have no husband:
18: For thou hast had five husbands; and he whom thou now hast is not thy husband: in that saidst thou truly.
19: The woman saith unto him, Sir, I perceive that thou art a prophet.

This entire passage addresses the morality of the woman at the well. Moreover, this passage addresses the lack of effective change on behalf of the woman at the well. The number five has typically been associated with grace. However, morality and grace have a relationship. Show me an immoral and decadent society and I will show you a society lacking grace. Our morals have a direct impact on the display of grace we show our fellow man.

Concerning the woman at the well, Jesus knows that she does not have a Husband but he asked her to invite him outside anyway. She tells Jesus that she does not have a husband, which is true. Jesus gave her credit for not lying, but she is living a lie because the truth is, she had five failed marriages for whatever reason, and she has opted for shacking. Jesus told her she had five Husbands. We can speculate if she would have offered that information. For whatever reason, the woman and the man in the house are not married. The woman at the well does not feel good about this, so she tries to get Jesus off the topic by getting into this "you must be a Prophet thing", but Jesus did not fall for this verbal distraction. Here, we witness her living the lie by trying to distract Jesus instead talking to him about her lifestyle. She had enough reason to think he was a prophet, but let us say he was a prophet, was she interested in what he could offer? No, she wanted to keep living her lie (worrying about her image), and talk about something else when she could get a blessing and some real personal direction.

The number five in this passage symbolizes self-deception, self-sabotage, and moral corruption. This passage also represents the need for positive change in our lives. The lady at the wanted to keep her privacy and this was another form of self-deception. She was living a lie because she overlooked that Jesus knew her entire story anyway. Five, in this passage also shows that grace and change was available for the woman at the well because she was in the presence of Jesus. Think of the change, chance, opportunity and grace when one is confronted with the number five. How many stones did David use against Goliath? He picked up five smooth stones but only one was needed to bring about change.

6

SERVICE - WORK – RESPONSIBILITY - FAMILY

IN REVERSE

TYRANNY - IRON FIST - UNACCOUNTABILITY

The number six comes in four flavors which are 6, 15 and 24.

This is known as the six line or two family.

6 is a single digit number which cannot be reduced.

15 is a compound number which can be reduced by adding 1 + 5 which equals 6.

24 is a compound number which can be reduced by adding 2 + 4 which equals 6.

THE NUMBER SIX (6)

SCRIPTURE
GENESIS
1:24 And God said, Let the earth bring forth the living creature after his kind, cattle, and creeping thing, and beast of the earth after his kind: and it was so.

1:25 And God made the beast of the earth after his kind and cattle after their kind, and every thing that creepeth upon the earth after his kind: and God saw that it was good.

1:26 And God said, Let us make man in our image, after our likeness: and let them have dominion over the fish of the sea, and over the fowl of the air, and over the cattle, and over all the earth, and over every creeping thing that creepeth upon the earth.

1:27 So God created man in his own image, in the image of God created he him; male and female created he them.

1:28 And God blessed them, and God said unto them, Be fruitful, and multiply, and replenish the earth, and subdue it: and have dominion over the fish of the sea, and over the fowl of the air, and over every living thing that moveth upon the earth.

1:29 And God said, Behold, I have given you every herb bearing seed, which is upon the face of all the earth, and every tree, in the which is the fruit of a tree yielding seed; to you it shall be for meat.

1:30 And to every beast of the earth, and to every fowl of the air, and to every thing that creepeth upon the earth, wherein there is life, I have given every green herb for meat: and it was so.

1:31 And God saw every thing that he had made, and, behold, it was very good. And the evening and the morning were the sixth day.

BIBLICAL KEYWORDS:
Made, Good, Image, Created, Male and Female, Given, Bearing Seed, Living, Very Good.

DESCRIPTION:
By design, the number six is an incomplete eight. When writing the number the six, you start from the right, moving down a curve, and while in the motion of moving up off the curve, it stops. This geometric description describes why the number six is a number of incompletion or the number of humanity.

If the six was tilted up right and the motion was completed, it would be an eight, which is a number of new beginnings. This number reminds us that they are incomplete without good relations with ourselves and the Father. We must move to new beginnings (8) and stages (9) in all things to become whole or wholly. The number 15 uses the Devil as a symbol in the world of the occult. This means more than just being a Devil with a tail, and horns and hoofs. The nature of the Devil is to maintain incompleteness and confusion by being an adversary. Six shows the Devil in our lower nature. Six reminds us to not solely focus on external demonic forces, but to pay attention to the devil in each of us. Six symbolizes the need to be responsible because it is incomplete by design. This is why six represents responsibility love, and service. As Disciples of Christ, we are challenged to incorporate the constructive qualities of this number into our lives.

BIBLICAL EXAMPLES:

EXAMPLE 1
GENESIS 31:41
41: Thus have I been twenty years in thy house; I served thee fourteen years for thy two daughters, and six years for thy cattle: and thou hast changed my wages ten times.

The number six is associated with the verb **serve**; six is a number of work and service. Six in this passage represents the need to be responsible, domestic and demonstrate good work ethics. How could one be domestic and responsibly provide if there is no food (cattle). Also, the number 14 represents two sevens, one for each daughter. The two sevens form the Hebrew letter "Z" or *Zayin*. The symbol of "Z" is the arrow. The arrow symbolizes Jacob's focus. The number seven means to be satisfied, full or it's enough. The daughters were enough for a man living in a polygamous culture.

Jacob is satisfied, focused on his work, the task of providing service and being responsible.

EXAMPLE 2

EXODUS 35:2:
1: And Moses gathered all the congregation of the children of Israel together, and said unto them, these are the words which the LORD hath commanded, that ye should do them.
2: Six days shall work be done, but on the seventh day there shall be to you an holy day, a sabbath of rest to the LORD: whosoever doeth work therein shall be put to death.

The number six symbolizes work, responsibility, domestication and service. Work and service are key definitions for this number. What is work? Work is a service, it may be for profit or not but it is a service. Moreover, what happens when we fail to work? We become incomplete and eventually irresponsible. A person who is able to work and does not work is a danger to himself or herself and their entire family. Why? Irresponsibility and laziness opens the door to scandalous behavior that eventually leads to crime and incarceration. We must ensure we are not working from our lower nature as described by the destructive side of the number six.

NOTES ON GENESIS 31:41
20 symbolizes the awareness needed to maintain a family. He observed this in the Fathers house.
Ten symbolizes the on and off, and potluck nature of the "Wheel of Fortune". What will one have gained when the wheel stops. In this case, his wages went up and down (ten times).

7

ANALYLZE - REST - BRIDGE - SATISFY

IN REVERSE

DOUBT- FAITHLESS – ALOOFNESS - HESISTANT

In the Bible, seven comes in four flavors which are 7, 16, and 25.

This is known as the seven line or seven family.

7 is a single digit number which cannot be reduced.

16 is a compound number which can be reduced by adding 1 + 6 which equals 7.

25 is a compound number which can be reduced by adding 2 + 5 which equals 7.

THE NUMBER SEVEN (7)

SCRIPTURE:
GENESIS
2:1 Thus the heavens and the earth were finished, and all the host of them.
2:2 And on the seventh day God ended his work which he had made; and he rested on the seventh day from all his work which he had made.
2:3 And God blessed the seventh day, and sanctified it: because that in it he had rested from all his work which God created and made.

BIBLICAL KEYWORDS:
Finished, Ended, Rested, Sanctify.

DESCRIPTION:

In Hebrew, the number Seven derived from the Hebrew word *shevah* which comes from the root word *savah*. It means to be full, satisfied or have enough. God rested on the 7th day because it was enough. Seven represents analytical thought. God was analyzing his work from day one. We read that he "saw that it was good." This implies a review or a double check took place. Be not deceived, God did not check to see if it was good everyday, take a look for yourself. What would have God done if he saw that it was not good? How would he know that is was not good? Almighty God checked, and reviewed his work, and saw that it was good. Seven represents analytical thinking, unlike three which represents creative thinking and processes. Seven does not represent completion because rarely is anything complete. Just because something is finished does not mean it is complete. Only the Father is complete. This number means to be full satisfied or enough not complete. I cautiously use the word *complete*. The number seven is also a number of perfection. We see this in Joshua 20:16 *Among all these soldiers there were seven hundred chosen men who were left-handed, each of whom could sling a stone at a hair and not miss.*

BIBLICAL EXAMPLES:

EXAMPLE 1
GENESIS 7: 2-5
2: Of every clean beast thou shalt take to thee by sevens, the male and his female: and of beasts that are not clean by two, the male and his female.
3: Of fowls also of the air by sevens, the male and the female; to keep seed alive upon the face of all the earth.
4: For yet seven days, and I will cause it to rain upon the earth forty days and forty nights; and every living substance that I have made will I destroy from off the face of the earth.
5: And Noah did according unto all that the LORD commanded him.

The above passage symbolizes the number *Seven* being enough. Also, striving for cleanliness is satisfying in the eyes of God. Uncleanliness represents "difference", the opposite of being clean. There were 14 doves (clean) and four Ravens (unclean) in the Ark. One of the unclean Ravens was used to determine the difference between land dryness before and after the flood. The Raven was not expected to return. Noah expected the Raven to keep flying back and forth until food was located. Noah would have known the land was dry if he never saw the Raven flying back and forth.

EXAMPLE 2
Genesis 7: 9-10
9: There went in two and two unto Noah into the ark, the male and the female, as God had commanded Noah.
10: And it came to pass after seven days that the waters of the flood were upon the earth.

There were seven days of drought. Seven means "enough" now it is time for water in the form of a flood. This occurred on the eighth day, but the seventh day was "enough", and represented the last day of "no water"

EXAMPLE 3
Genesis 8

1: And God remembered Noah, and every living thing, and all the cattle that was with him in the ark: and God made a wind to pass over the earth, and the waters assuaged;

2: The fountains also of the deep and the windows of heaven were stopped, and the rain from heaven was restrained;
3: And the waters returned from off the earth continually: and after the end of the hundred and fifty days the waters were abated.
4: And the ark rested in the seventh month, on the seventeenth day of the month, upon the mountains of Ararat.

In this passage, after the water finished its (work) in 150/6 days, it was "enough" and it was time to "rest" on the seventh month. (1+5=6)

EXAMPLE 4
Genesis 29

18: And Jacob loved Rachel; and said, I will serve thee seven years for Rachel thy younger daughter.
19: And Laban said, It is better that I give her to thee, than that I should give her to another man: abide with me.
20: And Jacob served seven years for Rachel; and they seemed unto him but a few days, for the love he had to her.
21: And Jacob said unto Laban, Give me my wife, for my days are fulfilled, that I may go in unto her.

The key word for this passage is <u>fulfilled</u>; again, seven means "enough". Jacob served seven years and it was enough. Now, give me the girl!

EXAMPLE 5
Exodus 25

37: And thou shalt make the seven lamps thereof: and they shall light the lamps thereof, that they may give light over against it.

Seven lamps will be enough, God is satisfied and the seven lamps represent the seven spirits of God.

EXAMPLE 6
Numbers 13:22

20: And what the land is, whether it be fat or lean, whether there be wood therein, or not. And be ye of good courage, and bring of the fruit of the land. Now the time was the time of the first ripe grapes.
21: So they went up, and searched the land from the wilderness of Zin unto Rehob, as men come to Hamath.
*22: And they ascended by the south, and came unto Hebron; where Ahiman, Sheshai, and Talmai, the children of Anak, were. (Now Hebron was built **seven** years before Zoan in Egypt.)*

Twelve spies went to survey the land of Canaan. Notice the key words: searched and built. These are key words describing the number Seven.

EXAMPLE 7
Leviticus 26

13: I am the LORD your God, which brought you forth out of the land of Egypt, that ye should not be their bondmen; and I have broken the bands of your yoke, and made you go upright.
14: But if ye will not hearken unto me, and will not do all these commandments;
15: And if ye shall despise my statutes, or if your soul abhor my judgments, so that ye will not do all my commandments, but that ye break my covenant:
16: I also will do this unto you; I will even appoint over you terror, consumption, and the burning ague, that shall consume the eyes, and cause sorrow of heart: and ye shall sow your seed in vain, for your enemies shall eat it.
17: And I will set my face against you, and ye shall be slain before your enemies: they that hate you shall reign over you; and ye shall flee when none pursueth you.
18: And if ye will not yet for all this hearken unto me, then I will punish you seven times more for your sins.

Seven times is enough, eight times would imply a new punishment will be administered.

8

NEW BEGININGS - CONTROL - EXECUTE - REFORM

IN REVERSE

OPPRESSION - INJUSTICE – STRAIN – STAGNATION - PRIDE

In the Bible, eight comes in three flavors, which are 8, 17 and 26.

This is known as the eight line or eight family.

8 is a single digit number which cannot be reduced.

17 is a compound number which can be reduced by adding 1 + 7 which equals 8.

26 is a compound number which can be reduced by adding 2 + 6 which equals 8.

THE NUMBER EIGHT (8)

In the Book of Genesis, the number eight was not used during Almighty God's creation of the world. Almighty God rested on the Seventh day, for everything was enough (7). Eight is the best number to follow seven because there was a new beginning on the horizon. Almighty God the Father set his creation in motion by letting it do what it is supposed do. Eight is represents execution, control, resurrection, vision, regeneration and lastly, new beginnings. The Hebrew number Eight comes from the Hebrew root word *shah'meyn* which means to *make fat or cover with fat or one who abounds in strength.* Eight is positioned between Seven and Nine; it is also a number of influence. Eight is the highest of the discernment and reformation numbers (2, 5). Eight is also a number of preparation. In the Chaldean number system, it represents the letters H, Q, and Z. In the Hebrew number system, eight represents the letters F and P. Eight represents the execution of a new step, process or order. Newness or new beginnings are always associated with this number in the Bible.

BIBLICAL EXAMPLES:

EXAMPLE 1
NOAH THE EIGHTH PERSON
II Peter 2:5
5: And spared not the old-world, but saved Noah the eighth person, a preacher of righteousness, bringing in the flood on the world of the ungodly;
Noah represents the **execution** of **new order** or a New World.

EXAMPLE 2
THE EIGHT SOULS
I Peter 3:20
20: Which sometime were disobedient, when once the long-suffering of God waited in the days of Noah, while the ark was a preparing, wherein few, that is, eight souls were saved by water.
In I Peter we see the biblical key word "prepare"; thus, eight souls were saved to be part of something new: A new beginning.

EXAMPLE 3
THE SIN OFFERING-Lev 9:1

1: And it came to pass on the eighth day, that Moses called Aaron and his sons, and the elders of Israel;
2: And he said unto Aaron, Take thee a young calf for a sin offering, and a ram for a burnt offering, without blemish, and offer them before the LORD.
3: And unto the children of Israel thou shalt speak, saying, Take ye a kid of the goats for a sin offering; and a calf and a lamb, both of the first year, without blemish, for a burnt offering.

The number eight in this passage symbolizes management and reformation of the people through the leadership of Moses and Aaron. There are two offerings mentioned in this passage: the sin offering and the burnt offering. We experience newness in our walk with God after we present an offering which is also a sacrifice. Our worship life will always carry us to a higher intimacy with Almighty God. Through Christ Jesus, we experience constant new beginnings with Almighty God. Worship, praise, sacrifice and our offerings will bring us into a New Beginning experience with the Father.

EXAMPLE 4
JOSIAH'S REIGN-II KING 22:1

1: Josiah was eight years old when he began to reign, and he reigned thirty and one years in Jerusalem. And his mother's name was Jedidah, the daughter of Adaiah of Boscath.

The emphasis for both examples is control and leadership of a group. In other words, an old fool can be a King or a young man with vision. It's not the age of the King per se but his ability to control and reform a group.

EXAMPLE 5
SOLEMN ASSEMBLY
2 Chr 7:8-9

8: Also at the same time Solomon kept the feast seven days, and all Israel with him, a very great congregation, from the entering in of Hamath unto the river of Egypt.
9: And in the eighth day they made a solemn assembly: for they kept the dedication of the altar seven days, and the feast seven days.

The execution of the solemn assembly began on the eighth day. God rested on the seventh day after creating the world. Though 'eight' is not mentioned per se, eight represents the execution of living out the entire creation event.

EXAMPLE 6
SOLEMN ASSEMBLY
Neh 8:18
18: Also day by day, from the first day unto the last day, he read in the book of the law of God. And they kept the feast seven days; and on the eighth day was a solemn assembly, according unto the manner.
The solemn assembly was held on the Eighth day.

EXAMPLE 7
THE LORD'S SORE DISPLEASURE
Zech 1:1
1: In the eighth month, in the second year of Darius, came the word of the LORD unto Zechariah, the son of Berechiah, the son of Iddo the prophet, saying,
2: The LORD hath been sore displeased with your fathers.
There are three sides to a number just as we live in three dimensional universe: length, depth and height. This scripture is revealing the abusive side of the eight regarding leadership and people. Eight can be tyrannical and deviant when negative.

EXAMPLE 8
Acts 7:8
CIRCUMCISION ON THE EIGHTH DAY & DELIVERANCE
7: And the nation to whom they shall be in bondage will I judge, said God: and after that shall they come forth, and serve me in this place.
8: And he gave him the covenant of circumcision: and so Abraham begat Isaac, and circumcised him the eighth day; and Isaac begat Jacob; and Jacob begat the twelve patriarchs.
The act of a new beginning regarding the circumcision is symbolically sealed by occurring on the eighth day.

9

STAGES - COMPASSION - MASS INFLUENCE

IN REVERSE

UNCOMPASSION - MATERIAL - GREED - STUCK

The number nine comes in four flavors which are 9, 18, 27.

This is known as the nine line or nine family.

9 is a single digit number which cannot be reduced.

18 is a compound number which can be reduced by adding 1 + 8 which equals 9.

27 is a compound number which can be reduced by adding 2 + 7 which equals 9.

THE NUMBER NINE (9)

DESCRIPTION

Completion or endings best describe the qualities of the number nine. Nine is the last of the single digit numbers (1-9). As well as nine ending the single digit numbers, it also escorts the end of all double and triple numbers: 19, 29, 109, 999, 5,999.

There are nine planets, nine systems in the human body: digestive, reproductive, muscular, urinary, endocrine, respiratory, circulatory, skeletal and cardiovascular. Jesus died in the ninth hour. Where eight speaks of new beginnings, nine speaks of endings, entrances and stages. Nine is associated with the planet Mars which is a plant of war, the red planet (mars/wars/men/women). The red planet denotes anger, blood and ill temperament. Nine is also an accelerated three (3): 3x3 = 9. In fact, multiplication is accelerated addition. Moreover, nine is a number of influences, and it should be, because it contains the essence of every number below it: 1-8 (1-alpha & 800-omega). Nine is more than just a number, sign, or symbol; it is a stage of existence. The numbers eight and nine were not mentioned in the story of creation in the book of Genesis, but they are there and in effect. After Almighty God rested on the seventh day (7), eight (8) marked a new beginning to execute the work of the first seven days. Nine (9) indicated the ending of the earth being without form and void. Thus the cycle of life was in motion. When nine is multiplied by any other number, it always reproduces itself.

BIBLICAL EXAMPLE

The Book of Job, the 18th book of the Bible. 1 plus 8 equals nine. The name Job totals nine: J1/O6/B2=9. And in the ninth chapter, Satan is suggesting to God that through material circumstance, he can get Job to curse God. In other words, Satan is suggesting he can get Job to operate on the negative side of his number. We do not have his birth date, but we do have Job's name number which is nine. Notice how wisely nine is encoded in this book. The definitions are in the stories and symbolically reinforced by book order, chapter and verse number.

EXAMPLE 1

Revelation 13:18
[18]This calls for wisdom. If anyone has insight, let him calculate the number of the beast, for it is man's number.

His number is 666. Many have been taught to pay attention to the three 6's but it is the number nine we should be watching. In fact, "THE BOOK OF REVELATION 13:18" equals 99/18/9. The name of Jesus has a value of nine. The word "Women" has a value of nine. However, the Dragon, which pursued the woman into the wilderness, has a numerical value of 4 that means the Dragon had a plan and the foundation to destroy the woman and her Child. Nine is a number of mass influences and a number of the people. Just as the ministry of Jesus appealed to women, this relationship is revealed in sign and symbol because Jesus and women share the same number which is nine. The value of a society is found in the character of its women.

    A Nation is destroyed when the women are tainted (influenced 9). Women as an institution have a numerical name value of nine. The name Jesus has a value of Nine. Jesus represents the constructive side of this number, which is

        compassion, love and mercy. Despite the individual name of any woman, all women are prophetically called to the constructive side of the Nine that is in Christ. The Beast mentioned in the Bible has a numerical value of nine. The beast represents the destructive side of the nine. There is a spiritual and physical battle currently taking place regarding the identity of all women. Unfortunately, many men have been agents of the enemy in oppressing the Godly ordained role of women worldwide.

10

TIMING AND ACCESS

THE NUMBER TEN (10)

TIMING AND ACCESS

The number ten, besides being a number of laws and commandments, represents timing and access. I will discuss Nehemiah, the ten gates, the ten spies, the ten virgins, and the ten lepers. Let us discuss the nature of this number before I use the scriptures. The number ten is a compound number composed of a"1" and "0". These two numbers, in appearance, are no different from the numbers 11-19. The number ten is different from most numbers because of the "1" and "0" because this number is not solely used for counting.

The number ten represents electrical current in the form of binary numbers. In computers, the number 10 appears similar to a binary number. Binary numbers are 1's and 0's. Binary numbers are either on or off, on = 1 and off =0. This may explain why the ancient Egyptians described the number ten as the wheel of fortune because the outcome could be good or bad, up or down. The Egyptian wheel of fortune probably appears similar to the wheel of fortune on Bob Barker's "The Price is Right". The wheel is spun and where it stops, nobody knows. Binary numbers represent electrical current used to power a computer. The entire computer processing cycle is based on the timing and access of data in the form of bits and bytes. In fact, without getting too technical, the control unit within the computer uses a system clock to synchronize instructions and data, by sending out electrical pulses. The number of these electrical pulses per second shows the speed of a processor.

EXAMPLE 1

Binary Numbers: What can binary numbers teach us about the number ten? The number ten is a number of timing, access, will and law. We often fail to follow God's will for our lives because of bad timing. Bad timing leads to missed opportunities. We will now see what we can learn about the number ten through the computer, specifically through binary numbers and the machine cycle process. The central processing unit (Often called CPU) is the brain of a computer and this is the location for processing data in the computer. The *cpu* is found on a circuit board or motherboard inside the PC. This control center is a complex and extensive set of electronic circuitry that executes stored program instructions. All computers, large and small, must have a central processing unit. A processor handles binary data in the form of bits and bytes. The processor will also retrieve data and perform processing on that data. The processor will also store the results in either its own internal memory, which is known as cache, or the systems memory. 8 bits make a byte. A **bit** refers to a digit in the base 2 binary numeral system. For example, the number 1001011 is 7 bits long. Binary digits are almost always used as the basic unit of information storage and communication in digital computing and digital information theory. Therefore, 8 bits make a byte. A **byte** is commonly used as a unit of storage measurement in computers, regardless of the data stored. In other words, letters and numbers represent bytes. A process called the machine cycle handles processing of bits and bytes

The Machine Cycle (personal computer)

Fetch -   get an instruction from Main Memory

Decode - translate it into computer commands

Execute - actually process the command

Store -   write the result to Main Memory

The Gospel of Numbers and Letters in Scripture

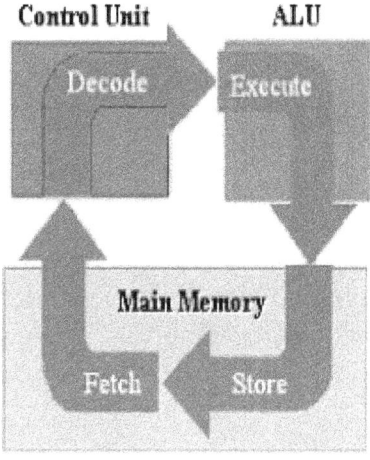

For instance, to add the numbers 1 and 2 and show the answer on the screen requires the following steps:

1. Fetch instruction: "Get number at address 1a2b3c"

2. Decode instruction.

3. Execute: The ALU finds the number. *(which happens to be 1)*

4. Store: The number 1 is stored in a temporary spot in Main Memory.

5 - 8 Repeat steps for another number (− 2)

9. Fetch instruction: "Add those two numbers" 1+2

10. Decode instruction.

11. Execute: ALU adds the numbers 1+2.

12. Store: The answer is stored in a temporary spot "3".

13. Fetch instruction: "Display answer on screen." "3"

14. Decode instruction.
15. Execute: Display answer on screen. "3"

In order for the end-user to have information appear on the screen, the computer must have proper timing so data can have access to system resources such as memory and storage,

EXAMPLE 2
The Ten Spies
NUMBERS 14:36-39

36Then the ten scouts who had incited the rebellion against the LORD by spreading discouraging reports about the land 37were struck dead with a plague before the LORD. 38Of the twelve who had explored the land, only Joshua and Caleb remained alive. 39When Moses reported the LORD's words to the Israelites, there was much sorrow among the people. 40So they got up early the next morning and set out for the hill country of Canaan. "Let's go," they said. "We realize that we have sinned, but now we are ready to enter the land the LORD has promised us."

In the passage above, we read about the ten spies in the book of Numbers in the Bible. Twelve spies were sent to Canaan to survey the land. The Amalekites and Canaanites are native inhabitants of Canaan. Yahweh is giving the land to the Israelites. The Israelites sent spies to survey the land before they went to war with the Amalekites and Canaanites. Twelve spies went but the group was split into two groups. Ten spies said there were giants in the land and provided a false report to Moses and Aaron. Two did not provide a false report. In fact, those two, Joshua and Caleb encouraged the Israelites by saying they could take the land despite the inhabitants who they did not see as giants. Again, we see the number two which is a number of *differences.* We talked about the number ten being a binary number where 1 is on and 0 is off. In the book of Numbers we see two reports, one is on (Caleb & Joshua) and the other off (ten spies).

What was the purpose of sending the spies? The purpose of using spies was to provide the Israelites with an idea about the conditions they would face when they waged war against the Amalekites and Canaanites. The two reports were critical. If the Israelites listened to the ten spies, the Israelites may have become filled with fear. The Israelites may have decided to not take the land and wage war against the Amalekites and Canaanites. The ten spies were also killed for their misuse of time:

Numbers:14:*34 "Because the men who explored the land were there for forty days, you must wander in the wilderness for forty years--a year for each day, suffering the consequences of your sins. You will discover what it is like to have me for an enemy.' 35I, the LORD, have spoken! I will do these things to every member of the community who has conspired against me. They will all die here in this wilderness!"*

The number ten teaches us to be aware of timing and the will of God for our lives. We must know his voice and be willing to move in the proper season. We must move at the proper time to have access to what belongs to us. If our timing is off, then we will miss a point of access and hit a wall or in the reverse a law or law.

EXAMPLE 3
Story of the Ten Bridesmaids
Matthew 25:1-13
1"The Kingdom of Heaven can be illustrated by the story of ten bridesmaids who took their lamps and went to meet the bridegroom. 2Five of them were foolish, and five were wise. 3The five who were foolish took no oil for their lamps, 4but the other five were wise enough to take along extra oil. 5When the bridegroom was delayed, they all lay down and slept. 6At midnight they were roused by the shout, `Look, the bridegroom is coming! Come out and welcome him!' 7"All the bridesmaids got up and prepared their lamps. 8Then the five foolish ones asked the others, `Please give us some of your oil because our lamps are going out.' 9But the others replied, `We don't have enough for all of us. Go to a shop and buy some for yourselves.' 10"But while they were gone to buy oil, the bridegroom came, and those who were ready went in with him to the marriage feast, and the

door was locked. 11Later, when the other five bridesmaids returned, they stood outside, calling, `Sir, open the door for us!' 12But he called back, `I don't know you!' 13"So stay awake and be prepared, because you do not know the day or hour of

The number ten in this passage reveals this number is not solely associated with laws and commandments. This passage is all about timing and access. We see the number 2 which is number of difference and preparation. There are ten bridesmaids but there two groups. One group is foolish and the other group is wise. The wise group brought extra oil for their lamps while the five foolish brides did not bring extra oil for their lamps. When the bridegroom appeared, the five foolish women started asking the five wise bridesmaids for some of their oil. The five foolish bridesmaids were not able to go with the bridegroom. The five foolish bridesmaids were standing in front of a locked door knocking and begging to get in. They missed an opportunity to have a husband and did not have ACCESS to the bridegroom. One group was on (Wise) and the other group was off (Foolish).

EXAMPLE 4
Ten Healed of Leprosy
Luke 17:11-19

11As Jesus continued on toward Jerusalem, he reached the border between Galilee and Samaria. 12As he entered a village there, ten lepers stood at a distance, 13crying out, "Jesus, Master, have mercy on us!" 14He looked at them and said, "Go show yourselves to the priests." And as they went, their leprosy disappeared. 15One of them, when he saw that he was healed, came back to Jesus, shouting, "Praise God, I'm healed!" 16He fell face down on the ground at Jesus' feet, thanking him for what he had done. This man was a Samaritan. 17Jesus asked, "Didn't I heal ten men? Where are the other nine? 18Does only this foreigner return to give glory to God?" 19And Jesus said to the man, "Stand up and go. Your faith has made you well."

We have talked about the number ten being a number of timing and access. This is also a number of laws commandments. We need an example of this number operating in the confines of timing and access. In Luke 17:11, we read about ten lepers who saw Jesus walking along the border between Galilee and Samaria. When they saw Jesus, they yelled out to him *"Jesus, Master, have mercy on us"*. Let us stop right here for one second. Jesus was on the border between Galilee and Samaria which means he could cross into either city at any moment. Supposed the men yelled to Jesus at the wrong time? Supposed they waited and Jesus was out of hearing range. The ten lepers were at the right place at the right time and they called out to Jesus for healing. After the cleansing of the ten lepers, Jesus told them to show themselves to the priest. Typically, the priest would walk by the lepers' everyday and do nothing to help. However, Jesus heard their cries while walking on the border and was able to cleanse them. One of the lepers came back to thank Jesus .The other nine lepers did not thank Jesus at all. Jesus states that he healed ten men. Where are the other nine lepers? We have two groups; the number two is a number of differences. One group is on (1 leper). The other group is off (9 lepers). In my view, they all were cleansed. However, because the other nine did not acknowledge God's goodness through Jesus, they were not completely healed. The one leper who did return to recognize God was completely healed. In this case, bad timing means the 9 lepers missed an opportunity to be completely healed. In conclusion, the number ten is an awesome number. This number teaches us how to pace and time our actions. This number teaches us how to be attentive to the hand and spirit of God. The number ten also explains what can occur if we fail to be attentive to his will for our lives.

11

REVELATION AND REFORMATION

THE NUMBER ELEVEN (11)

REVELATION AND REFORMATION

Disorder, disorganization, imperfection, disintegration and judgment describe the qualities of the number eleven. Throughout the Bible, the theme of judgment and lawlessness is obvious. The number eleven has become omnibus because of the attacks of September 11th. There is more to this number than judgment as seen in the 11 judgments brought upon Egypt. The number eleven is more than a number of disorder, disorganization and imperfection. All of the above are merely the results of one concept, which explains the inner meaning of this number. The word "Difference" best describes the number the eleven. The number 11 is a number of *difference*, which leads to disorder, disorganization, imperfection, disintegration and judgment.

What do you see when looking at this number? You will see two 1's. What do you see if two objects or persons which represent the same appearance, in this case, twins. What do most people do when they encounter a set of twins? Most people look for a difference between the two twins. With identical twins, if you look long enough, you will notice a difference in appearance and behavior. The number 11 represents the number two because there are two digits in the compound number 11. 1 + 1 = equals two. The number eleven has a strong bond and connection to the number two which is a number of communication, diplomacy, reformation and preparation. These same qualities are inherent in the number eleven. The primary definition of this number is "difference". Any difference in human affairs or following Godly instructions will lead to disorder, disorganization, imperfection, disintegration and judgment. I want you, the reader, to know that I took my time on this number. I prayed to Almighty God in the name of our Lord and Savior Jesus the Christ that he would take me to another level with this number. I prayed the people would know how to pace themselves and align themselves with the movement of the God's Kingdom. This number teaches us to avoid being at a difference with ourselves and the will of God. The number eleven requires humanity to be a group but to be as one in appearance just like the number eleven. This number is composed of two numbers but it is one in appearance.

The enemy will have to think twice when attacking those in the Body of Christ because we will be many but one in appearance and behavior. This number requires that we appear the same and act the same. We learn how to handle our affairs both physically and spiritually when we study the teachings of Jesus the Christ. This number calls us to higher level of discipleship. Eleven represents disorder, disorganization, imperfection, disintegration and judgment. We will prevent disorder, disorganization, imperfection, disintegration and judgment if we take ownership of our thoughts, words and deeds. The number eleven teaches us to never become at difference with ourselves or truth. We must pursue oneness of faith, oneness of speech, oneness of action. Oneness of speech produces either good speech or bad speech. Oneness of action produces either good deeds or bad deeds. The oneness of positive behavior will reduce sin and social error. Our appearance and actions should always be one. Our actions should not fluctuate in confusion and sin because this leads to death. This is probably why the occult describe 11 as a bad Number. Consider a set of twins, which is the evil twin? Many parents are familiar with the term "terrible two's". The number eleven represents "difference". What were the events of 911 all about? It was a difference that one group had with another. For whatever reason, the groups failed to become one in thought, word and deed. What was the result? Disorder, disorganization, imperfection, disintegration and judgment were the result.

12

THE VICTIM OR SACRIFICE

THE NUMBER TWELVE (12)

THE VICTIM OR SACRIFICE

TWELVE
Divine government, elections, apostolic fullness and spiritual government represent qualities of the number 12. There are plenty of references of this number in the Old Testament and New Testament. Several of these references include the 12 tribes of Israel and the twelve disciples. The number twelve is a number of sacrifices and its symbol is known as the victim. The victim symbol is an idea embraced by the ancient Egyptians. They showed the symbol of the number twelve as the hanged man or the sacrifice. The domestic and spiritual life of Jesus demonstrates the character of this number. Jesus recruited twelve disciples. The twelve disciples trained for discipleship. They dedicated their lives to the teachings of Jesus the Christ, the Son of God who would die for the sins of humanity.

The word disciple is related to the word discipline. The disciples were not expected to live normal lives as followers of Jesus. The twelve disciples would have to sacrifice their lives to follow Jesus. They could not be of this world. The 12 disciples could not walk and talk like average men. These 12 men had to sacrifice their personal dreams and desires for a higher cause. That cause represents a man who would serve as a bridge between two worlds (Physical & Spiritual) so those who accepted Christ as Lord and Savior would have eternal life. Whether by faith, belief or knowledge, this is a true and sacred process. In fact, it is so true, it appears impossible to many.

In the Old Testament, goats were sacrificed for the sins of the people hence the word scapegoat. In the book of Leviticus 16: 8-26, we read about the goat of Azazel. This goat was taken into the wilderness on the Day of Atonement. During this time period, atonement was made when he priest laid Israel's guilt upon the goat.

On the goat, it was written, "upon him all their iniquities unto a land not inhabited". The goat in this case is a victim and a sacrifice. Under the Law of Moses, the goat was taken to a mountain, which was ten Sabbath day's journey from Jerusalem. The person in charge of the goat would push the goat down a deep slope on the mountain. The poor goat could not survive such a fall. The idea was to make sure the goat did not return because if it did, the sins would return as well. This may sound like a bad idea. Some may say this task is useless or it is a silly idea. However, if you think about it, this is a very powerful ritual when you consider the power of words. The Israelites were invoking a blessing and negating the effects of negative causes. The manipulation of thoughts, words and deeds in this chapter rivals the powerful Balaam in Numbers 22. He cursed whomever he cursed and blessed whomever he blessed. He was so powerful that God himself had to intervene on behalf of the Israelites because Balaam was going to curse them. We must understand the power of atonement is real, the ritual is real and the outcome has everlasting effects.

The very same concept of sacrifice changes in the New Testament. Instead of using a goat or a lamb, a universal sacrifice is used to accomplish two tasks. The first task was for Christ to defeat death. The second goal is to exercise power over life and death through resurrection of the spirit. When you get past all of the religious overhead and theology, Jesus was able to operate in two worlds at the same time. He could operate in the dimension of the seen and the unseen. Jesus represents the number twelve because he was responsible for 12 disciples. In a sense, he was the 13th disciple of God the Father because his life was a living sacrifice. The number twelve calls everyone to a life of sacrifice. This number requires that we overcome the things of this world: drugs, alcohol, addiction, porn, masturbation, materialism, anger, wrath, hate, envy, jealousy, lying and greed. Let me provide another example, which will illustrate the basic concept of sacrifice.

In order for real sacrifice to take place, something has to go. Something must be taken, destroyed or used so another can exist. What Jesus did was nothing new when put it into perspective. I went to a social. I wanted to drink a cup of soda. There was a bag of ice in the sink but there was no scoop available to get the ice out of the bag.

So I used one of the plastic cups for the scoop. That cup would not be used for drinking but it would used to scoop ice. I placed that one cup next to the bag of ice so everybody could use the cup instead searching for a scoop. However, I went a little further. I wanted everyone to know the cup was not used or just sitting on the counter so I left a cup full of ice in the cup next to the bag so the next person would already have ice in the cup. All the next person had to do was put ice back in the cup and leave it filled with ice for the next person. A system was in place. Sadly, nobody picked up on my experiment. Everyone at the social used the cup but nobody placed ice back in the cup for the next person. I kept placing ice in the cup for the next person. This simple example explains what Christ did on the cross. One cup was used to invoke a process. There was no work for anyone. Nobody had to look for a scoop; nobody had to search for ice because I left ice in the cup for the next person. There was nothing for anybody to do. Sometimes, many cups with ice are placed next to the drinks. All one has to do is pour and drink, take the cup and enjoy. In this case, there was one cup, the ice and the drinks. Even though the cup with the ice was used, nobody put ice back in the cup for the next person. As a result, the cup sacrificed to be used as a scoop just looked like an empty used cup on he counter. Nobody recognized the purpose of having ice in the one cup. So it was with Jesus. He was the only one walking in his shoes and many missed who he was. Jesus claiming to be the Son God did not make any sense to what many people perceived.

With the sacrifice of one cup, there was a process in place. With Jesus, one sacrifice, a process for everlasting life was put in motion for the salvation of humanity. All we have to do have faith and know that Jesus is the Son of God. We must have faith and know that Jesus has all power in his hands. In order for this process to work, we must understand protocol. The proper protocol in this case is sealed in a process called the Holy Trinity. We go through Jesus to have access to the Father. Jesus has victory over death. He has all power in his hands. All who accept him as Lord and Savior will benefit from his victory. The benefits of accepting Jesus are reaped in both worlds of the seen and unseen and that is a blessing. Following Christ is about surviving in one world and properly transitioning into another with assurance.

For many, religion and theology can be very overwhelming and discouraging. The number 12 symbolizes what Jesus did in Calvary is real. Sacrifices are performed so that something or someone can live more abundantly.

When we talk about divine government, we are talking about a working, tried and true institution that has been singled out for a specific purpose. This is why the scriptures says "thy kingdom come, thy will be done, on earth, as it is in Heaven". The arrival of Jesus to this world was more than a dry run; it was something that had to be done. The arrival of Jesus had to be one time for all time. Twelve represents this one time payment because twelve is a number of sacrifice. We must understand the plan of salvation and eternal life has been worked out. All we have to do is go along with the program. The number twelve will help us see the role of Jesus and the plan of the Heavenly Father and the comfort provided the Holy Ghost. There can be no divine government without a sacrifice. Life teaches that one cannot get something for nothing. The entire Universe operates on the premise of sacrifice.

Jesus died so that we may have life more abundantly on earth but with spiritual assurance in the hereafter. All of you who have accepted Christ will reap the majority of your benefits when you leave this plane of existence. To others, please do not let tradition, theology and the negative side of organized religion prevent you having spiritual assurance and insurance. The number 12 is all about sacrifice. There can be no divine government or apolostolic fulfillment without a sacrifice. The role of the disciples is mute without the act of sacrifice. Jesus embodies the number twelve which is a number of sacrifices.

Let us do a little numerology. The Hebrew letter Lamed is the twelfth letter of the Hebrew alphabet. The symbol of Lamed is the Ox goad which is used by the shepherd to guide the sheep along the pastures. The Ox goad is shaped like the letter Lamed. Lamed means *to learn and to teach* and this is what Jesus did with the disciples. He taught by using parables. Jesus led by example but he was a teacher. How fitting is it for the letter Lamed to be the 12th letter of the Hebrew alphabet. The number 12 reduces to the single digit 3 because $1 + 2 = 3$. Lamed has a numerical value of 30 which reduces to 3 because $3 + 0 = 3$.

Three is symbolic of the Holy Trinity. Therefore, 12, 3, lamed, the Ox goad, Divine Government and the Trinity are all related to the idea and act of sacrifice.

The number twelve calls us to a higher level of service and sacrifice for a higher cause. Regarding the number twelve, you will see words such as rule, servant, subject, rule and allot throughout the entire Bible: Gen 14:4, Gen 17:20, Gen 25:16, Gen 42:13, Ex 28:21, Num 17:6. This number requires service for something new and everlasting (Exodus 15:27). The life of Jesus embodies the character and nature of the number twelve. The number twelve is a number of sacrifice and divine selection.

13

AUTHORITATIVE PLANS, REBELLION, REFUGE, MEASUREMENT AND RULE.

THE NUMBER THIRTEEN (13)

Authoritative Plans, Rebellion, Refuge, Measurement and Rule.

The number thirteen has been given a bad image. This may be because of the Egyptian series symbol of the skeleton using a scythe to plow a field. This symbol represents hard work, real hard work, no handouts. Thirteen is rooted with (1) *begin* and (3) *ideas*. Therefore, begin + ideas = plans and methods or 1+3=4. This number appears to be a bad luck number because of many negative associations: Friday the 13th, The Jason Movies, 13 moons on the old Proctor & Gamble logo. In a way, it is a bad luck number. However, authoritative plans, violence, rebellion, revenge and vengeance represent the qualities of the number 13. The bad luck comes into play after the fact. The scriptures are clear on the role of this number.

This number will used to describe plans, rule, measurement and authoritative plans throughout the Bible. Thirteen may appear as a bad luck number because it is associated with rebellion, refuge and revenge. The scriptures reveal there is more than rebellion and refuge. There is an underlying theme of authoritative plans and measurement operating in the scriptures. The number thirteen can be a bad luck number depending on what end of the rope you are holding. This number teaches us to humble ourselves and wait on God's favor. If not, we run the risk of being on the opposite end of the Lord's authoritative plans. In this case, the number 13 will appear as a bad luck number. We can be on the favorable side of the Lord's authoritative plans if we are hear, obey and finish what we are instructed to do.

Example 1
ESTER 8:11
11 The king's edict granted the Jews in every city the right to assemble and protect themselves; to destroy, kill and annihilate any armed force of any nationality or province that might attack them and their women and children; and to plunder the property of their enemies.

12 The day appointed for the Jews to do this in all the provinces of King Xerxes was the thirteenth day of the twelfth month, the month of Adar. 13 A copy of the text of the edict was to be issued as law in every province and made known to the people of every nationality so that the Jews would be ready on that day to avenge themselves on their enemies.

The number thirteen in this passage is symbolic of two themes. First, the king passed an edit which gave the Jews the right to avenge themselves. The Jews avenged their enemies but why did that happen? It happened because the king passed an edit on Ester's behalf. An authoritative plan was allowed by the King. The Jews would probably not have avenged their enemies without the authoritative plan or the edit from the King.

Example 2
GENESIS 17:24-26
Foundations to adulthood
24 Abraham was ninety-nine years old when he was circumcised in the flesh of his foreskin. 25 And Ishmael his son was thirteen years old when he was circumcised in the flesh of his foreskin. 26 That very same day Abraham was circumcised, and his son Ishmael;

The name Ishmael has a numerical value of = 31/4. If you notice, thirty one is the opposite of thirteen. 13 is related to 31 just like Ishmael was related to Jacob. Regarding 13 year old Jewish boys, the age thirteen is an age of passage. This is known as the Bar Mitzpah. The boy becomes responsible for himself under Jewish Law. Ishmael was expected to responsible for himself or have the right to exercise authoritative plans concerning his affairs. There is no need for him to become a rebellious teenager because he is recognized as being responsible for himself according to Jewish Law. Girls reach this age of passage at the age of 12 and this is known Bat Mitzvah.

Example 3
GENESIS 14: 3-5

3 All these latter kings joined forces in the Valley of Siddim (the Salt Sea For twelve years they had been subject to Kedorlaomer, but in the thirteenth year they rebelled. 5 In the fourteenth year, Kedorlaomer and the kings allied with him went out and defeated the Rephaites in Ashteroth Karnaim, the Zuzites in Ham, the Emites in Shaveh Kiriathaim

The number thirteen is associated with rebellion, refuge and revenge. This passage of scripture, the number thirteen is used to indicate rebellion.

Example 4

Jeremiah 1-9: Authoritative Plans

The Call of Jeremiah

4 Then the word of the LORD came to me, saying:
  5 " Before I formed you in the womb I knew you;
  Before you were born I sanctified you;
  I ordained you a prophet to the nations."
6 Then said I:
  " Ah, Lord GOD!
  Behold, I cannot speak, for I am a youth."
7 But the LORD said to me:
  " Do not say, 'I am a youth,'
  For you shall go to all to whom I send you,
  And whatever I command you, you shall speak.
  8 Do not be afraid of their faces,
  For I am with you to deliver you," says the LORD.

This passage shows the number thirteen operating in a very unique and divine manner. The people of Israel have proven to be unfaithful in the eyes of the Lord. Judah has rebelled against the Lord and Jeremiah was called by the Lord to warn Judah about their unfaithfulness. The Lord wants Judah to live right, observe the law and become a people of faith. The number thirteen in this case is not emphasizing the spiritual rebellion of Judah because the children of Israel have been demonstrating faithlessness throughout the entire Bible. The number thirteen in this passage is symbolic of God's authoritative plans. Notice how Jeremiah starts out in verse 4. The Lord is saying that before Jeremiah was formed in his mother's womb, the Lord already knew him. Jeremiah was already set apart. Jeremiah was appointed to be a prophet to the nations before was born. Jeremiah said that he did not know how to speak. The Lord had authoritative plans in mind for Jeremiah. The number thirteen speaks to authoritative plans by God and man. This number may appear as a bad luck number but it could be good depending if you are operating with authoritative plans from a higher power.

    Our role as brothers and sisters in the Body of Christ is to not avoid thirteen but to watch the movement of God's hand. This number teaches us to stay out of God's way. This number is like the third rail on a set of train tracks. If you are backsliding, watch out for the number thirteen on your way back home. This number shows how God will use people to carry out his plans.

14

DIVINE SELECTION, EXCLUSION BY GRACE, PASSOVER

THE NUMBER FOURTEEN (14)

Divine Selection, Exclusion by Grace, Passover

Fourteen is rooted with a (1) which means *begin,* and (4) which means *organize things,* this suggest effective coordination, accommodation, and selection. Fourteen is often associated with Passover, which is true, however; there is additional information. Fourteen represents the celebration of Passover. This number also symbolizes divine selection and exclusion by grace. According to Webster's dictionary, exclusive means *not to share or without others*. This number is rooted by the number 1 and 4 which equals 5. Five on the constructive side means grace, change, movement and moral correctness.

The number 14 displays the qualities of five which is grace. Observing the number 14, this number is composed of two 7's or $7 + 7 = 14$. Seven comes from the Hebrew shevah meaning to be satisfied, full or enough. 14, as it relates to people, events, God will show acts of exclusion and selection. This number will show God acting on behalf his people. This number will show God intervening in the affairs of his children. We see the number fourteen in the form of a day (Chr 30:15), year (Gen 14:5) or numerical quantity (Job 42:12). 14 cannot be categorized as a good or bad number. This number is close to the hand of God. Fourteen is in the same company of deliverance and revelation. I would not exclude this number in this modern day of prophecy and fulfillment. The number fourteen is referenced 48 times in the entire Bible.

EXAMPLE 1

We are familiar with the idea of Passover in Exodus 12. We understand the children of Israel sprinkled blood on their doorpost so the Lord would Passover their dwelling unit. If not, each child or animal alive, which was the first-born, would be killed. God stated he would pass judgment on the gods of Egypt.

The first-born animals are killed as well. Exodus 12:14 states: *This a day you are to commemorate, for the generations to come you shall celebrate it as a festival to Lord.* The Passover theme does not fully express the acts of God in regards to interacting with his people. In the Book of Exodus 12:6, the animals were to be kept until the fourteenth night. Afterwards, they were to be slaughtered. The blood of the slaughtered animals was sprinkled on the door post

EXAMPLE 2
This number represents exclusion by grace. In the book of Acts 27:27-33, we read about Paul who is a prisoner on a ship from Adramyttium. He was being taken to Caesar the Emperor of Rome to stand trial. During the voyage, the ship encounters a "northeaster" (Acts 27:13). The ship was pulled to the lee of a small island called Cauda. The men were unable to eat or drink because of the violent storm which was tossing the ship. After fourteen days, Paul, the prisoner, urged the men to eat 'you have been in constant suspense and have gone without food". Paul goes on to say "Not one of you will lose a single hair from his head": Acts 27:33-35.

This is another version of the Passover because the men on the ship were able to escape death. However, this is more than Passover. In this specific passage, we are dealing with exclusion by grace. Paul was told by an Angel that he would have to stand trial before Caesar and *"God has graciously given you the lives of all who sail with you": Acts 27:23-25.* In other words, if you were in the same storm on another boat, your safety was not guaranteed. The number 14 in this passage is symbolic of the exclusive grace granted to the men on the ship simply because it was ordained that Paul go before Caesar in Rome. The concept of Passover does not directly apply to Acts 27:27 because there is no blood, lamb, sacrifice or door post involved. God has decided to exclusively show his grace to the men on the ship because Paul was on the ship. This passage is almost the opposite of Jonah and the Big Fish. We can be blessed by being around the right person or be cursed by being around the wrong. Seek out the Ordained man or woman of God.

EXAMPLE 3
We read about exclusiveness operating in the book of 2 Corinthians 12:2. Paul is discussing how he is strong through bragging about his weaknesses and not his strengths. He is not bragging about himself. Paul does not see any benefit in boasting about himself because there is nothing to be gained. Paul does know of a man he can boast about and this man was caught up to the third heaven. While this man was in paradise, he heard inexpressible things that man is not permitted to tell. According to Paul, this man was taken up to the third heaven Fourteen years ago. The number fourteen is symbolic of God exclusively selecting a man to be taken up to the third Heaven. Even though Paul was talking about having a substantive reason to boast, I am looking at the numbers which apply to the man who was exclusively selected for this blessing. In this case, it is the number fourteen.

EXAMPLE 4
The first chapter of Matthew provides the genealogy of Jesus Christ. Matt 1:17 states "Thus there were fourteen generations in all from Abraham to David, fourteen from David to exile to Babylon, and fourteen from the exile to the Christ". Many people may agree or disagree with the entire genealogy. However, my concern is the hidden message within the scripture and the number fourteen. Matt 1:17 clearly reveals the exclusive works of God by working through a selected bloodline, an exclusive blood line. Again, the Godly act of Passover is not present in this passage of scripture. However, the number fourteen is present as a symbol of exclusion. In other words, this bloodline is sacred.

EXAMPLE 5
Let the sinner beware. Isaiah 36, "In the fourteenth year", shows the number fourteen working against Sennacherib the King of Assyria who attacked and captured Judah.
Sennacherib also spoke against the power and the presence of God while addressing the people of Judah in Ezekiel 36:15 *"do not let Hezekiah mislead you when he says the Lord will deliver us. Has the god of any nation ever delivered his land from the hand of the King of Assyria?*

In Isaiah 37:7, the Prophet Isaiah speaks the word of the Lord to Hezekiah's men *"Listen, I (God) am going to put a spirit in him so that when he hears a certain report, he will return to his country, and there, I will have him cut down with the sword"*. In Isaiah 37:38, Sennacherib is killed by his sons while worshipping his god Nisroch. Sennacherib was about to possess the land of Judah and things looked pretty bad for Hezekiah and Judah. However, Hezekiah had enough sense to consult the great prophet Isaiah to get a word from the Lord. The hand of exclusion is working against Sennacherib. Almighty God exclusively put a spirit in Sennacherib that would make him return to his country when he heard a certain report. God could have killed him on the spot but what fun would that have been? Almighty God told the prophet show how Sennacherib would be killed. Sennacherib was exclusively selected for death. This number reminds us that God can become exclusive with us if we turn his wrath upon us. Exclusion can be a good thing or a bad thing, depending if you are on God's good side.

EXAMPLE 6

Ezekiel 40:1 provides the supreme example of Divine Selection in regards to the inner meaning of the number fourteen. Ezekiel was taken to the land of Israel to a very high mountain in the fourteenth year after the fall of Jerusalem. He also saw a man whose appearance was like bronze. This man also had a measuring rod in his hand. The prophet was given a vision to share with the children of Israel. Ezekiel saw the East gate to the Outer Court, the North Gate, the South Gate, the Gates to the Inner Court, the Rooms for preparing Sacrifices, the Temple, Rooms for the Priest, the Altar, the Prince, the Levites, the Priest, Instructions for Division of the Land, Instructions for Offerings and Holy Days, the River From the Temple, Instructions for Boundaries for the Land and the Gates to the City. Ezekiel was a prophet but this vision was not a prophecy. Ezekiel was divinely selected to ensure that a direct request from Almighty God was carried out to the letter.

Through the number fourteen, God is calling us to have an exclusive relationship with him. The number fourteen requires that we put ourselves in a position to be excluded from the things of this world. The number fourteen puts us in a position to encounter a miracle and a blessing before the eyes of the world. We can expect to be selected for divine exclusion when we fast and offer our lives as a living sacrifice, exercise a of spirit of expectancy, hold on for 14 days, 14 months and even 14 years. I challenge you to petition Almighty God for an act of exclusive grace or divine selection in your life.

15

DIVINE INSTRUCTIONS AND PASSIONS

THE NUMBER FIFTEEN (15)

DIVINE INSTUCTIONS AND PASSIONS

The following definitions describe the nature of this number: divine instructions, celebrations and feasts. This number teaches us how to pace ourselves when chasing the presence of God. Fifteen teaches us how to listen for direction. Let us see what happens in the Book of Exodus 16 which is all about the Israelites following instructions. You will have to read the entire chapter to see what God is doing with the Israelites.

Example 1
Exodus16:1-8
The whole Israelite community set out from Elim and came to the Desert of Sin, which is between Elim and Sinai, on <u>the fifteenth day</u> of the second month after they had come out of Egypt. 2 In the desert the whole community grumbled against Moses and Aaron. 3 The Israelites said to them, "If only we had died by the LORD's hand in Egypt! There we sat around pots of meat and ate all the food we wanted, but you have brought us out into this desert to starve this entire assembly to death." 4 Then the LORD said to Moses, "I will rain down bread from heaven for you. The people are to go out each day and gather enough for that day. <u>In this way I will test them and see whether they will follow my instructions.</u> 5 On the <u>sixth</u> day they are to prepare what they bring in, and that is to be twice as much as they gather on the other days." 6 So Moses and Aaron said to all the Israelites, "In the evening you will know that it was the LORD who brought you out of Egypt, 7 and in the morning you will see the glory of the LORD, because he has heard your grumbling against him. Who are we, that you should grumble against us?" 8 Moses also said, "You will know that it was the LORD when he gives you meat to eat in the evening and all the bread you want in the morning, because he has heard your grumbling against him. Who are we? You are not grumbling against us, but against the LORD."

In a nutshell, the Israelites were given instructions on when and how to eat the quail at night and the bread in the morning. The number fifteen is working in two forms. The two forms are found in the double-digit form 15 and in the single digit form which is the number six because 1 + 5 = 6. The number six is symbolic of work, service and responsibility. The Lord needed the Israelites to accomplish three expectations. The first expectation was to follow instructions. The second expectation was to gather the quail at night and the bread in the morning. The third expectation was to gather a double portion on the sixth day because the seventh day was the Sabbath. God was breaking the Israelites out of bad pagan habits of looking to other gods as a source. He wanted to provide for them personally so they would know there is only one true and living God despite their complaints. In a pagan environment, they typically would make a sacrifice to the god in question to get what they needed. In this case, the true and living God is not interested in their offerings or sacrifices. God wants their obedience. The group can be in position to be obedient if the leaders are at least hearing from God. However, if the man or woman of God is hearing from the Lord, the people must be willing to do their part by demonstrating obedience.

EXAMPLE 2
***LEV 23:6** On the fifteenth day of that month the LORD's Feast of Unleavened Bread begins; for seven days you must eat bread made without yeast.*

15 symbolizes feasts and celebrations. We read about this in Lev 23:6. The theme of divine instructions is working with the celebration of feast. While we are here, we see the number seven at work. The number Seven means to be satisfied, full or enough. For seven days the Israelites received instructions to eat bread without yeast. They were given these instructions on the fifteenth day. The emphasis on feasts can also be seen in the 15th verse which begins with "Feast of Weeks".

EXAMPLE 3
NUM 28: 16-20

16 'On the fourteenth day of the first month the LORD's Passover is to be held. 17 On the fifteenth day of this month there is to be a festival; for seven days eat bread made without yeast. 18 On the first day hold a sacred assembly and do no regular work. 19 Present to the LORD an offering made by fire, a burnt offering of two young bulls, one ram and seven male lambs a year old, all without defect. 20 With each bull prepare a grain offering of three-tenths of an ephah of fine flour mixed with oil; with the ram, two-tenths;

The number fifteen is typically associated with passion and celebration. So it is with this passage, the feast took place on the 15th day. The children of Israel are not celebrating what they have done. They are celebrating what the Father has done concerning Passover. How awesome, celebrating an act of God. Today, we hold many celebrations but they are primarily for what a man or woman has accomplished. Fifteen reminds us to celebrate the things of God, let us celebrate what has been done and what he is doing. Can we celebrate the acts of God without padding the pockets of corporate America or some greedy Church and or church leader?

16

STEWARDSHIP, WORRY, SERVICE

THE NUMBER SIXTEEN (16)

Stewardship, Worry, Service

Sixteen is rooted by (1) *begin, leadership* and (6) *commerce, service*, which totals seven (7) *enough*. This number teaches us how to relax and smell the roses. Like an aging boxer in denial, we must know when to retire. Sixteen reminds us of the valleys and peaks we encounter in life. We must learn to slow ourselves down while at the height of any success because it will lessen the blow if change is brought about through unexpected events. The number sixteen is a call to effective leadership and service. Through this number, we learn about consistent responsibility and accountability. Let us review the first example of this number at work in 2 Chr 26: 1-5. To bring emphasis to the nature of this number notice what happens in verse 16.

EXAMPLE 1
2 Chr 26: 1-5.
Uzziah King of Judah
1 Then all the people of Judah took Uzziah, who was sixteen years old, and made him king in place of his father Amaziah. 2 He was the one who rebuilt Elath and restored it to Judah after Amaziah rested with his fathers. 3 Uzziah was sixteen years old when he became king, and he reigned in Jerusalem fifty-two years. His mother's name was Jecoliah; she was from Jerusalem. 4 He did what was right in the eyes of the LORD, just as his father Amaziah had done. 5 He sought God during the days of Zechariah, who instructed him in the fear of God. As long as he sought the LORD, God gave him success. 16 But after Uzziah became powerful, his pride led to his downfall. He was unfaithful to the LORD his God, and entered the temple of the LORD to burn incense on the altar of incense. 17 Azariah the priest with eighty other courageous priests of the LORD followed him in. 18 They confronted him and said, "It is not right for you, Uzziah, to burn incense to the LORD. That is for the priests, the descendants of Aaron, who have been consecrated to burn incense. Leave the sanctuary, for you have been unfaithful; and you will not be honored by the LORD God."

The above example shows the nature of the sixteen at work during the reign of Uzziah. He became powerful as a leader but his pride led to his downfall.

EXAMPLE 2
2 Chronicles 28
Ahaz King of Judah
1 Ahaz was twenty years old when he became king, and he reigned in Jerusalem sixteen years. Unlike David his father, he did not do what was right in the eyes of the LORD. 2 He walked in the ways of the kings of Israel and also made cast idols for worshiping the Baals. 3 He burned sacrifices in the Valley of Ben Hinnom and sacrificed his sons in the fire, following the detestable ways of the nations the LORD had driven out before the Israelites. 4 He offered sacrifices and burned incense at the high places, on the hilltops and under every spreading tree.

In this example, Ahaz reigned for 16 years and his reign was ominous because he made idols to Baal. The number twenty means awakening and he became King of Judah at the age twenty. After his awakening as King of Judah, he fell by not doing what is right in the eyes of the Lord which is symbolized by the number 16.

EXAMPLE 3
2 Kings 15
Azariah King of Judah
1 In the twenty-seventh year of Jeroboam king of Israel, Azariah son of Amaziah king of Judah began to reign. 2 He was sixteen years old when he became king, and he reigned in Jerusalem fifty-two years. His mother's name was Jecoliah; she was from Jerusalem. 3 He did what was right in the eyes of the LORD, just as his father Amaziah had done. 4 The high places, however, were not removed; the people continued to offer sacrifices and burn incense there. 5 The LORD afflicted the king with leprosy until the day he died, and he lived-in a separate house. Jotham the king's son had charge of the palace and governed the people of the land.

King Azariah was 27 when he began to reign as King of Judah.

Twenty-Seven reduces to the number 9, which is a number mass influence and stages. He was a good king but he failed to remove the idols from being worshipped in high places. In this case, we are talking about the Asherah poles. The people were not focused on the true and living God. King Azariah was unable to influence the worship lives of the people. Sadly, he was afflicted with leprosy even though he did what was right in the sight of the Lord. The number sixteen is critical to those in leadership. This tells us that we must become effective in leading the people of God or suffer consequences. Every leader should study this number before claiming to be led by the Lord.

17

MANAGEMENT AND ADMINISTRATION

THE NUMBER SEVENTEEN (17)

MANAGEMENT AND ADMINISTRATION

Control, management and administration represent the qualities of the number 17. This number can be studied by analyzing the single digit 8 because 1 + 7 = 8. This number teaches us to handle our responsibilities so we can complete spiritual challenges. Number one means to begin, lead or pioneer. The number seven means *"to be satisfied, full or enough"*. Combining 1 and 7 produces the number 8 which means new beginnings and execution. This is a prophetic and administrative number. The number one is a number of thought and the number seven is a number of influence. Combining thought and influence can only produce a vision which must be executed and controlled but under the guidance of the Lord if one desires true success. Let us see how this number is described in the scripture.

EXAMPLE 1
Jeremiah 32 8-15

8 "Then, just as the LORD had said, my cousin Hanamel came to me in the courtyard of the guard and said, 'Buy my field at Anathoth in the territory of Benjamin. Since it is your right to redeem it and possess it, buy it for yourself." I knew that this was the word of the LORD; *9* so I bought the field at Anathoth from my cousin Hanamel and weighed out for him seventeen shekels of silver. *10* I signed and sealed the deed, had it witnessed, and weighed out the silver on the scales. *11* I took the deed of purchase—the sealed copy containing the terms and conditions, as well as the unsealed copy- *12* and I gave this deed to Baruch son of Neriah, the son of Mahseiah, in the presence of my cousin Hanamel and of the witnesses who had signed the deed and of all the Jews sitting in the courtyard of the guard. *13* "In their presence I gave Baruch these instructions: *14* 'This is what the LORD Almighty, the God of Israel, says: Take these documents, both the sealed and unsealed copies of the deed of purchase, and put them in a clay jar so they will last a long time. *15* For this is what the LORD Almighty, the God of Israel, says: Houses, fields and vineyards will again be bought in this land.

Jeremiah 32: 8-15 describes the purchase of field in Anathoth which is in Benjamin. The prophet Jeremiah is confined to the courtyard guard at the royal palace in Judah. The king of Babylon has taken siege of Jerusalem. Jeremiah is being imprisoned by King Zedekiah, the King of Judah. Zedekiah wants to know why Jeremiah is prophesying against him by saying that Judah will be given to the King of Babylon. Thus, Zedekiah will see Nebuchadnezzar face-to-face. Meanwhile, Jeremiah receives a word from the Lord that his cousin Hanamel will offer to sell him a field found in Anathoth which is in Benjamin. The word of the Lord proved to be accurate. The Lord commanded the sealed and unsealed copy of the deed be placed into a clay jar so the seals will be preserved. The Lord said "Houses, fields and vineyards will again be bought in this land".

God allowed Judah to be taken by Babylon because they continued to sacrifice their children to Molech and they worshipped Baal. The Lord has a change of heart and prepares to bless the Israelites and make an everlasting covenant with his children. The number 17 is the only number mentioned in this chapter. The Lord is moving in the prophetic by placing the deed of the sale to Jeremiah in a clay jar and says "Houses, fields and vineyards will again be bought in this land". The field was sold for seventeen shekels of silver and how fitting because this number is symbolic of prophecy, new beginnings, administration, management, vision and affairs. This number is associated with new beginnings because seventeen is the compound form of the single digit eight which means new beginnings. The number seventeen is associated with infinity. Notice the geometric design of the number eight, it is closed and looped. For years, many have been taught the single digit eight is a number of new beginnings. However, the definition of 8 applies to the entire eight line which includes the numbers 8, 17, 26, 35, 44, 53 and so on.

EXAMPLE 2
Genesis8
1 But God remembered Noah and all the wild animals and the livestock that were with him in the ark, and he sent a wind over the earth, and the waters receded. 2 Now the springs of the deep and the floodgates of the heavens had been closed, and the rain had stopped falling from the sky. 3 The water receded steadily from the earth. At the end of the hundred and fifty days the water had gone down, 4 and on the seventeenth day of the seventh month the ark came to rest on the mountains of Ararat. 5 The waters continued to recede until the tenth month, and on the first day of the tenth month the tops of the mountains became visible.

How fitting is it for this example to be located in the eighth chapter. Noah and his Ark were floating in the water for 150 days. On the seventeenth day of the second month, the ark rested on Mt Ararat. There are several numbers at work. The seventeenth day is symbolic of the new beginning for Noah, his family and the animals. 17 is symbolic of the execution, management and exercise of control required to unload the Ark once they are ready to step on dry ground. The second month is symbolic of the reformation and the preparation God put into preserving humanity through Noah. The 150 days is symbolic of the number fifteen which represents the divine instructions received by Noah. The scriptures state that at the end of 150 days the water receded. The disappearance of the water signals the end of Noah following the divine instructions of the Lord to build an Ark.

18

WARNING, REPENTENCE, UNKOWN, READINESS

THE NUMBER EIGHTEEN (18)

The Unknown, Repentance

Eighteen is a material, physical and spiritual number. It is rooted by (1) leadership, and (8) influence, discernment and control which totals (9) which is a number compassion, influence and power. Eighteen represents two struggles. First, this number represents the struggle between the higher nature of humanity, which leans towards spirituality, and enlightenment. Second, eighteen represents the lower nature of humanity that craves the things of this world. This number represents the results of the mind and spirit. The scriptures do not offer many passages about this number. This number is a warning that we should continue to rise in our recognition and worship of Almighty God the Father.

Nine is a material number. Nine can be worldly and this can seen in the numerical value of the words: *Use* (9) and *Money* (9). I found something of particular interest in the scriptures. The book of Luke happens to use this number in two passages in the same chapter. Luke Chapter 13 discusses repentance opposed to perishing. Repentance is a way of reconciling with the Father about our sinful deeds. Repentance provides us with another opportunity to try to walk in our higher self. The question is, "what happens if we fail to repent?" The answer is obvious, we perish. There is no compassion in perishing.

The book of Luke emphasizes this point by using the number eighteen twice in chapter 13 of Luke. The number thirteen represents hard work and authoritative plans. In Luke 13:4 we read about the eighteen men who were killed. Jesus says *"I tell you, Nay, but except ye repent, ye shall all likewise perish. Or those eighteen, upon whom the tower of Siloam fell and slew them, think that they were sinners above all men that dwelt in Jerusalem"*. The numerical value of the word "Tower" equals 9. Jesus was saying that unless we repent for our sins, we maybe caught off guard.

Eighteen reminds us to keep a compassionate and forgiven heart because one never knows when their time on this earth will come to an end. If it is your time, one would want to leave in good standing. When you see the number eighteen, cry out to God, beg for forgiveness and know that He is God. This number is hard to find in the scriptures. Thirteen represents hard work. We must work hard to govern our thoughts, words and deeds. The number 3 is critical in building up to the number nine. I will discuss the role of the 3 in building up to the number 9 shortly. The next time we encounter the number 18 is in Luke Chapter 13. There is a woman who has a spirit of infirmity for 18 years and she was unable to stand straight. She could not stand upward and look up. If one cannot look up, how can one think up, act up and grow up. The woman was unable to heal herself. She was unable to stand straight on her own. She needed the love and compassion of a loving savior to deliver her from her sickness. Eighteen reminds us of God's everlasting power and compassion.

The definition of the number 18 is embedded in Chapter 13 of Luke. In verse 13, Jesus heals the woman and she is able to stand straight. The aching pains of this world no longer drag down her body. She can concentrate on upward things. Nine is a number of compassion when positive and represents a lack of compassion when negative. The number 18 is a reminder about doing what is right and pleasing in the eyes of God Almighty. We see the number 18 again in judges 3:12. The Israelites did evil in the sight of the Lord and they had to serve Eglon for 18 years as result. The number eighteen represents the absence of God's compassion concerning the Israelites. However, it was not until the children of Israel cried unto the Lord (repentance), the Lord raised them up a deliverer (Ehud). Will we choose light or darkness, height or depth for ourselves? Or, will be caught off guard? In the book of Judges 20:25, the scriptures talk about the children of Israel being defeated twice by the Benjamites. Verse 25 states eighteen thousand men from the Israelites were killed. The Israelites went before God each time after they were defeated. The second time, they fasted, offered burnt offerings, and peace offerings. The children of Israel did not defeat the Benjamites until the third attempt.

18 is also call to repentance. This number reminds us to stay in communion with the Father, especially while dealing with the cares of this world. Eighteen shows us that if we repent, if we stay before God, even in defeat, we can rise. We will rise to fight another day. Earlier in this chapter, I talked about the number three and how 3 builds up to nine: 3 + 3 + 3 = 9 by addition. Or, we can use accelerated addition which is multiplication to do the following: 3x3 is nine. Nine could not exist without three. This is true when you also consider that 1 + 1 + 1 = 3 or 3x1 =3 or 1x3=3. The number three plays a key role in the construction of the number nine. Let us look at the number three in the book of Luke. The book, chapter and verse of Luke 13:4 has a value of 3 (Book: L3, U3, K2, E5 =13, 1+3 = 4 : Chapter 13: Verse 4 = 8, 4 = 8 – 12, 1+2 =3). The book, chapter and verse of Luke 13:13 has a value of 3. Luke 13:4 mentions the 18 men which were killed at Siloam. In Luke 13:13, Jesus heals the woman who was sick with a bad back for eighteen years. In the book of Judges 20:25, the Israelites defeated the Benjamites after the third attempt. We use the power of the three in recognizing the Father, Son, and Holy Ghost. The number 18 is a number which provides a warning about the movement and wrath of God. This number reminds to be ready and to repent.

19

ATTAINMENT, EXPECTANCY, SUCCESS

THE NUMBER NINETEEN (19)

ATTAINMENT, EXPECTANCY, SUCCESS

The number nineteen is a blessed number. This number is not associated with any major upheavals or danger. In fact, this is a number of attainment. This number is made up a "1" which means to begin and "9" which represents mass influence. The number nine is a powerful number which affects every number in the number system. Nineteen is what I call an escort number because it escorts every many number above or below its position. For example, any number containing a 9 in the last position is a number of assistance. 19 leads to 20; 39 leads to 40, 49 leads to 50 and so on. The number nineteen is not just a number but it is a stage where something enters and something exits. Nineteen will always take one to the next level.

The number nineteen represents attainment and success. There are not too many references of this number in the Bible; at best there may be 6 or seven passages of scripture which use this number. David inherited the land of Judah in Joshua 19:38, David was made King over Judah in 2 Samuel 2:30, Judah fell to Nebuchadnezzar in 2 Kings 25:8. You say "hey Judah fell", yes but The Babylonian King attained a victory, land and people. This reaffirms that God is no respecter of people. In life, we rise and fall. In fact, rising and falling is a lesson taught by the nature of this number. Often, when one person gains something another person loses. The number 19 reduces to a 1 which makes this a number of leadership, innovation and inheritance.

20

REJUVENATION, REBIRTH AND AWARENESS

THE NUMBER TWENTY (20)

REJUVENATION, REBIRTH AND AWARENESS

Twenty is a number social change, reformation and awareness. The number twenty teaches us to watch our minds and heart and also watch for the wrath of God. This number teaches us the Lord will move against us with no warning. Twenty also represents awareness and discernment.

EXAMPLE 1
Consider the demise of Sodom mentioned in Genesis 18. The city of Sodom and Gomorrah was a wicked city in the eyes of the Lord. God plans on destroying the town and the people. While Abraham is talking with the Lord, he decides to cut a deal for the people. Abraham starts with the number fifty and works his way down to the number ten. The idea was to have the Lord spare the people if the Lord found at least 50 righteous people. Each time the Lord agrees to spare the town, Abraham lowers the number because he knows there are not too many good people in this town. Hey, do not take my word. If you notice, his number is not going up, the number is going down. He eventually gets to the number ten. The Lord agreed to spare the town if he could find at least ten righteous people. Abraham was aware of what the Lord was going to do and he was aware of the condition of the people. In this case, The Lord was determined to destroy Sodom and there would be no chance of rejuvenation or rebirth for the people of this town.

There are six important numbers mentioned in Genesis **18: 28-33:** 50, 45, 40, 30, 20, and 10. Fifty represents, grace: 5 + 0 =5. Forty Five represents plans and organizing people, 4 and 5. Thirty represents carelessness and lawlessness: 3 + 0 = 3, the negative side of the number three. The number ten represents timing and access because time is out for the people of this town. Ten is also symbolic of Lot and his wife leaving the town and not looking back (timing). The number twenty represents awareness, judgment, reformation and preparation. If one reads to the end of chapter 19, one will find out exactly what God did in the end. He destroyed Sodom and Gomorrah. God judged this town and it was reformed later in time.

About awareness, lots wife was turned into salt because of her lack of awareness. Lots wife was not focused on the future, her mind remained in the past. Abraham tried to save the town based on his awareness. I guess there was not one righteous person in the town because it was destroyed.

EXAMPLE 2

In Genesis 31:38, we see judgment, awareness and reformation taking place. Laban is accusing Jacob of stealing. Laban decides to pursue Jacob into Canaan. Laban eventually catches up with the Jacob and goes through all his possessions. Laban's daughter Rachael hid Laban's images from his sight by sitting on them when her father Laban came into to her tent. Laban does not find anything. Jacob reminds Laban that he has been with him for *twenty years*. Laban is unaware that his own daughter was the one who stole his images. Laban passed judgment on Jacob by thinking Jacob stole his images when it was his daughters who stole his images. Twenty is a number of reformation, preparation, awareness and judgment. This number also teaches us to not assume based on our perceived awareness. Twenty teaches us how to approach God for awareness. Sometimes we may need to hold a situation in prayer for twenty minutes or twenty days. We may have to prepare 20 days to have insight on a specific issue. The number nineteen dealt with attainment but the number twenty addresses decisions and soundness of judgment based on our awareness.

21

RELEASE, FREEDOM FROM OPPRESSION AND BONDAGE.

THE NUMBER TWENTY ONE (21)

REJUVENATION, REBIRTH AND AWARENESS

Twenty One represents freedom and release from oppression, struggle and bondage. This number is not hard to examine. This number is the reverse of 12 which is known as the sacrifice or victim. These numbers carry the same energy. This number suggests someone will be held in bondage or face a struggle. The number 12 represents struggle and oppression for the sake of sacrifice with the idea of discipline looming in the background. The number 12 represents a sacrifice with the idea of an offering, where Jesus is the offering or the new lamb. The blood of Jesus represents the vehicle for Passover. The number twenty one does not have any elements of an offering or sacrifice. The number 12 leads to death. Without victory, the number 21 leads to continued oppression, struggle and bondage. Jesus represents the perfect price for 12 and 21 because these numbers are the same but they are in reverse. If you are facing a struggle, bondage or oppression, consider Daniel's technique. He humbled himself and he waited on God for 21 days to provide spiritual backing.

This number teaches us how to have an intimate relationship with God. The number 21 calls us to have an intensive life of praise, worship and faith. Twenty One reminds us that we can hear from God and we can have an Angelic encounter. Twenty One encourages us to raise our game when prayer, worship and devotion are concerned. The following examples show how this number is used in the Bible.

EXAMPLE 1

Exodus 12

The Passover

1 The LORD said to Moses and Aaron in Egypt, 2 "This month is to be fore you the first month, the first month of your year.

3 Tell the whole community of Israel that on the tenth day of this month each man is to take a lamb for his family, one for each household. 4 If any household is too small for a whole lamb, they must share one with their nearest neighbor, having considered the number of people there are. You are to determine the amount of lamb needed in accordance with what each person will eat. 5 The animals you choose must be year-old males without defect, and you may take them from the sheep or the goats. 6 Take care of them until the fourteenth day of the month, when all the people of the community of Israel must slaughter them at twilight. 7 Then they are to take some of the blood and put it on the sides and tops of the doorframes of the houses where they eat the lambs. 8 That same night they are to eat the meat roasted over the fire, along with bitter herbs, and bread made without yeast. 9 Do not eat the meat raw or cooked in water, but roast it over the fire—head, legs and inner parts. 10 Do not leave any of it till morning; if some is left till morning, you must burn it. 11 This is how you are to eat it: with your cloak tucked into your belt, your sandals on your feet and your staff in your hand. Eat it in haste; it is the LORD's Passover. 12 "On that same night I will pass through Egypt and strike down every firstborn—both men and animals—and I will bring judgment on all the gods of Egypt. I am the LORD. 13 The blood will be a sign for you on the houses where you are; and when I see the blood, I will pass over you. No destructive plague will touch you when I strike Egypt. 14 "This is a day you are to commemorate; for the generations to come you shall celebrate it as a festival to the LORD -a lasting ordinance. 15 For seven days you are to eat bread made without yeast. On the first day remove the yeast from your houses, for whoever eats anything with yeast in it from the first day through the seventh must be cut off from Israel. 16 On the first day hold a sacred assembly, and another one on the seventh day. Do no work at all on these days, except to prepare food for everyone to eat—that is all you may do. 17 "Celebrate the Feast of Unleavened Bread, because it was on this very day that I brought your divisions out of Egypt. Celebrate this day as a lasting ordinance for the generations to come. 18 In the first month you are to eat bread made without yeast, from the evening of the fourteenth day until the evening of the twenty-first day.

19 For seven days no yeast is to be found in your houses. And whoever eats anything with yeast in it must be cut off from the community of Israel, whether he is an alien or native-born. 20 Eat nothing made with yeast. Wherever you live, you must eat unleavened bread."

There are several numbers at work in this passage. We will look at the number 7, 8 and 21. In the above passage, the Lord is going to deliver the Israelites from the Egyptians. However, the Lord needed the people to do a few things in advance. On the 10th of the first month, the family was instructed to take a lamb and take care of it until the fourteenth day of the month. The people would have to be together in the evening to slaughter the lambs. The blood from the slaughter was sprinkled on the doorposts of all the houses of the Israelites. The Lord would Passover each house that was covered with the blood. The Lord struck down every firstborn male and firstborn animal if there was no blood on the doorposts. Besides the roasted lamb meat, the Israelites were instructed to prepare unleavened bread, but why? The Lord was going to have Passover on the 14th, if the Israelites prepared leavened bread; they would waste a day waiting for the bread to rise which would put Passover on the 15th. Leavened bread was comfort food and this was not the time for comfort, it was time for business. In fact, timing (10) was critical because it was time to be delivered from the Egyptians. It is easier to carry unleavened bread (crackers) because it last longer than fermented bread which contains yeast.

    The scriptures teach the Israelites were not to have any bread with yeast for seven days which is the 14th to the 21st. Seven means to be satisfied, full or enough. The Israelites had enough and that all is they needed to get through Passover. The Lord wanted to move on the 14th and he was not going put his plans off for a bread baking recipe. The Israelites did not have time to make leavened bread, if so, they would have had to make the bread on the 13th. How is the number seven being used? The number seven is being used in multiples all the way up to the number twenty one. Afterwards, there is a release and freedom from oppression ($7 \times 2 = 14$ and $7 \times 3 = 21$). What happens after the seventh day? We can assume they start using yeast on the 8th day.

Eight is symbolic of new beginnings for the Israelites because they will no longer be under the rule of Egypt. The number Twenty One represents freedom, deliverance and release. There is a little more to unleavened bread than rising yeast. Typically, we are taught the "unleavened bread" represents the "seven days of coming out of sin". We should consider that leavened bread represents Sin. Yeast is compared to sin because it grows. The word "sin" is a Roman word used in the game of archery. One sinned if the mark was missed (bulls eye). We are human and we are prone to "sin". Often, sin can lead to addiction and bondage. This is why sin is compared to leavened bread because it grows. The "unleavened bread" represents the body of Jesus the Christ. Through Jesus, we have victory over sin because we are covered by the blood of Jesus. The blood of Jesus represents his life which was anointed by God.

Passover affirms our baptismal covenant mentioned in Acts 2:38 and 5:32 with Jesus the Christ. When we repent and come out of sin, there will be a void where sin resided. What does God instruct his children to do for seven Days? God commands them to consume unleavened bread (Lev.23:6), which represents the body of Jesus the Christ, (John 6:51).

"I am the living bread which came down from heaven: if any man eat of this bread, he shall live for ever: and the bread that I will give is my flesh, which I will give for the life of the world."

We are to put the leavened bread or sin out of our houses and our lives (Exodus: 12:14-20) before the Days of "Unleavened Bread" begin. We also learn about removing sin from our lives by the account provided in Matt.12:43-45. An unclean spirit went out of a man. The man did not fill the void with righteousness. Seven more spirits came to possess the same man. So we must take sin seriously. The number 21 reminds us to be mindful of sin and how to look for the release from bondage in our lives.

EXAMPLE 2
Daniel 10:12-14
12 Then he continued, "Do not be afraid, Daniel. Since the first day that you set your mind to gain understanding and to humble yourself

before your God, your words were heard, and I have come in response to them. 13 But the prince of the Persian kingdom resisted me twenty-one days. Then Michael, one of the chief princes, came to help me, because I was detained there with the king of Persia. 14 Now I have come to explain to you what will happen to your people in the future, for the vision concerns a time yet to come."

Daniel saw a man in his vision. This man was to respond to Daniel's prayers. This man was held up by the Price of Persia, which is a dominion level demon (Eph 6:12). This Prince of Persia held up this man for 21 days and it took the help of the Chief Arch Angel Michael to free this man from his struggle with the Prince of Persia. We can assume that if Michael did not intervene, this man would have taken longer to arrive to respond to Daniel's prayers. This man was not oppressed but he was tied up. The number twenty one represents a release from struggle. The number 3 is at work in this passage because Daniel had this vision in the 3rd year of Cyrus's reign as King of Persia. Daniel mourned and fasted for three weeks. 3 x 7 = 21, this number is symbolic of freedom from struggle and oppression and bondage. This also represents self bondage in the form drugs, alcohol, porn, strip clubs, prostitution, cigarettes, cursing, gossip, dependency, pride, falsehood and deceit. Often, we are our own worst enemy.

22

ERRONEOUS THINKING, DECISIONS, METHODS, PLANS

THE NUMBER TWENTY TWO (22)

ERRONEOUS THINKING, DECISIONS, METHODS, PLANS

TWENTY TWO
Preparation, diplomacy and relations describe the qualities of this number. This number involves people (2) and things (4). In the Bible, the number twenty two represents erroneous thinking, decisions, gains and losses. The number 22 reduces to a single digit 4 which is a number planning, methods and structure. This number also possesses the qualities of the 2: $2 + 2 = 4$ and $2 \times 2 = 4$.

EXAMPLE 1
Joshua 19:29-31
29 The boundary then turned back toward Ramah and went to the fortified city of Tyre, turned toward Hosah and came out at the sea in the region of Aczib, 30 Ummah, Aphek and Rehob. There were twenty-two towns and their villages.
31 These towns and their villages were the inheritance of the tribe of Asher, clan by clan.
The keyword in this passage is *boundary* because 22 is a number of planning and structure. A boundary was established for twenty two towns and villages. Regarding gains and losses, these towns were inherited by Asher.

EXAMPLE 2
Judges 7:2-8
2 The LORD said to Gideon, "You have too many men for me to deliver Midian into their hands. In order that Israel may not boast against me that her own strength has saved her, 3 announce now to the people, 'Anyone who trembles with fear may turn back and leave Mount Gilead.' "So twenty-two thousand men left, while ten thousand remained.

4 But the LORD said to Gideon, "There are still too many men. Take them down to the water, and I will sift them for you there. If I say, 'This one shall go with you,' he shall go; but if I say, 'This one shall not go with you,' he shall not go."

5 So Gideon took the men down to the water. There the LORD told him, "Separate those who lap the water with their tongues like a dog from those who kneel down to drink." 6 Three hundred men lapped with their hands to their mouths. All the rest got down on their knees to drink.

7 The LORD said to Gideon, "With the three hundred men that lapped I will save you and give the Midianites into your hands. Let all the other men go, each to his own place." 8 So Gideon sent the rest of the Israelites to their tents but kept the three hundred, who took over the provisions and trumpets of the others. Now the camp of Midian lay below him in the valley.

The Lord is demonstrating his power in the lives of the Israelites. They are about to war against the Midians but Israel has too many men. Through an offer by God, the faithless and fearful men of Israel have an opportunity to avoid war and leave town. Twenty two thousand men accept the offer and exit the town. A lack of faith is an error in judgment. Failing to not trusting God is erroneous thinking and leads to loss and death. This entire passage speaks to the idea of decisions and methods. There was devil at work in this passage, all God had to do was observe the habits of 10,000 men. In othe words, all of us are prone to excercising erroneous technique in the trials of life. In verse 5, God wanted to reduce the number men who will war against the Midians. God instructs Gideon to take the men to the river and God is observing how the men drink water. God is looking at the *method* used by each man to drink water from the river. God wanted to see which men would drink water by lapping water like a dog. Anyone wth a dog knows that a dog drink water without kneeling. The Lord was also looking to see who knelt down to drink, like a camel. A camel can afford to kneel while drinking because they have no natural predators in the desert. Even the mighty Lion knows not to kneel while drinking at a water source. Kneeling down to drink is not ideal because the men must be ready to respond to any sudden attacks. If you are kneeling down, you are already in position to be defeated.

So it is with our decisions, he watches our technique as well. A dog has four feet but never kneels to drink. Rarely will you see a four-legged animal (Lion, Tiger, and Zebra) kneel down at a water well. Kneeling down at water well is erroneous thinking and could cost you your life. If a dog has enough sense to stand on all four feet while drinking near a water source, what can we say of a man who kneels down to drink at a river? Anything can happen to him in that position. He will not be in position to respond to any sudden events. This number teaches us to put ourselves in a position to respond to the enemy and to avoid erroneous thinking. In this passage, there was no mention of generational curses or demonic activity. This numbers reminds to take ownership for our actions and how we handle our business opposed to blaming the Devil or somebody else for our mistakes.

EXAMPLE 3
2 Chronicles 7:4-6
4 Then the king and all the people offered sacrifices before the LORD. 5 And King Solomon offered a sacrifice of twenty-two thousand head of cattle and a hundred and twenty thousand sheep and goats. So the king and all the people dedicated the temple of God. 6 The priests took their positions, as did the Levites with the LORD's musical instruments, which King David had made for praising the LORD and were used when he gave thanks, saying, "His love endures forever." Opposite the Levites, the priests blew their trumpets, and all the Israelites were standing.

This passage represents the offering made by Solomon. Let us put 21st century spin on this passage. In church, the Pastor may say it is time for tithes and offering. What do most of us do? We start thinking and we make a DECISION on whether we are going give an offering. We make a decision on how much we are going to offer. Ten percent of the gross is expected for the tithe. The offering is a freewill decision. Solomon decided to offer twenty two thousand heads of Oxen. He could have offered a lesser amount. There was no error in his thinking and he showed faith in God by his offering. Solomon understands that one must be in position to offer sacrifices. He also understands the power of the freewill offer and Solomon was known as a wise man.

EXAMPLE 4

Judges 20:20-22

20 The men of Israel went out to fight the Benjamites and took up battle positions against them at Gibeah. 21 The Benjamites came out of Gibeah and cut down twenty-two thousand Israelites on the battlefield that day. 22 But the men of Israel encouraged one another and again took up their positions where they had stationed themselves the first day.

Erroneous thinking leads to bad plans, methods and plays. In Judges 20, the Israelites executed bad plays. They lost the first time but eventually they got it right by looking at how they went to war. In the other words, the Israelites reviewed their methods and plans. This requires methodic planning for events and personal plans. This numbers reminds us to be methodic and effective in all things.

23

OBEDIENCE, FORMATION, GROUP FAITH

THE NUMBER TWENTY THREE (23)

Obedience, Formation, Group Faith

In the Bible, the number twenty three is used with various themes in the scripture. The first examples are found in 1 Chronicles 2:21-23, 1 Corinthians and Jeremiah 25:2-4. The other examples are used in the context of longevity for the Kings of Judah and Israel. This number is specialized and is not used as often as the number seven or twelve. Twenty Three is composed of the number 2 (preparation) and 3 (creative thought). Twenty Three is related to the number 5 (2+3) and 6 (2x3, 3x2, 2x2x2). Reformation, discernment and preparation represent the qualities of the number Twenty Three. The number two is the driving force behind the number twenty three. The number twenty three symbolizes the ability to follow established rules and guidelines. The numbers 5 (organize people) and 6 (commerce, domestication, responsibility) are associated with the twenty three as well. This means that people will be organized and managed.

EXAMPLE 1

The 23rd Psalm is the best example to describe the definition of this awesome number. Obedience, formation and the proper organization is vital regarding this number. 2 + 3 = 5. Five deals with the movement and organization of people. The shepherd is responsible for moving and organizing the sheep. However, the sheep must be obedient by listening and following. The sheep can easily be attacked or destroyed by predators if they fail to listen and be obedient. To whom must the sheep listen and follow? The sheep must listen and follow the shepherd. Who is our shepherd? Our shepherd is Jesus the Christ, the Son of God. This is where the number twenty three becomes critical. This number addresses the mobilization and organization of people.

In other words, twenty three is a number of group faith and behavior. Specifically, $2 + 3 = 5$ and five represents the movement and change of people. The number five represents obedient groups of people seeking the guidance of God the Father through his Son Christ Jesus. The very core of this number reveals this fact. A man and a woman both provide 23 chromosomes to procreate life. Without the act of procreation, humanity would not be able to organize to take dominion of the earth. The Word of God stresses the importance of these two numbers in the following Books of the Bible:

GROUP FAITH AND BEHAVIOR

Deuteronomy 19: 15: 2 or 3 witnesses
Joshua 7:3: 2 or 3 witnesses
Isaiah 17:6: 2 or 3 grapes
Matthew 18: 20: 2 or 3 gathered

Twenty Three is a number which should be studied by church leaders because of its close relationship to the number five (2+3=5). This is one of those numbers that require in depth study and reflection. Some numbers such as the number two and three are very mystifying. I was very excited when the movie "23" starring Jim Carey was released. The movie was mysterious in the beginning but it lost substance towards the middle of the movie. About the movie and my quest of studying numbers and letters, I did not find "it". For trivial purposes, I included some very interesting facts concerning this mysterious number. Of all the numbers, I find two, three, twenty three and twenty eight the most intriguing because they have geometric, anatomical and mathematical significance.

Consider the following concerning the number twenty three:

Human sex cells have 23 chromosomes.

The planet Earth has an axial tilt of 23.5 degrees

The number of joints in the human arm is 23.

$2/3 = .666$

The earth rotates on an axis of 23 and a half degrees.

Each parent contributes 23 chromosomes to start a new human life during reproduction.

It takes 23 seconds for blood to circulate through the body.

Alphabet: The W is the 23 letter of this alphabet. The letter W symbol for that letter is two points down and three points up.

BCE, the term meaning "Before Common Era", or before the birth of Christ. B, C, E: the 2nd, 3rd, and 5th letters of the alphabet.

Bible Daniel 8:14 And he said unto me, Unto two thousand and three hundred days; then shall the sanctuary be cleansed.

Bible: There is no 23rd Chapter to Revelations. Revelations

In ancient Israel, every city had a local Sanhedrin each which had 23 judges.

In Japanese, "ni" is 2, and "san" is 3 which spells Nisan or Nissan (the car). Nisan is also a Hebrew month adopted from Babylonians.

LeBron James wears the number 23 shirt.

Chicago Bull's basketball star Michael Jordan's retired shirt number is 23, which is also the day of his father's death.

WILLIAM Shakespeare was born and died on April 23.

The comet Hale-Bopp was first sighted on July 23, 1996.

ROMAN Emperor Julius Caesar was stabbed 23 times when he was assassinated.

The average smoker gets through 23 cigarettes a day.

December 23, Birth date of Joseph Smith, founder of The
1805 Church of Jesus Christ of Latter-day
Saints (Mormons).

Adolf Hitler organized the National
Socialist Congress on January 23.
On November 23 he tried to take over.

There are 23 buildings on the Microsoft
campus in Redmond, Washington.

September 23 is the Fall Equinox.

September 23 is Yom Kippur.

There are exactly 23 visible letters and numbers on the
front of the U.S. Coins. Some coins have a single letter under the year.

URLs for the web contain 2 "/"s and 3 W's (http://www)

Washington D.C starts with the letter "W", the 23rd letter of the
alphabet. The Pentagon (5 sides) is located in Washington D.C.

24

WORSHIP, HIGH PRAISE

THE NUMBER TWENTY FOUR (24)

WORSHIP, HIGH PRAISE

The number twenty-four embodies the fullness of high praise and the worship of Almighty God. The number twenty-four is composed of a 2 (preparation, social reformation) and 4 (organizing things). Six is a number of commerce and passion, domestication and service: (2 + 4 = 6). Applying mathematics, we will analyze the numbers 2, 4, and 6 to understand the nature of the number 24. This number is a step beyond organizing things (4) and organizing people (5). Twenty Four is a number of service, protocol and passion. The number 12 plays an important role in building the number twenty four because 12 x 2 = 24 and 12 + 2 = 24. Twelve is a number sacrifice. One must be willing to offer something to make a sacrifice. The number twenty four is a number of worship and high praise for God Almighty. This number teaches us to offer a sacrifice of praise. Twenty Four reminds us to offer time from our busy schedules and give God time through praise and worship. Do you have time for God the Father?

EXAMPLE 1
Numbers 7: 87-89
87 The total number of animals for the burnt offering came to twelve young bulls, twelve rams and twelve male lambs a year old, with their grain offering. Twelve male goats were used for the sin offering. 88 The total number of animals for the sacrifice of the fellowship offering came to twenty-four oxen, sixty rams, sixty male goats and sixty male lambs a year old. These were the offerings for the dedication of the altar after it was anointed. 89 When Moses entered the Tent of Meeting to speak with the LORD, he heard the voice speaking to him from between the two cherubim above the atonement cover on the ark of the Testimony. And he spoke with him.
There are four type offerings which are the burnt offering, grain offering, sin offering and the fellowship offering. Twelve young bulls, rams and male lambs were offered for the burnt and grain offering. Pork was not on the menu.

The number twelve is a number of sacrifices but a sacrifice has no real purpose without something of value to offer. Whatever we offer must have value or it is a not a sacrifice. Was this a real sacrifice or just a Holy dinner? Sure this was a real sacrifice if you consider that killing too many animals at the wrong time was not ideal in those days. The idea is to kill what you need based on the population of your tribe. If there was not enough rain and poor crops and few animals, the sacrificial ceremony still had to be completed. The number twelve reveals a sacrifice will be required. Twelve plus twelve equals twenty four which means that a sacrifice is a critical part of worshipping God. If we are not willing to make an offer or offers then how can we be obedient to Gods will for our lives? If we are not willing to make an offer to God then how can we expect to God to make an offer to us?

The fellowship offering required twenty four oxen, sixty rams, sixty male goats and sixty 1-year old male lambs. Twenty Four in this passage reminds us that fellowship is another critical part of worship. Fellowship is critical because it allows us concentrate on the presence of God and places us on God's turf. Fellowship reinforces group behavior which leads to unification of faith in the spirit. The two most intelligent decisions that any person can make are to accept Christ and engage in group fellowship in Christ. That is powerful insurance and assurance. The number 24 calls us to high worship and accountability. Twenty Four is a higher vibration of 12 which is a number of sacrifices. This is just one phase of worship.

EXAMPLE 2
Nehemiah 9: 1-3
The Israelites Confess Their Sins
1 On the twenty-fourth day of the same month, the Israelites gathered together, fasting and wearing sackcloth and having dust on their heads. 2 Those of Israelite descent had separated themselves from all foreigners. They stood in their places and confessed their sins and the

wickedness of their fathers. 3 They stood where they were and read from the Book of the Law of the LORD their God for a quarter of the day, and spent another quarter in confession and in worshiping the LORD their God.

Worshipping God requires more than prayer. Confession and repentance are critical parts of worship. The idea of worship is to stay in covenant relationship with Almighty God. Confession allows us to realign ourselves with God when we fall short of the glory. Confession demonstrates that one is aware of sinful behavior. This also includes the sins of your fathers. The Israelites had to separate themselves from all foreigners. They did not bring the influences of other people to the place of worship. The Israelites came to God as clean as possible.

EXAMPLE 3
Revelation 4
The Throne in Heaven
4Surrounding the throne were twenty-four other thrones, and seated on them were twenty-four elders. They were dressed in white and had crowns of gold on their heads. 5From the throne came flashes of lightning, rumblings and peals of thunder. Before the throne, seven lamps were blazing. These are the seven spirits of God. 6Also before the throne there was what looked like a sea of glass, clear as crystal. In the center, around the throne, were four living creatures, and they were covered with eyes, in front and in back. 7The first living creature was like a lion, the second was like an ox, the third had a face like a man, the fourth was like a flying eagle. 8Each of the four living creatures had six wings and was covered with eyes all around, even under his wings. Day and night they never stop saying: "Holy, holy, holy is the Lord God Almighty, who was, and is, and is to come." 9Whenever the living creatures give glory, honor and thanks to him who sits on the throne and who lives for ever and ever, 10the twenty-four elders fall down before him who sits on the throne, and worship him who lives for ever and ever. They lay their crowns before the throne and say: 11"You are worthy, our Lord and God, to receive glory and honor and power, for you created all things, and by your will they were created and have their being.

John is taken to Heaven in the spirit where he saw someone sitting upon a throne. Twenty-Four other thrones with twenty four elders surrounded the throne. He also saw seven lights which represent the seven spirits of God.

There were four living creatures around the throne and what are they doing? They were worshipping the One on the throne. The four creatures worship the one the throne day and night by saying "Holy, holy, holy is the Lord God Almighty, who was, and is, and is to come". How magnificent it would be to have a 24-hour worship service! The number twenty-four is symbolic of true worship and high praise for God Almighty. This number teaches us how to stay focused in our pursuit of the Holy Spirit. The number two represents thoughts and emotions. The number four handles the organization of things. The "things" are the offerings: sin offering, grain offering, burnt offering and the fellowship offering.

EXAMPLE 4
Haggai 2:9-16
Blessings for a Defiled People

10 On the twenty-fourth day of the ninth month, in the second year of Darius, the word of the LORD came to the prophet Haggai: 11 "This is what the LORD Almighty says: 'Ask the priests what the law says: 12 If a person carries consecrated meat in the fold of his garment, and that fold touches some bread or stew, some wine, oil or other food, does it become consecrated?' "

The priests answered, "No."

13 Then Haggai said, "If a person defiled by contact with a dead body touches one of these things, does it become defiled?"

"Yes," the priests replied, "it becomes defiled."

14 Then Haggai said, " 'So it is with this people and this nation in my sight,' declares the LORD. 'Whatever they do and whatever they offer there is defiled.

15 " 'Now give careful thought to this from this day on —consider how things were before one stone was laid on another in the LORD's temple. 16 When anyone came to a heap of twenty measures, there were only ten.

When anyone went to a wine vat to draw fifty measures, there were only twenty. 17 I struck all the work of your hands with blight, mildew and hail, yet you did not turn to me,' declares the LORD. 18 'From this day on, from this twenty-fourth day of the ninth month, give careful thought to the day when the foundation of the LORD's temple was laid. Give careful thought: 19 Is there yet any seed left in the barn? Until now, the vine and the fig tree, the pomegranate and the olive tree have not borne fruit. " From this day on I will bless you. "

We read in the 18th verse about the day the Foundation of the Lord's temple is laid. We may not be able to be in the company of the twenty four elders in Revelation 4. However, we can get a similar thrill in the church if we worship God in spirit and truth. How can we truly worship Almighty God if we are unclean? Sin separates us from God. I am convinced the power of God's anointing in our lives is directly related to the level of cleanliness in our lives. Therefore, we strive for righteousness, not just any righteousness but righteousness in Christ where we are covered by the blood of Jesus (his life). If we fall, then we should get up and continue to strive for righteousness, sanctification and cleanliness. The number twenty-four is about worshipping Almighty God. This number calls us to pay attention to what we worship or what we make into a god. This number reminds us to worship our God in spirit and truth. The Body of Christ should be watchful and mindful of this number. This number can symbolically be used for fasting (24 hour or days). The number 24 reminds us to keep our eyes on Father, the Son and the Holy Ghost. This number reminds us that praise is paramount in each of our lives. Lastly, when we get weary in prayer, remember the four beasts mentioned in Revelation 4 who praise God 24 hours a day.

25

THE BRIDGE OF LIFE, JOINING, CONNECTIONS

THE NUMBER TWENTY FIVE (25)

THE BRIDGE OF LIFE, JOINING, CONNECTIONS

Faith, discernment, analysis, joining, connections and spiritual devotion represent the qualities of the number twenty five. Twenty five teaches us that faith is designed to combat the harshness of reality. Faith reveals our true zest for the Holy presence of God. It takes devotion to praise Almighty God day and night as in the number 24. Twenty-Five teaches us to have a high faith in Almighty God. Twenty-Five reduces to the number seven because $2 + 5 = 7$. The number seven is associated with the letter Z or zayin/zain. Looking closely at the letter Z, notice the two 7's. The first seven is in the up position. The other seven is in the down position. The number twenty five represents the connection between the spirit world (up) and the physical world (down). 7 and the entire seven line (7, 16, and 25) is known as the *bridge* because the seven connects the physical to the spiritual.

The 25th is associated with the birth of Jesus. He is our bridge to the spiritual realm but we must accept him as Lord and savior to have special access between both worlds. If you do not choose him then you will go to a spiritual realm but not with Christ Jesus present. **Twenty-Five teaches us to be concerned about the migration of the spirit upon death.** Most people are not concerned about death until a loved one transitions from this life. Wisdom suggests that we should take an interest in what happens to our spirit upon death because the spirit lives on. The first law of thermodynamics confirms this fact: Energy cannot be created nor destroyed. Jesus had the power to cross both worlds of the seen and the unseen. He knows the way so why not choose him. Why go into uncharted area when you can go with someone who knows the way. Twenty Five represents the entire crossing from the physical world to a specific place in the spirit world. Trust me; the spirit world is another ball game. It is best to have an ambassador at death. When we accept Christ, we have access to a specific area in the spirit world. There is no hanging around or being lost in the spirit world. The physical world is temporary, it is very short, but it appears long to five senses.

We enter another existence when we transition from this physical plane. The definitions of many letters and numbers clearly points to the existence of another world and twenty five is one of those numbers. Was Christ born on 12/25? Who knows? However, he is associated with the number twenty five and that is good enough for me. This number is symbolic of his role as the Son of God but serving as a bridge for humanity. Jesus came to earth that we would have life more abundantly. Twenty Five is symbolic of a bridge which carries the spirit from inside the physical realm to the spiritual realm. Twenty Five is a reminder of the devotion required to be connected to Almighty God the Father.

EXAMPLE 1
Revelation 4
The Throne in Heaven
1After this I looked, and there before me was a door standing open in heaven. And the voice I had first heard speaking to me like a trumpet said, "Come up here, and I will show you what must take place after this." 2At once I was in the Spirit, and there before me was a throne in heaven with someone sitting on it. 3And the one who sat there had the appearance of jasper and carnelian. A rainbow, resembling an emerald, encircled the throne. 4Surrounding the throne were twenty-four other thrones, and seated on them were twenty-four elders. They were dressed in white and had crowns of gold on their heads. 5From the throne came flashes of lightning, rumblings and peals of thunder. Before the throne, seven lamps were blazing. These are the seven spirits of God. 6Also before the throne there was what looked like a sea of glass, clear as crystal

I used Revelation 4 for the number twenty-four. However, we can also use this verse for the number twenty-five. Verse 2 states there was one throne, the main throne. Verse four states there were twenty-four thrones. Actually, there are twenty-five thrones. Consider the following: $24 + 1 = 25$ and $2 + 5 = 7$ and 7 means to be full, satisfied or enough. In other words, this is where many may never go or see. This location mentioned in the scriptures is the other side of the bridge or twenty-five.

Twenty five is a higher vibration of the number *seven*. In verse five, there are *seven* spirits of God. About the number 25, the number two represents reformation of the people. In this case; we are discussing heavenly affairs about the twenty four elders and the four living creatures. The number five represents the organizing people. The number five is a number of communication and grace. The four living creatures worship Almighty God day and night. The twenty four elders were worshipping Almighty God as well. Imagine that! We as humans offer a few hours of worship at best. However, there other creatures in heaven that worship Almighty God day and night.

EXAMPLE 2
Nehemiah 6 14-16: Faith, Devotion

14 Remember Tobiah and Sanballat, O my God, because of what they have done; remember also the prophetess Noadiah and the rest of the prophets who have been trying to intimidate me from the completion of the Wall 15 So the wall was completed on the twenty-fifth of Elul, in fifty-two days. 16 When all our enemies heard about this, all the surrounding nations were afraid and lost their self-confidence, because they realized that this work had been done with the help of our God.

This is a wonderful story of faith and discernment. Nehemiah was determined to rebuild the wall in Jerusalem. Sanballat, Geshem did not want Nehemiah to rebuild the wall. Because Nehemiah wanted to rebuild the wall, there was a plan to kill Nehemiah. The idea was to plan a meeting and kill Nehemiah when he arrived. Nehemiah discerned what was in the hearts of his opposers. He did not go the meeting despite the five attempts offered by Sanballat and Geshem. Nehemiah was asked by Shemaih to meet with him inside the house of God so Nehemiah could hide from Shaballat and Geshem because they wanted to kill him. However, Nehemiah knew that a man of his calling should not run or hide in the house of the Lord. He discerned that Shemiah was paid by Shaballat and Geshem so they could spread cowardly rumors about Nehemiah. The prophet knew that he could run and hide. But, running would not look good and would cause the people to lose faith him and God.

The number twenty-five is a number of faith, discernment and spiritual devotion. This number reminds us to never run from the enemy. Notice how Nehemiah respected his office as a prophet. Jeremiah ensured that he "walked it the way he talked it". He discerned that Shemiah was not sent by God. Nehemiah knew that Almighty God is mighty in battle and would not have him run, duck or hide from the enemy.

The number Twenty Five is a reminder that we should always walk in our identity as the children of Almighty God. We should know who we are in Christ Jesus, the Son of God. Shaballat and Geshem went through all of this so Nehemiah would not rebuild the wall in Jerusalem. But why? What is the big deal? If you notice, the wall was built in the month of Elul. This is an important month for the Jews. The wall was completed on the 25th day of Elul and it was completed in 52 days. If you notice, 52 is the opposite of 25. Both numbers reduce to the number seven, which means to be satisfied, full, or enough. I talked about the number 25 being a number of faith and devotion. Elul is the twelfth month of the ecclesiastical year. Elul is a time of repentance for the high Holidays of Rosh Hashanah and Yom Kippur. This is the time to ask for forgiveness from others and God. During this month, several rituals are conducted which lead up to the High Holy days. For example, the *shofar* is blown every morning from Rosh Hodesh Elul to the day before Rosh Hashanah. These blasts are designed to awaken our spirits and urge us to look at our inner selves and prepare for the High Holy Days. If you notice, the 25th of Elul is similar to the 25th of December. Elul is the 12th month of the Hebrew calendar. This is a little food for thought concerning the Christian during Christmas in this western culture.

EXAMPLE 3
Numbers 8:23-25
23 The LORD said to Moses, 24 "This applies to the Levites: Men twenty-five years old or more shall come to take part in the work at the Tent of Meeting, 25 but at the age of fifty, they must retire from their regular service and work no longer.

We need to discuss the Levites to understand how the number 25 is being used in this passage. Who were the Levites? The Levites were the only Israelite tribes who received cities and no tribal land when Joshua led the Israelites into the land of Canaan. The Tribe of Levi served particular religious duties for the Israelites. The landed tribes were expected to give tithes to the Levites. In Number 18:2 and Genesis 29:34, the name *Levi* is interpreted as "joined" or "attached to". We talked earlier about the number 25 being associated with a bridge which connects the physical to the spiritual. In the book of Numbers 8, the Levites were set aside to perform devotional duties as Priest. They were appointed in the Mosaic Law for the service of the Tabernacle and of the Temple. The number 25 is symbolic of the service of the Tabernacle and of the Temple. This is a physical version of the four creatures who praised Almighty God day and night in Revelation 4:4. The beginning of Numbers 8 talks about 7 lamps. The 7 lamps represent the 7 spirits of God mentioned in Revelation 4. The number twenty five stresses the importance of Godly devotion, praise and the connection to Christ Jesus that we may have access to a specific place in the spirit world.

EXAMPLE 4
Ezekiel 8:15-17
15 He said to me, "Do you see this, son of man? You will see things that are even more detestable than this."
16 He then brought me into the inner court of the house of the LORD, and there at the entrance to the temple, between the portico and the altar, were about twenty-five men. With their backs toward the temple of the LORD and their faces toward the east, they were bowing down to the sun in the east.

17 He said to me, "Have you seen this, son of man? Is it a trivial matter for the house of Judah to do the detestable things they are doing here? Must they also fill the land with violence and continually provoke me to anger? Look at them putting the branch to their nose!

The house of Judah did detestable things in the eyes of the Lord. In this example, we see a lack of devotion, the house of Judah is not in a position to deal with a lack of faith. How can you devote yourself to the Lord when you have no faith in the Lord? Devotion demands faith.

26

MOBILIZATION, SPECIALIZATION AND ORGANIZATION

THE NUMBER TWENTY SIX (26)

MOBILIZATION, SPECIALIZATION AND ORGANIZATION

The Bible does not offer too much information on this number. Twenty Six is a member of the eight family which includes the numbers 8, 17. Twenty-Six contains all the inherent qualities of the number eight which represents new beginnings, execution, control, reformation, vision and management. However, twenty-six is a little more specialized because it is rooted by the number two (preparation, reformation, communication) and six (commerce, domestication, service, work). This makes 26 a powerful number and it will always be found working to reform and manage the masses. Twenty-Six knows how to organize the people. This is a number of war and politics because the number 2 represents people. The number 6 represents commerce, work and service. Twenty-Six is a specialized number, which organizes people.

EXAMPLE 1
Judges 20:14-16
14 From their towns they came together at Gibeah to fight against the Israelites. 15 At once the Benjamites mobilized twenty-six thousand swordsmen from their towns, in addition to seven hundred chosen men from those living in Gibeah. 16 Among all these soldiers there were seven hundred chosen men who were left-handed, each of whom could sling a stone at a hair and not miss.

The number twenty-six is mobilizing the men of Benjamin to fight against the Israelites. There are two numbers at work in this passage: 26 and 7. I talked about twenty six as being a number of specialization. In this case, the twenty six thousand men were mobilized to fight. There were twenty six thousand swordsmen (specialization) and there were seven hundred left-handed men who were gifted with the use of the slingshot. The number seven means to be satisfied, full or enough and it is also a number of perfection. In other words the seven hundred left-handed men were perfect in their specialization.

EXAMPLE 2

2 Chronicles 35:7-9

Josiah provided for all the lay people who were there a total of thirty thousand sheep and goats for the Passover offerings, and also three thousand cattle—all from the king's own possessions.

8 His officials also contributed voluntarily to the people and the priests and Levites. Hilkiah, Zechariah and Jehiel, the administrators of God's temple, gave the priests twenty-six hundred Passover offerings and three hundred cattle. 9 Also Conaniah along with Shemaiah and Nethanel, his brothers, and Hashabiah, Jeiel and Jozabad, the leaders of the Levites, provided five thousand Passover offerings and five hundred head of cattle for the Levites.

I talked about the root numbers of 26, which are 2 and 6. The number six represents domestication, work and service. Josiah is providing the lay people with sheep and goats for the Passover offering. In verse 8, we read the officials also contributed voluntarily to the people. Imagine that! This is like a group of politicians using government funds to help people without all the bureaucratic confusion. The number twenty-six represents the mobilizing of people for a cause. In this case, it is for an offering.

27

STAGES, ENTRANCES, EXITS, MASS INFLUENCE, COMPASSION

THE NUMBER TWENTY SEVEN (27)

STAGES, ENTRANCES, EXITS, MASS INFLUENCE, COMPASSION

The number twenty seven is an awesome number. This number is part of the 9 line which includes the numbers 9 and 18. Twenty Seven is a higher vibration and expression of the number nine. Nine is a number of mass influence and compassion. It is a staging number which means something will end and something will begin. This number typically indicates an ending in the Bible. An ending can be anything from death to the rising of a new King. The number nine is an escort number. This number is used to enter another level. For example, 9 exits 1-8 and enters 10-19. 19 exits 10-18 and enters 20. 29 exits 20-28 and enters 30. In the number 27, the number two (reformation, preparation) is partnered with the number 7 (to be satisfied, full or enough, finish, perfection). Therefore, twenty-seven represents people, phases and endings. Twenty-Seven is a number of mass influences because of the 2 and 7 rooting. In other words, 2 (reformation, preparation) is working with 7 (perfection, enough, fullness) and the result is the staging area of the nine which leads to the next level.

Consider the name of Jesus, which has a value of 9 in the Hebrew numbering system. Also, the name Jesus Christ has a numerical value of nine in the Hebrew numbering system. The Book of Revelation reveals the number nine will play a major role concerning the battle between the Christ and the Anti-Christ. The number of the Christ is 9 and the number of the beast is 9 (666), 6 x 3 = 18, 1 + 8 = 9. Also, notice the word "women" equals nine. This means the woman will be the object of the final battle between good and evil. Humanity does not have a chance at survival when all the women are corrupted. Men can always be procreated as long as there are women on the planet. Women represent the number nine (mass influence). Women are the salvation of man and civilization.

The forces of evil know this is true and the Angels know this is true. Too much emphasis has been placed on watching the destructive behavior of men.

However, we should direct our attention to the worldwide condition and treatment the woman. Men will probably succeed in depleting the earth of its resources but an elevated feminine presence will balance the unruly nature of the male. Think of the woman when you think of the number nine. Most people think of the devil or the beast when we think of the number 666, which is a nine. We need to start thinking about Jesus when we hear any flavor of the number nine: 9, 18 and 27. Also, we need to remember the mass influence of the constructed woman when we think of the number nine. Twenty-Seven is a higher vibration of the number nine. This is an entrance and exit number. This is a staging number of influences. If you think I am making this up, consider what happens when a woman gives birth to a child. The child progresses from one stage to another. The child travels from the womb into the stage of life. At the end of this life, the spirit of that child migrates to another realm and it all starts in the womb of the mother. The woman was the chosen vessel to handle this awesome task. All women are corporately under the influence of the number nine.

EXAMPLE 1
Genesis 8:13-15
13 By the first day of the first month of Noah's six hundred and first year, the water had dried up from the earth. Noah then removed the covering from the ark and saw that the surface of the ground was dry. 14 By the twenty-seventh day of the second month the earth was completely dry.
The earth was completely dry by the 27th day of the second month. In other words, prior to the 27th of the second month, the earth was still wet or soggy. The end of the earth's wetness came on the 27th day of the second month. The dryness of the land represents a new stage.

EXAMPLE 2
1 Kings 16: 9-11

9 Zimri, one of his officials, who had command of half his chariots, plotted against him. Elah was in Tirzah at the time, getting drunk in the home of Arza, the man in charge of the palace at Tirzah. 10 Zimri came in, struck him down and killed him in the twenty-seventh year of Asa king of Judah. Then he succeeded him as king. 11 As soon as he began to reign and was seated on the throne, he killed off Baasha's whole family. He did not spare a single male, whether relative or friend.

The above passage indicates that Elah was killed by Zimri in the 27th year of the reign of Asa. The number 27 is symbolic of the ending of Zimri's life. Again, when you see the number 27 or any flavor of the nine: 9, 18, look for an ending or a new stage.

EXAMPLE 3
1 Kings 20 29-31

29 For seven days they camped opposite each other, and on the seventh day the battle was joined. The Israelites inflicted a hundred thousand casualties on the Aramean foot soldiers in one day. 30 The rest of them escaped to the city of Aphek, where the wall collapsed on twenty-seven thousand of them. And Ben-Hadad fled to the city and hid in an inner room. 31 His officials said to him, "Look, we have heard that the kings of the house of Israel are merciful. Let us go to the king of Israel with sackcloth around our waists and ropes around our heads. Perhaps he will spare your life."

A wall collapsed and ended the life of twenty seven thousand men. Look for an ending whenever you see this number in the scripture. The ending could be good or bad.

EXAMPLE 4
1 Chronicles 26:31-33
31 As for the Hebronites, Jeriah was their chief according to the genealogical records of their families. In the fortieth year of David's reign a search was made in the records, and capable men among the Hebronites were found at Jazer in Gilead. 32 Jeriah had twenty-seven hundred relatives, who were able men and heads of families, and King David put them in charge of the Reubenites, the Gadites and the half-tribe of Manasseh for every matter pertaining to God and for the affairs of the king.

Nothing bad happened in the above passage. However, Josiah was put in charge of the Rebenites and the Gadites and half the tribe of Manasseh. Twenty Seven is symbolic of the beginning of Jeriah's new position of leadership. Twenty-Seven is a staging number representing beginnings, endings and stages.

EXAMPLE 5
Ezekiel 29: 10-25
10 therefore I am against you and against your streams, and I will make the land of Egypt a ruin and a desolate waste from Migdol to Aswan, as far as the border of Cush. [a] 11 No foot of man or animal will pass through it; no one will live there for forty years. 12 I will make the land of Egypt desolate among devastated lands, and her cities will lie desolate forty years among ruined cities. And I will disperse the Egyptians among the nations and scatter them through the countries. 13 " 'Yet this is what the Sovereign LORD says: At the end of forty years I will gather the Egyptians from the nations where they were scattered. 14 I will bring them back from captivity and return them to Upper Egypt, the land of their ancestry. There they will be a lowly kingdom. 15 It will be the lowliest of kingdoms and will never again exalt itself above the other nations. I will make it so weak that it will never again rule over the nations. 16 Egypt will no longer be a source of confidence for the people of Israel but will be a reminder of their sin in turning to her for help. Then they will know that I am the Sovereign LORD.' "

17 In the twenty-seventh year, in the first month on the first day, the word of the LORD came to me: 18 "Son of man, Nebuchadnezzar king of Babylon drove his army in a hard campaign against Tyre; every head was rubbed bare and every shoulder made raw. Yet he and his army got no reward from the campaign he led against Tyre. 19 Therefore this is what the Sovereign LORD says: I am going to give Egypt to Nebuchadnezzar king of Babylon, and he will carry off its wealth. He will loot and plunder the land as pay for his army. 20 I have given him Egypt as a reward for his efforts because he and his army did it for me, declares the Sovereign LORD. 21 "On that day I will make a horn grow for the house of Israel, and I will open your mouth among them. Then they will know that I am the LORD."

In the above passage, The Lord is ending the reign of Egypt's power and glory and he is giving all of Egypt's wealth to Nebuchadnezzar. This is and ending for Egypt and a beginning for this King.

28

SOCIAL REFORMATION, JUSTICE,

THE NUMBER TWENTY EIGHT (28)

SOCIAL REFORMATION, JUSTICE,

Twenty Eight is one of the strongest numbers from 1 through 31. The Bible does not mention too much about this number. The great E.W Bullinger (1837-1913) probably put a lot thought in expressing this number in the scripture. Like all other numbers in the Bible, the definition of a number is revealed by how it is used. The Bible is considered divine and inspired because it is often by guidance of Holy Spirit and Revelation that many writers are led to higher levels of wisdom. Bullinger (Number in Scripture) did not cover this number in great detail and I may understand why. I consider Bullinger to be ahead of his time and our time because of the depth of his work. I reviewed his work to get an idea on how he handled the number twenty eight. To my surprise, he described this number in terms of multiples of 4 and 7 or 4x7. This means that he used the qualities of 4 and 7 to describe the number twenty eight. Through inspiration of the Holy Ghost, I was led to take another route. Again, I am convinced this route was revealed to me by guidance of the Holy Spirit of God. Otherwise, I would have never come to see this number based on what little the scriptures offered about this powerful number. I assume Bullinger probably dug very hard over 90 years ago to discuss many of the double digit numbers. Therefore, as an ardent admirer of Bullinger, I am eager to present additional information regarding the number twenty eight.

    The number twenty eight is a compound number composed of two single digit numbers which are the numbers 2 and 8. Even though Twenty Eight reduces to the single digit "1" it is part of the reformation and discernment line: 2, 5, 8. Justice and reformation represent the number twenty eight. We know that two represents preparation, diplomacy, communication, and reformation. Eight is a number of execution, control and new beginnings. The numbers 2 and 8 gave birth to the number Twenty Eight. Twenty Eight is a number of the people. This number fights for justice. It is also a number of contradictions because the number 2 has the opposite qualities of the eight.

For example, the number two can be weak and indecisive and the number Eight can be over bearing and controlling. Yet, these numbers are used to reform the masses.

JEHU

To understand the number Twenty-Eight, we must study the life and character of Jehu. He was the ultimate religious, political figure I have ever studied. Jehu personifies the number Twenty-Eight because this numbers fights for social reformation and justice for the little man. This number cannot tolerate a bully. Jehu personifies this number because of his name number and the number of years he served as King of Judah which is Twenty Eight. Oddly, this is only time I have been able to find this number in the scriptures. 2 Kings 9-10 provides the entire story of Jehu's mission. The number Twenty-Eight is mentioned in 2 Kings 10:36. I will highlight what is mentioned in the scriptures. However, I need to cover the number of his name to illustrate how the eight played out in his life. We will examine the numbers 8 and 28. The name *Jehu* has a numerical value of 8 in Hebrew System and the Pythagorean system.

Hebrew System
J=1 E=5 H=5 U=6 = 17, 1 + 7 =8

Pythagorean (Greek) System
J=1 E=5 H=8 U=3 = 17, 1 + 7 = 8

The number eight is a number of execution, control, leadership and new beginnings. The number eight is the highest and strongest of the reformation and discernment numbers: 2, 5, and 8. The number eight describes the character of Jehu. His mission is revealed in the number 28 which was used to describe the number of years he was King of Judah which is Twenty Eight. This number represents justice, serving a higher power and fighting on behalf of the Father. Twenty-Eight reduces to the number 1: 2+8 = 10, 1 + 0 = 1. The number one is a number of leadership and authority.

However, twenty-eight is composed of the numbers 2 and 8. The number 2 is a number diplomacy, politics, communication, preparation, difference, decisions and relationships. The number eight is number of influence, power, authority, vision, control, execution and new beginnings. The nature of Twenty Eight can be observed if the qualities of 2 and 8 are combined. Let us read what the scriptures provide about the work of Jehu and compare it to the description provided for the number Twenty-Eight.

SUMMARY OF JEHU'S MINISTRY

Jehu anointed king Judah: 2 Kings 9
Jehu kills Joram king of Israel: 2 Kings 9:14
Jehu kills Ahaziah king of Judah 2 Kings 9: 27
Jehu orders the death of Jezebel 2 Kings 9:30
Jehu destroys the house of Ahab 2 Kings 10
Jehu slays the worshipers of Baal 2 Kings 10:18

Jehu, the son of Nimshi, was an army captain who was anointed King over Israel during the time of Jezebel. Jehu was anointed by Elisha to bring judgment to the entire house of Ahab in Israel. Jehu reigned over Israel for 28 years. During his reign as King of Israel, he completely destroyed the house of Ahab. He eradicated the worship of Baal and Asherah in Israel. While he was anointed King of Israel, it was prophesied "and the dogs shall eat Jezebel in the portion of Jezreel, and none shall bury her. And he (the prophet) opened the door and fled."(II Kings 9:10). The prophecy came to fruition after Jehu rode up to Jezreel, where Jezebel was living. Jezebel knew of Jehu's arrival and she "painted her eyes and beautified her head and looked out of an upper window."(2 Kings 9:30). After Jehu entered into the gate of Jezreel, Jezebel asked if he had come in peace. Jehu lifted up his face to her window and asked "Who is on my side? Who? Moreover, two or three eunuchs looked out at him."(2 Kings 9:32). The eunuchs threw her down out of the window. Afterwards, Jehu drove her body into the city and ate and drank. He then ordered that she be buried because she was a king's daughter. However, when the servants went to bury her they only found her skull, feet and the palms of her hands.

The number Twenty-Eight is clearly brought out in this passage of scripture. This probably explains why the number Twenty-Eight is only mentioned once in the entire Bible. Twenty is a true number of God and a true number of leadership. All the qualities of the number Twenty-Eight are depicted in the ministry and life of Jehu. He is a true man of the people who fought for justice, did the will of God and he did not take any prisoners. Nor did he compromise. He was merciless when dealing with Jezebel. To be on his side was to be on God's side. There is so much we can learn from the leadership style of Jehu who personifies the number twenty-eight. It is rare to for someone to have the same name number in the Greek and Hebrew numbering system.

29

BETRAYAL, REFORMATION, WEAKNESS

THE NUMBER TWENTY NINE (29)

BETRAYAL, REFORMATION, WEAKNESS

Danger, trial, warnings, tribulation, treachery and deceit in the face of faith describe the number Twenty-Nine. Hezekiah, who was the King of Judah for Twenty-Nine years, provides an example about the nature of this number (II kings 18-21). Hezekiah is considered one of Judah's greatest Kings who did "what was pleasing before the eyes of the lord". Hezekiah was able to prevent Sennacherib from attacking Jerusalem. Sennacherib was the treacherous King of Assyria.

God told Elijah to tell Hezekiah to get his house in order because he was going to die and not recover. Hezekiah then went before God to discuss his life for himself. As result of his faith, God told Elijah to tell Hezekiah that 15 years will be added to his life. The number Twenty-Nine, as represented by Hezekiah, demonstrates that we can overcome diversity through having a personal relationship with the Father. Twenty-Nine reminds us that we need God to guide us through the trials and tribulations of life.

Twenty-Nine represents the highest number of social reformation. King Hezekiah reformed Judah by tearing down anything that had to do with polytheism: the Asherah poles, the Nehustan (Snake staff) and smashing sacred stones. Twenty-Nine is designed to reform people. If Dracula needs blood then (29) needs people. This number is famous for attracting enemies. Twenty-Nine reduces to a single digit (2) which is a member of the two line: 2-11-22-29. Twenty-Nine is rooted: (2) *union, diplomacy, communication* and (9) *power, influence, materials.* Twenty-Nine is a close neighbor to Twenty-Eight. However, there is huge difference between these numbers. For instance, if someone was trying to steal your hamburger, Twenty-Eight would fight to ensure you received your hamburger. Twenty-Nine would convince you that you need to have the hamburger in your life. Also, Twenty-Nine would devise a way for you to get the hamburger.

Twenty-Eight would fight for your rights to have the hamburger and ensure the hamburger is never taken from you. This number requires obedience to God. Twenty-Nine is a reminder for leaders to walk in righteousness. Twenty-Nine also reminds us that we can communicate directly with God approaching him with humble and broken heart.

30

VALUE AND SIGNIFICANCE

THE NUMBER THIRTY (30)

Value and Significance

The number thirty represents value, significance and importance. The 3 is a number of manifestation, unity, accomplishment, creativity and processes (The Trinity). The number zero is a number of infinity and represents the dark womb of space. Zero is also symbolic of the womb from which life comes forth. Life was designed to come through the dark space of the womb. So it is with numbers, all numbers come out of zero or nothingness. Thirty is often associated with morning and sorrow; this is the case with the death of Moses and Aaron. However, I encourage you to look further into this number and ask one question. Why do we mourn the lives of loved ones who have transitioned from this world? We mourn because our loved ones have value in our lives. We mourn because our loved ones are important to us. We often mourn when we lose items of significance.

EXAMPLE 1
Genesis 18:29-31
29 Once again he spoke to him, "What if only forty are found there?" He said, "For the sake of forty, I will not do it." 30 Then he said, "May the Lord not be angry, but let me speak. What if only thirty can be found there?" He answered, "I will not do it if I find thirty there." 31 Abraham said, "Now that I have been so bold as to speak to the Lord, what if only twenty can be found there?" He said, "For the sake of twenty, I will not destroy it."

This entire passage was about value because Abraham kept lowering the number of righteous people which could be found in Sodom because he knew there were few if none. The Lord eventually destroyed the town. This passage has nothing to do with mourning or sorrow per se. This passage represents the idea of value, significance and importance. No found value was found in Sodom.

EXAMPLE 2
Genesis 32:14-16
14 two hundred female goats and twenty male goats, two hundred ewes and twenty rams, 15 thirty female camels with their young, forty cows and ten bulls, and twenty female donkeys and ten male donkeys. 16 He put them in the care of his servants, each herd by itself, and said to his servants, "Go ahead of me, and keep some space between the herds. The number thirty is associated with the female camels. The female animals are of more value than the males. The male animals cannot exist If you lose of all the female animals. The number thirty is used in this verse and there is no reason to mourn.

EXAMPLE 3
Genesis 41:45-47
45 Pharaoh gave Joseph the name Zaphenath-Paneah and gave him Asenath daughter of Potiphera, priest of On, to be his wife. And Joseph went throughout the land of Egypt. 46 Joseph was thirty years old when he entered the service of Pharaoh king of Egypt. And Joseph went out from Pharaoh's presence and traveled throughout Egypt. 47 During the seven years of abundance the land produced plentifully.
Who can deny that Joseph was a valuable asset to Pharaoh. Joseph was the reason Egypt experienced seven years of abundance.

EXAMPLE 4
Numbers 4:3
3 Count all the men from thirty to fifty years of age who come to serve in the work in the Tent of Meeting.
Men starting at the age of thirty we were to serve in the work of the Tent of Meeting. The Tent of Meeting is a significant event. The number thirty is symbolic of value and importance.

EXAMPLE 5
Numbers 20:28-30
28 Moses removed Aaron's garments and put them on his son Eleazar. And Aaron died there on top of the mountain.

Then Moses and Eleazar came down from the mountain, 29 and when the whole community learned that Aaron had died, the entire house of Israel mourned for him thirty days.

The people mourned thirty days because Aaron was a man of significance in addition to his death.

EXAMPLE 6
1 Samuel 13

1 Saul was thirty years old when he became king, and he reigned over Israel forty-two years.

2 Saul chose three thousand men from Israel; two thousand were with him at Micmash and in the hill country of Bethel, and a thousand were with Jonathan at Gibeah in Benjamin. The rest of the men he sent back to their homes.

3 Jonathan attacked the Philistine outpost at Geba, and the Philistines heard about it. Then Saul had the trumpet blown throughout the land and said, "Let the Hebrews hear!"

Saul became King of Israel for 42 years and he was thirty years old when he became King. Saul is one of the most significant men in the long line of Kings of Israel. We would not appreciate David if it was not for Saul. He is significant because the Israelites wanted Saul to be their King and the Lord wanted David to be King. Therefore, the Lord gave the Israelites what they wanted. Saul proved to be a wicked King. He is significant for many reasons; Saul propels the character of David. Saul was a valuable learning lesson for the Israelites. Saul taught the Israelites a valuable lesson between knowing your wants and needs which comes back to idea of importance.

EXAMPLE 6
DUETERONOMY 34:7-9

7 Moses was a hundred and twenty years old when he died, yet his eyes were not weak nor his strength gone. 8 The Israelites grieved for Moses in the plains of Moab thirty days, until the time of weeping and mourning was over. 9 Now Joshua son of Nun was filled with the spirit of wisdom because Moses had laid his hands on him. So the Israelites listened to him and did what the LORD had commanded Moses.

Finally, we have an example of mourning, but why are the people mourning for Moses? They are mourning because he was a man of value, importance and significance. The Israelites are not crying for the sake of crying. If so, thirty would be a number of death.

31

OPPORTUNITY, READINESS AND YOUTHFUL GUIDANCE.

THE NUMBER THIRTY ONE (31)

Spiritual Opportunity, Readiness and Youthful Guidance.

The number Thirty One is the number 13 in reverse. Thirteen represents authoritative plans. What is an authoritative plan? An authoritative plan is produced by someone with authority. Many of Biblical figures operated with Authoritative power and this includes Moses, Jeremiah and Ezra. About the numbers 13 and 31, the number thirteen has the number "1"as its foreground number and this symbolizes the <u>one</u> God and the <u>one</u> individual operating with authority. The <u>one</u> God worked through the one Jeremiah that he would become a prophet to the nations. In the number 13, the number three is the background number. Three is a number of unity, manifestation and processes. The number thirteen represents a person who walks into authority, power and direction. The number thirty one has the number three as the foreground number and the number one as the background number. Thirty One symbolizes walking with God to carry out his will.

The number thirty one teaches us to seek the presence of God. This is a masterful number of plans, methods and structure. Jeremiah was anointed as a prophet before he was born. His spiritual office as a prophet preceded his physical office as a prophetic leader. For many of us, we are searching for God's will in our lives so we can walk in proper office. The number one, the background number of 31, reminds us to exercise independence for the will of God in our lives. You must demonstrate the ability to operate independently and responsibly if God is calling you to a position of leadership in the church. Thirty One reminds us to maintain structure, organization and independence in all things. Independence shows God that we are able to carry on the weight of his will at any moment. Spiritual warfare is guerrilla warfare.

This number reminds us that we must have the form and structure to be spiritual guerrilla warfare warriors for the Kingdom. Thirty one demands organization and structure. This number will help be in the worlds but not of the world.

EXAMPLE 1
2 Chronicles 34
1 Josiah was eight years old when he became king, and he reigned in Jerusalem thirty-one years. 2 He did what was right in the eyes of the LORD and walked in the ways of his father David, not turning aside to the right or to the left. 3 In the eighth year of his reign, while he was still young, he began to seek the God of his father David. In his twelfth year he began to purge Judah and Jerusalem of high places, Asherah poles, and carved idols and cast images.

Josiah became King of Judah at the age of eight which is a number of control, management, vision and new beginnings. He was King for 31 years. The number 31 is symbolic of his Godly walk with the Lord. Josiah did what was in the eyes of the Lord. In this passage, we read about Josiah having enough sense to seek the Lord at an early age. This passage teaches there is spiritual opportunity in youth. This is a number that should be heavily impressed upon children in the Church. Josiah should a Biblical figure that should be preached about on the same level as Moses and Joshua. Josiah should become an icon for the youth. This number and this man will inspire the youth to seek and stay with God at an early age.

Chapter 6:
The 31 Daily Categories of Prayer and Observance

Days of the Month

1-Prayers of independence, leadership
2-Prayers of preparation, discernment, reformation
3-Prayers of revelation
4-Prayers of structure, foundation and plans
5-Prayers of direction, righteousness, communication
6-Prayers of service and responsibility
7-Prayers of release
8-Prayers of execution
9-<u>Watch Sign:</u> Entrance and Exit Stage, prayers of compassion and love
10-Prayers of timing and access
11-Prayer of relationships and unity
12-Prayers of habit and behavior
13-<u>Watch Sign:</u> Finger of God, Prayers of Planning
14-Prayers of defense and protection
15-Prayers for focus and passion
16-Watch Sign: Falling down, prayers of humility and submission to God
17-Prayers of execution and implementation
18-<u>Warning Sign:</u> Entrance and Exit, Prayers of compassion and influence
19-Prayers of expectancy
20-Prayers of awareness
21-Prayers of freedom and deliverance
22-Prayers of planning and foundation

23-Prayers of obedience and self-control
24-Prayers of order
25-Prayers of devotion and observation
26-Prayers of reformation for people and the masses
27- <u>Warning Sign:</u> Entrance and Exit, Prayers of unconditional love
28-Prayers of justice, leadership and direction
29-Prayers of discernment and righteousness
30-Prayers of remembrance and proclamations
31-Prayers of Opportunity

There are many ways we can pray to Almighty God. We are taught to pray constantly and to me this can be every second or every ten minutes. The categories listed above were revealed to me while visiting a Church. This list helped me expand the areas of my prayers. This list also added flavor and purpose to my prayer life.

Prior to this revelation, I used each number as a sign. For example, whenever I saw the number eighteen, I knew a warning was coming forth. If I saw any member of the nine line: 9, 18 and 27, I knew something was going to end or expect a new stage. If I saw the number 5, 14, and 23, I knew to watch for change and events. Each day has its own meaning and significance. Also, we can maximize each day by knowing the meaning of that day. For example, if you are looking for a job, consider the number nineteen, which is a number of expectancy and attainment.

Numbers and letters can be used for symbolic gestures in our prayer life. Maybe you could fast for nineteen days. In other words, the number of you fast can reflect the meaning of that day. Or, pray constantly every 19 minutes for eight days about a specific need. Lastly, one could conduct the interview on the 19th of any month. Time is critical and time is relatively short. Time can be defined in terms of years, months, weeks, days, hours, minutes and seconds. The time has come for us to utilize prayer as it relates to time.

Each day would have the same number if the days were the same but this is not the case. Each day offers its own hand and we should be mindful of this simple truth. These type of routines will not change the heart per se but serve as methods of disciplining the flesh. Moreover, these categories can help you following the hand of God through sign and symbol.

The 28 Seasons: **Ecclesiastes 3**

Solomon possessed a wise understanding of time. Also, we should be mindful of our use of time "watch as well as pray". In other words, each day is different and we should approach each day with wisdom so we can get the most out of each day. Ecclesiastes 3 stresses the importance of making decisions and paying attention to the time. Often, it is not what we do but it when we do it. It is one thing to walk by faith and not by sight. However, it is another thing when a blessing is sitting right in your face and no action is taking place because one is still waiting on the Lord. The study of numbers and letters teaches the power of choice, timing and consequences. Twenty Eight is number of "Social Justice". This is also a number of discernment and leadership. This number requires action and decisive leadership. These seasons are not for God but these seasons are for the people of God to be cautious about how we use time.

Ecclesiastes 3

A Time For Everything

1. **There is a time to be born.**

2. **A time to die.**

3. **A time to plant.**

4. **A time to pick what is planted.**

5. There is a time to kill.

6. A time to heal.

7. A time to break down.

8. A time to build up.

9. There is a time to cry.

10. A time to laugh.

11. A time to have sorrow.

12. A time to dance.

13. There is a time to throw stones.

14. A time to gather stones.

15. A time to kiss.

16. A time to turn from kissing.

17. There is a time to try to find.

18. A time to lose.

19. A time to keep.

20. A time to throw away.

21. There is a time to tear apart.

22. A time to sew together.

23. A time to be quiet.

24. A time to speak.

25. There is a time to love.

26. A time to hate.

27. A time for war.

28. A time for peace.

Again, we run into the number twenty eight which is a number social reformation and discernment. Solomon, who is considered to be a very wise man, understood the importance understanding days and the time. The scriptures require us to be discerning concerning people but for the time and the day as well. May Almighty God bless you and keep you.

Chapter 7:

THE HISTORY OF LANGUAGES

It is only fair to provide a brief background on languages to understand how alphanumerical values came into existence. Each language has its own alphanumeric values and this includes Hebrew, Aramaic, Hindi, English, Greek and German. I will discuss the Afro-asiatic languages and the Indo-European languages. The Afro-asiatic languages include the Berber languages, Semitic languages, Chadic languages, Omotic languages and Cushitic languages. The Indo- European Languages includes the Hittie Language, Indo-Iranian Languages, Greek, Italic languages, Armenian Languages, Germanic Languages, Albanian Languages, Slavonic Languages, Celtic Languages, Tocharian Language and the Baltic Languages.

THE AFRO-ASIATIC LANGUAGES
Our focus will be on the Semetic, Hebrew, Greek, German, Hindi and English Languages of the Afro-asiatic and Indo-European Languages. According to the Dictionary of Languages *"It is because of the great length of time involved here that proto-asiatic has been more difficult to work on than proto-Indo-European. There is another difficulty. All the Afroasiatic languages are built on word roots consisting of consonants, between which vowels are inserted to create various verb and noun forms. The Semitic languages have three consonant roots.*

The others have mainly two consonant roots, and it has not been clear how the Semetic forms could be in practice and have developed out of these. Ehret has presented persuasive evidence that single consonant suffixes, with various fixed meanings are still found in some of the Afroasiatic languages, became attached invariably to word roots in 'Pre-Proto-Semetic", thus resulting in the well known three consonant roots of modern Semetic Languages".

A.L. Schlozer created the term Semetic in 1781 because he needed a way to group the Arabic, Hebrew, and Aramaic languages. Schlozer saw that each language group were descendents of Noah's son Shem. With all of this in mind, I will first discuss the Phoenician and Hebrew languages. History teaches the ancient Hebrews did not use the vowels "A" and "E" in pronouncing the name of God, YHWH. The Hebrews borrowed their language from the Phoenicians. The Phoenician language did not use vowels. Before one can appreciate Hebrew, one must understand the Phoenician Language. Known as the mother of all languages, it is a Consonantal Language.

CUNIFORM SCRIPT

Cuneiform is a pictographic or syllabic script used by many languages and by several Sumerian empires in ancient Mesopotamia and Persia (3300 BC to 500 BC). Cuneiform is not a specific language but it is comprised of several language scripts used in Western Asia. The word "Cuneiform" comes from the Latin Cuneus which means "wedge". In addition, these languages assigned their own word sounds to the symbol. So any script that uses wedges can be called cuneiform but the individual signs must be made up of wedges. The following is a list of languages that used cuneiform.

Sumerian
Old Persian-
Akkadian (Eastern Semetic/Afroasiatic)
Assyrian (Eastern Semetic/Afroasiatic)
Babylonian (Eastern Semetic/Afroasiatic)
Elamite
Eblalite
Hurrian
Utarian
Ugaritic

THE EGYPTIAN HIEROGLYPHIC SCRIPT

The Egyptian Script existed in several periods throughout history:
Old Egyptian: 3100-2200 BC
Middle Egyptian: 2200 to 200 BC
Late Egyptian: 1600 to 700 BC
Demotic: 700BC to 400 AD
Coptic 200 AD to 1400 AD

This script belongs to Afroasiatic language family and is the second oldest of all written languages with Cuniform probably being the oldest. The Egyptians used a hieroglyphic script which was used on stone as early as 3000 BC or earlier. The Egyptians were eventually conquered by the Persians and then the Macedonians in the 4th century B.C.

THE PHOENICIAN SCRIPT

The Phoenician script is a Proto-Sinatic language originating in West Asia between 1200 - 1000 B.C. Many languages such as Hebrew, Latin and Greek descended from the Phoenician script. The Phoenician script is a descendent of the Proto-Sinatic script. Both scripts are known as consonantal scripts because they only contain consonants, thus vowels were not used. The Proto-Sinatic and Phoenician scripts contained 22 letters, which were adopted by the Hebrews. The Phoenician script is read from right to left, just like the Hebrew script. The major difference between the Proto-Sinatic languages and the Phoenician was seen in the graphical expressions of the letters. The Phoenician letters grew to be more linear, and abstract in appearance. The images of the Proto-Sinatic languages were pictorial.

The Phoenician script remained in use until about 200AD, but it was in a cursive or Punic form. Therefore, one can infer the Phoenician script was part of the Afroasiatic languages or Northern Semetic. In addition, the Proto-Sinatic script is part of the Afroasiatic language family as well-being that it originated in West Asia.

THE HEBREW SCRIPT

The Hebrew language came out of the Proto-Sinatic language family found in West Asia. The time period for Hebrew dates to 10th century, BCE (800 B.C) to present in the form of the Gezer calendar. Old Hebrew looks similar to the Phoenician script from where it originated. The word Hebrew comes from the Aramaic *'Ebraya'*. The original ancient Hebrew form is 'ibri', which means, "from the other side of the river". Many linguists prefer to use the name *Ivrit* to classify Modern Hebrew. This language belongs to the Semetic language family.

The early Jews of the Old Testament used the Hebrew language. Aramaic replaced Hebrew, the Babylonian language, Franca of the Persian, and Babylonian empires after the early Jews captivity into Babylonian. The Hebrew alphabet is also known as the *Alefbt* because of its first two letters: Aleph & Beth. The Hebrew vocabulary uses three three-consonant roots, which is a direct inheritance from the Phoenician script, which in turn, came from the Proto-Sinatic script. The square Hebrew letters of classical and Modern Hebrew came out from an Aramaic script, which was based on the Phoenician script or Northern Semetic.

The act of correct pronunciation was for religious, mystical, and magical reasons that include the practice of Jewish Mysticism (Kabbalah). This is where the names of God come into focus, particularly the name Yahweh or YHWH. The first letter of YHWH (Y) Yod was adopted by the Greeks and they changed it to I (Iota). The English J came from the Hebrew (Y) and Greek (IOTA) by means of the Germanic Anglo-Saxons. The English letter J came into existence about 500 years ago. Historically (J) is linked to the Afroasiatic languages and through the Indo-European Languages. In the Hebrew numbering system, A, IQ, J, and Y all have a numerical value of one. This is not the case in the Greek numbering system or the Pythagorean system where (Q) has a value of eight and I has a value of nine.

The Hebrews began to use Aramaic for everyday use and the Old Hebrew script was for religious use. As a result, the Aramaic script became known as the Jewish script. Hebrew was also known as the square script or the *ketab- merubba* because of the square shape of its letters. Some of the letters have two forms. This occurs when that letters appears at the end of a word. This includes letters such as kap, mem, pe and tzzadi. Though adopted from the Phoenician script, all the sounds were not reproduced. Some letters like *bet* have multiple sounds: (b) and (v), *pe* is both (p) and (f), and *kap* can be (k) and (x).

THE GREEK SCRIPT

The Greek language is listed as part of the Indo-European language family but in reality it comes from the Afroasiatic tree because they adopted their letters come from the Phoenicians. Some historians say they adopted their letters from the Hebrews, but we know where the Hebrews adopted their script (Phoenicians). The Greek script can dated back to 800-750 BCE in the Mediterranean region. They probably adopted the Phoenician script during the 9th century BCE. In the 5th century BCE, a Greek historian referred to the Greek letters as "*phoinikea grammata*", which means Phoenician letters. One problem with the Greek language was the Phoenician language was all consonants-no vowels. Therefore, there were letters that did not reflect Greek sounds (Tzaddai-Ts sound). In other words, some of the letters did not have a place in the Greek language because of sound. As a result, the Greeks changed some of those letters to represent vowels. The other choice would have been to not use those letters. This was the case for the Phoenician letter, Aleph, which became the Greek vowel Alpha (The English A).

There were various versions of the Greek language: Ionian, Athenian, Corinthian, Argosian and Euboean. The Ionian alphabet was adopted in all the Greek speaking states. Before the statewide adoption of the Ionian alphabet, the Euboean version, used in the Italic peninsula, and adopted by the Etruscans, and then the Romans. History teaches the Athenians were in disagreement with the Alexandrian's about the Holy Trinity.

I never understood why until I read information showing how Greeks had a problem with volumetric thinking. I will cover this issue in this chapter.

The Greeks were the first Europeans to use an alphabet. They were taught first by the Egyptians (Africans). According George G.M. James's, " Stolen Legacy", the Greeks would send their top scholars such as Plato and Pythagoras to Egypt to enroll in the Egyptian Mystery systems, one of the oldest learning institutions to ever exist. The Curriculum took 42 years to complete. Moses, though raised as an Egyptian, allegedly completed 27 years; thus, he would be considered a dropout by today's standards. Pythagoras completed 22 years. Pythagoras attended other mystery systems and temples as well, but his main body of learning came from the Egyptian Mystery systems.

It is no secret the Egyptians taught the Greeks everything they understood.

The Greeks were not the only students. There were Chaldeans, Phoenicians and Hebrews as well. Many historians and numerologist call Pythagoras the father of numerology, or numbers, but this is not true for he was a student as well. In fact, many of the Greeks were not considered good students. The Egyptians referred to the Greeks enrollees as children and little boys. Pythagoras was taught everything he knew that is why he attended the mystery systems- to learn. What did the Greeks learn from the Egyptians? The following is from George G. M. James "Stolen Legacy" on pages 135-136:

THE EGYPTIAN MYSTERY SYSTEM 42 YEAR CURRICULUM

(i) The Seven Liberal Arts: Grammar, Arithmetic, Rhetoric, Dialectic, Geometry, Astronomy and Music.
(ii) The Sciences of the 42 books of Hermes
(a) The singer or Odus-the two books of Hermes
(b) The Horoscopus-Four books of Hermes dealing with Astronomy
(c) Hierogrammat-hieroglyphics, cosmography, astronomy, and the topology of Egypt & Land surveying.
(d) The Stolistes-The books of Hermes that deal with proper animal slaughter and the embalming process.

(e) The Prophets-The Ten books of Hermes that deal with higher esoteric theology and the education of the Priest.
(f) The Pastophori- The Six Medical books of Hermes dealing with physiology, diseases of male/female, anatomy, drugs and instruments.
(iii) The Sciences of the Monuments (Pyramids, Temples, Libraries, Obelisks, Sphinxes, Idols.
(iv) The Secret Science of numerical symbolism, geometrical symbolism, magic, the book of the Dead, myths and parables
(v) The Social Order and its Protection-Law.

MORE ON THE GREEKS

The following is a lengthy excerpt from R.A.Schwaller de Lubicz, "A Study of Numbers". About the Greeks, he expressed views on the Greeks regarding language and Mathematics. His views line up with George G.M James in his book "The Stolen Legacy. These two authors were born almost 100 years apart and James did not reference any of Schwaller's material, yet they had the same views.

The following is an excerpt from page 21:
Translator's Note

Rene Schwaller, in fact, left emphatic instructions that this essay on the study of numbers, written early in his career, should not be published without a note explaining the passages concerning point, line, plane, and volume must be corrected in the light of his subsequent research into Egyptian Mathematics.

Schwaller came to believe the metaphor of creation as images by the point engendering a line, the line engendering a surface, and a surface engendering a volume was an arbitrary, misleading adaptation of Greek thought (Euclid and Aristotle). In contrast to this view, he presented his interpretation that the entirety of Egyptian mathematics was based on the notion that the primary express of being is not the philosophical "point", but the three dimensional volume. Hence he wrote in Le Temple de l' Homme, "Everything that exists is a volume... therefore, a point is the apex of volume, a line is the edge of a volume, and surface is the face of a volume."

These three components (point, line and plane), when considered by themselves, are abstract concepts expressive only of mental ideation with no basis in the three dimensional world of physical embodiment. By accepting the "original state" as volumetric, the physical world, which is also exclusively three dimensional, then reflects the essential nature of its creative origins. Saint Bernard restated this Egyptian philosophical theme: "What is God"? God is length, width, and depth. Schwaller considered, furthermore, that Greek philosophy, in adopting the image of "Original Being" as point rather than volume-like, had helped to "deviate" the primary paradigms of Western thought toward the reductionisms and mechanist assumptions that so plague modern man's relations to the natural world. All our thinking, designing, and engineering, practices follow this model of using two dimensional diagrams of points, lines, and planes, which are then superimposed on to the physical world of volume. In reality of the natural world its exclusively three-dimensional. Moreover; like a volume, inseparably binds opposed states: surface and interior; front and back; inside and outside; and top and bottom.

Much of Schwaller's subsequent work demonstrates the adherence of the ancient Egyptian mind to a volumetric model of reality, creating a "technique of thought" and mathematics of an entirely different character and more directive than our present ones derived from Euclidean and Aristotelian forms.

This difference, Schwaller felt, has lead Western mathematics, science, and philosophy in the direction of predominately abstract mental games, lacking the vitality and paradox necessary to create a harmonic dialogue between mind and nature.

For these reasons, Schwaller warns against the "error of youth" contained in this other wise insightful and informative exposition.

GERMAN

Why am I going into German? English came out of Indo-European Germanic language by the West Germanic script then the Anglo-Frisian languages, not Greek. The Germanic speakers include: Germany, Austria, Switzerland, Russia, Kazakhstan, Romania, and the United States. The earliest records of a German language come from the 8th century. They refer to the so-called Song of Hildebrand (few lines of an epic poem). Germania was the Roman name for the country and Germani for the people. German refers to the origin of language of the tribes that lived east of the Rhine and north of the upper Danube.

Historically, English and German are closely related but an English reader may not be able to understand the German text because the words do not look the same. This is because of two reasons. First, the high German sound shift changed the consonant sounds in the German form of words shared by both English and German languages: apple/aphel, help/helfen, make/machen.

Second, English heavily borrowed from Old French and Latin and this was not the case for the German script. English borrowed from other languages to make new words. The German script compounds its words. For example, The English word television is a Greek and Latin word, which means "far" and "vision". This corresponds to the German Fernseher, a compounded meaning that means "far-seer".

In German, each noun starts with a capital letter; also, adjectives based on proper names do not have capitals: das deutsche Buch "the German book". I discussed the German language so the reader can understand the relationship between English and German and English/Greek/Latin. Many English words were borrowed from the Greek and Latin languages to create new words. What does this mean? For one, it means that English, because of the borrowing factor, is derived from both Indo-European and Afroasiatic Languages. This is why it is important to understand the history of other languages. Concerning our children, the comprehensive and objective study of human languages will need to be employed in the form of Christian Education and Workshops. The depth of this subject matter is beyond the scope of public education. Sorry Charlie! This is why I subscribe to the school of thought that public education can make you dumb. I recall an international educational survey that described American Education as being "A mile wide and an inch deep".

The purpose of this chapter is to provide an overview of concerning languages and the evolution of popular English words I encourage you to study any and all languages because it will broaden your view of the world and yourself. I specifically, encourage you learn Biblical Hebrew, Aramaic, and Greek.

Chapter 8:
The meaning of names in the Bible

A

Abba From the Arabic, Syrian, and Aramaic, which means "father."

Abir -derived from the Hebrew, which means "strong."

Abiri -derived from the Hebrew, which means "courageous, gallant."

Achi -derived from the Hebrew, which means "my brother." In the Bible (1 Kings 5:15), a leader of the tribe of Gad.

Achiezer -derived from the Hebrew, which means "my brother is my helper." In the Bible (Numbers 1:12), a leader of the tribe of Dan.

Achimelech -derived from the Hebrew, which means "the king (God) is my brother." In the Bible (1 Samuel 21:2), a Priest who befriended David.

Achinoam -derived from the Hebrew, which means "my brother is a delight, sweet." Used in the Bible as a feminine name (1 Samuel 4:13).

Achishia -derived from the Hebrew, which means "my brother is a gift" or "my brother's gift."

Achitzedek -derived from the Hebrew, which means "my brother is just."

Adam -derived from the Hebrew, which means "earth." Also ascribed to Phoenician and Babylonian origins, which means" man, mankind." In the Bible (Genesis 2:7), the name of the first man.

Adar, Addar -derived from the Hebrew, which means "noble, exalted." The name of the Hebrew month that ushers in springtime. In the Bible (1 Chronicles 8:3), the son of Bela and a grandson of Benjamin.

Adir -derived from the Hebrew, which means, "noble, majestic."

Adon -derived from the Hebrew and Phoenician, which means "lord" or "master." In Hebrew literature, the name is often used as a synonym for God. In Greek mythology, Adonis was a young man of godlike beauty.

Aharon -derived from the Hebrew, which means, "teaching" or "singing." Also, -derived from the Hebrew, which means "shining" or mountain." Or, from the Arabic, which means "messenger." In the Bible (Exodus 4:14), the older brother of Moses and Miriam.

Akavya The Aramaic form of Akiva. Akavya ben Mehalalel was a leading first century talmudic Palestinian scholar. Akavia and Akaviah are variant spellings.

Akiva A variant form of the Hebrew name Yaakov (Jacob), which means "to hold by the heel." The famous Rabbi Akiva (ben Joseph) was a talmudic scholar of the first century.

Alexander From the Greek name Alexandros, which means "protector of men." According to legend in the Talmud (Tamid 31b), when the Greek monarch Alexander the Great conquered Palestine in 333 B.C.E. all Jewish boys born in that year were named Alexander in his honor.

Alon -derived from the Hebrew, which means, "oak tree." In the Bible (1 Chronicles 4:37), one of the sons of Simeon.

Alter From the Old English and the Old High German, which means "old, old one." Among Jews, a supplementary name given to a critically ill young man so as to confuse the angel of death into thinking that the man called "old one" could not possibly be the young sick person he was after.

Aluph -derived from the Hebrew, which means, "master, prince, ruler." Also -derived from the Hebrew, which means "loyal friend" or scholar."

Ami -derived from the Hebrew, which means "my people." In the Bible (Ezra 2:57), a servant of King Solomon whose descendants were among the Babylonian Exile returnees. Also, from the Aramaic, which means "mother."

Amiel -derived from the Hebrew, which means, " "God of my people." In the Bible (ll Samuel 9:4), the father of Machir, who befriended King David.

Amir -derived from the Hebrew, which means, ""mighty, strong." Also, -derived from the Hebrew, which means "sheaf of corn."

Amnon -derived from the Hebrew, which means, "faithful." In the Bible (ll Samuel 3:2) the eldest son of King David.ldest son of King David.

Amos -derived from the Hebrew, which means, "to be burdened, troubled." In the Bible (Amos 1:1), one of the twelve Minor Prophets (eighth century B.C.E.)

Amram -derived from the Hebrew, which means, "mighty nation." Also, from the Arabic, which means "life." In the Bible (Exodus 6:18), the father of Moses.

Anshil A Yiddish form of Asher.

Arel -derived from the Hebrew, which means, "lion of God."

Ariel -derived from the Hebrew, which means, "lion of God." In the Bible (Ezra 8:16), a leader who served under Ezra. Also, a symbolic name for Jerusalem, David's city (Isaiah 29:1). Used also as a feminine name.

Arik. A pet form of Arriel and Aryeh.

Arye, Aryeh -derived from the Hebrew, which means, "lion." In the Bible (ll Kings 15:25), an officer in the army of Pekach.

Asa From the Aramaic and Arabic, which means "to heal" or "healer." In the Bible (l Kings 15:8), a king of Judah.

Asher -derived from the Hebrew, which means, "blessed, fortunate, happy." In the Bible (Genesis 30:13), a son of Jacob and Zilpah.

Atid -derived from the Hebrew, which means, "timely, prepared, ready" or "future time."

Av -derived from the Hebrew, which means, "father."

Avi -derived from the Hebrew, which means, "my father."

Avichayil -derived from the Hebrew, which means, "father of strength" or "my father is strong." In the Bible (Esther 2:15), the father of Queen Esther.

Aviezer -derived from the Hebrew, which means, "my father is salvation." In the Bible, (Joshua 17:2), a member of the tribe of Manasseh.

Aviezri -derived from the Hebrew, which means, "my father is my help." Based on Judges 6:11, where Joshua is called Avi Haezri.

Avigal -derived from the Hebrew, which means, "father of waves (the sea)" or "father of joy," (God)

Avimelech -derived from the Hebrew, which means, "father of the king" or "my father is the king." In the Bible (Judges 9:1), a son of Gideon, one of the Israel's Judges.

Avinadov -derived from the Hebrew, which means "father of a prince" or "princely father." In the Bible (1 Samuel 16:8), the second son of Jesse and a brother of David. Also a son of King Saul and brother of Jonathon (1 Samuel 31:2).

Avinatan -derived from the Hebrew, which means, "my father has given."

Aviner -derived from the Hebrew, which means, "my father is a lamp." In the Bible (1 Samuel 14:50), a variant form of Avner, Saul's uncle and chief of staff.

Avinoam -derived from the Hebrew, which means, "father of delight." In the Bible (Judges 4:6), the father of Barak of the tribe of Naftali.

Aviram -derived from the Hebrew, which means, "my father is mighty." In the Bible (Numbers 16:1), a co-conspirator with his brother Dathan against Moses.

Avishai From the Aramaic which means "my father is my gift" or "gift of God." In the Bible (1 Samuel 26:6), a grandson of Jesse, a brother of Joab.

Avishalom -derived from the Hebrew, which means, "my father is peace" or "father of peace." In the Bible (1 Kings 15:2), Maacha, the daughter of Avishalom, was the mother of Aviyam, king of Judah.

Aviv -derived from the Hebrew, which means, "spring."

Avner -derived from the Hebrew, which means, "father of light" or father's candle," connoting strength and inspiration. In the Bible (l Samuel 17:55), Avner ben Ner was the uncle of King Saul and commander of his army.

Avraham -derived from the Hebrew, which means, "father of a mighty nation" or "father of a multitude. In the Bible (Genesis 11:26), the first Hebrew. His name was Avram, which was later changed to Avraham (Genesis17: 5).

Azriel -derived from the Hebrew, which means, "God is my help." In the Bible (I Chronicles 27:19), the father of a leader of the tribe of Naftali.

B

Baal -derived from the Hebrew, which means "master." In the Bible (l Chronicles 5:5), a member of the tribe of Reuben.

Bani From the Aramaic, which means "son" or "build." In the Bible (Ezra 10:29), an ancestor of a family of Babylonian Exile returns.

Bar From the Aramaic, which means "son," "natrual," "pure," or "grain"

Baruch -derived from the Hebrew which means "blessed"

Ben -derived from the Hebrew, which means "son." In the Bible, (l Chronicles 15:18), the name of a Levite. Used occasionally as an independent name, but most often as the pet form of names whose first syllable is "ben."

Ben Ami -derived from the Hebrew, which means "son of my people." In the Bible (Genesis 19:38), the son of one of Lot's daughters.

Ben Baruch -derived from the Hebrew, which means "son of Baruch."

Ben Chanan -derived from the Hebrew, which means "son of grace, gracious." In the Bible (1 Chronocles 4:20), a member of the tribe of Judah. Ben Hanan is a variant spelling.

Ben Ezra -derived from the Hebrew, which means "son of salvation." (1 Chronicles 4:17)

Ben Tov -derived from the Hebrew, which means "good son."

Ben-Tziyon -derived from the Hebrew, which means "excellence" or "son of Zion."

Ben-Yishai -derived from the Hebrew, which means "son of Yishai."

Ber A Yiddish name from the German Baer, which means "bear." Also, from the Anglo- Saxon, which means "boundary."

Beryl From the Greek, which means "a sea green precious stone." Also considered an acronym for Ben Rabbi Yehuda Leib, "which means the son of Rabbi Yehuda Leib.

Betzalel -derived from the Hebrew, which means "shadow of God," signifying God's protection. In the Bible (Exodus 31:2), the builder of the Tabernacle.

Binyamin -derived from the Hebrew, which means "son of my right hand," having the connotation of strength. In the Bible (Genesis 35:18), the youngest of Jacob's twelve sons.

Binyamin-Ze'ev A hybrid of Binyamin and Ze'ev (Zev).

Bivi A variant form of Bivai. In the Talmud (Sanhedrin 66b), a fifth century Babylonian scholar, the son of Abaye.

Boaz -derived from the Hebrew, which means "strength" or "swiftness." In the Bible (Ruth 2:1) the second husband of Ruth.

Bunim From the Yiddish, which means "good."

C

Chacham -derived from the Hebrew, which means "wise man."

Chadad -derived from the Hebrew, which means "sharp." In the Bible (Genesis 25:15), the sixth son of Ishmael, and a grandson of Abraham.

Chagai - From the Aramaic and Hebrew, which means "my feast, festive." In the Bible (Haggai 1:1), one of the twelve minor prophets.

Chagi - A variant form of Chagai. In the Bible (Genesis 46:16), a son of Gad and grandson of Jacob.

Chanan -A variant form of Chanina. In the Bible (1 Chronicles 8:23), a leader of the tribe of Benjamin.

Chananel -derived from the Hebrew, which means "God is compassionate." In the Bible (Jermiah 31:37), reference is made to the "tower of Chananel."

Chananya -derived from the Hebrew, which means "the compassion of God." In the Bible (Jermiah 28:1), a prophet during the reign of Zedekia, king of Judah.

Chanoch -derived from the Hebrew, which means "educated" or "dedicated." In the Bible (Genesis 5:18), the father of Metushelach.

Chatzkel A Yiddish form of Yechezkel

Cheifer -derived from the Hebrew, and Aramaic which means "to dig." In the Bible (Numbers 26:33), the father of Zalophehad, who had five daughters and no sons.

Chen -derived from the Hebrew, which means "charm, grace." In the Bible (Zechariah 6:14), a Babylonian Exile returnee.

Chizkiyahu - a variant form of Chizkia.

Choni - derived from the Hebrew, which means "gracious."

D

Dan -derived -derived from the Hebrew, which means "judge." In the Bible (Genesis 30:6), the fifth of the twelve sons of Jacob.

Daniel Babylonia. -derived -derived from the Hebrew, which means "God is my judge." In the Bible (Daniel 1:6), a Hebrew official in the court of Nebuchadnezzar, king of the Babylonia.

David -derived -derived from the Hebrew, which means "beloved." In the Bible (1 Samuel 17:12), the son of Jesse and the second king of Israel.

Deror -derived -derived from the Hebrew, which means "a bird (swallow)" or "free, free flowing."

Dov -derived -derived from the Hebrew, which means "bear."

Dubi -derived -derived from the Hebrew, which means "my bear."

E

Eden -derived -derived from the Hebrew, which means "delight, luxuriate." In the Bible ll Chronicles 31:15), a Levite in the time of King Hezekiah.

Efrat -derived -derived from the Hebrew, which means "honored, distinguished." In the Bible (1 Chronicles 2:50), the son of Caleb, a member of the tribe of Ephraim.

Efrayim -derived -derived from the Hebrew, which means "fruitful." In the Bible (Genesis 41:52), the second son of Joseph and a grandson of Jacob.

Ehud -derived -derived from the Hebrew, which means "love." In the Bible (Judges 3:15), a descendant of Benjamin and one of the Judges of Israel.

Eichi -derived -derived from the Hebrew, which means "my brother." In the Bible (Genesis 46:21), a son of Benjamin.

Eitan -derived -derived from the Hebrew, which means "strong." In the Bible (1 Chronicles 2:6) a son of Zerach and a grandson of Judah.

Eizer - In the Bible (Nehemiah 3:19), an officer in the time of Nehemiah.

Eizik - A Yiddish form of Isaac.

Elazar -derived -derived from the Hebrew, which means "God has helped." In the Bible (Exodus 6:23), a son of Aaron the High Priest.

Elchanan -derived -derived from the Hebrew, which means "God is gracious." In the Bible (ll Samuel 23:23), a warrior in King David's army.

Elezri -derived -derived from the Hebrew, which means "God is help."

Eli -derived from the Hebrew, which means "ascend" or "uplifted." In the Bible (1 Samuel 1:14), a High Priest and the last of the judges in the days of Samuel.

Eliezer - A variant form of Elazar. -derived -derived from the Hebrew, which means "my God has helped." In the Bible (Genesis 15:2), Abraham's servant.

Elimelech -derived -derived from the Hebrew, which means "my God is King." In the Bible (Ruth 1:2), the husband of Naomi and father-in-law of Ruth.

Elinatan -derived -derived from the Hebrew, which means "my God has given." In the Talmud (Eduyot 6:2), the father of Nechunya, a second century talmudic scholar.

Eliram -derived -derived from the Hebrew, which means "my God is mighty."

Eliran -derived -derived from the Hebrew, which means "my God is joy" or my God is song.

Elisha -derived -derived from the Hebrew, which means "my God is salvation." In the Bible (1 Kings 19:16), a Prophet, a disciple of Elijah.

Elituv -derived -derived from the Hebrew, which means "my God is goodness."

Eliyahu -derived -derived from the Hebrew, which means "the Lord is my God." In the Bible (1 Kings 17:1), one of the earliest of the Hebrew Prophets.

Elkana -derived -derived from the Hebrew, which means "God bought" or "God is jealous." In the Bible (Exodus 6:24), one of the son's of Korach of the tribe of Levi.

Elkayam -derived -derived from the Hebrew, which means "God lives."

Elyakim -derived -derived from the Hebrew, which means "God will establish." In the Bible (ll Kings 18:18), the steward of King Hezekiah's palace.

Elyashiv -derived -derived from the Hebrew, which means "God will respond." In the Bible (Nehemiah 3:1), a High Priest in the days of Nehemiah.

Emanuel -derived -derived from the Hebrew, which means "God is with us, God is our protector."

Erez -derived -derived from the Hebrew, which means "ceder."

Even -derived -derived from the Hebrew, which means "stone."

Evenezer -derived -derived from the Hebrew, which means "foundation stone."

Ezekiel -derived -derived from the Hebrew, which means "God will strengthen."

Ezer -derived from the Hebrew, which means "help." In the Bible (1 Chronicles 7:21), a member of the tribe of Ephraim.

Ezra -derived from the Hebrew, which means "help." In the Bible (Nehemiah 12:1), a Priest who returned to Judah after the Babylonian Exile.

F

Feivel -A Yiddish form of Phoebus, from the Latin and Greek, which means "bright one."

Fichel, Fishel From the Yiddish, which means "fish."

G

Gabai, Gabbai From the Aramaic, which means "collector of taxes" or synagogue attendant." In the Bible (Nehemiah 11:8), a leader of the tribe of Benjamin who was among the Babylonian Exile returnees.

Gabi - A pet form of Gabriel.

Gabriel -derived from the Hebrew, which means "God is my strength." Gavriel is the exact Hebrew form.

Gad -derived from the Hebrew and Aramaic, which means "happy, lucky, fortunate" or "a warrior." In the Bible (Genesis 35:26), one of the sons of Jacob from his wife Zilpah.

Gafni -derived from the Hebrew, which means "my vineyard."

Gai -derived from the Hebrew, which means "valley."

Gal -derived from the Hebrew, which means "wave" or "heap, mound."

Gamliel -derived from the Hebrew, which means "God is my reward." In the Bible (Numbers1:10), a leader of the tribe of Manasseh.

Gavriel -derived from the Hebrew, which means "God is my strength." In the Bible (Daniel 8:16), the angel seen my Daniel in a vision.

Gedalya -derived from the Hebrew, which means "God is great." In the Bible (Zephaniah 1:1), the governor of Judah appointed by Nebuchadnezzar, king of Babylonia.

Gedalyahu - A variant form of Gedalia.

Gershon- A variant form of Gershom.

Gever -derived from the Hebrew, which means "man." Or from the Aramaic, which means "to be strong." In the Bible (1 Kings 4:19), one of the twelve men who supervised the household of King Solomon.

Gidon -derived from the Hebrew, which means either "maimed" or "a mighty warrior." In the Bible (Judges 6:11), one of the Judges of Isreal, the warrior hero who defeated the Midianites."

Gil -derived from the Hebrew, which means "joy."

Gil–Ad -derived from the Hebrew, which means ""eternal joy."

Gilad -derived from the Hebrew, which means "mound of testimony."

Gili -derived from the Hebrew, which means "my joy."

Gur–Ari A variant form of Gur – Arye.

H

Henech -A Henech – A Yiddish form of Heinrich.

Hersh -From the Yiddish, which means "dear."

Hershel Hershel – A pet form of Hersh.

Herz - A pet form of Hersh. The name became popular as a result of the activity of Theodor Herzl (1860 – 1904), who worked for the establishment of a Jewish state.

Hillel -derived from the Hebrew, which means "the shining one" or praised, famous." In the Bible (Judges 12:13), the father of one of the judges of Israel.

Hosheia -derived from the Hebrew, which means "salvation." In the Bible (Hosea 1:1), an eight century B.C.E. Prophet who prophesied in the Kingdom of Israel during the reign of King Jeroboam.

I

Iezer I -A contracted form of Aviezer. In the Bible (Numbers 26:30), one of the sons of Gilad.

Isaac -derived from the Hebrew, which means "he will laugh." In the Bible (Genesis 21:3), Isaac was the second of the three Patriarchs. Yitzchak is the exact Hebrew form.

Israel - The Anglicized form of the Hebrew, which means either "prince of Gog" or "wrestled with God." The name was given to Jacob, the third of the three Patriarchs, after wrestling with the angel of God (Genesis 32:28).

Issachar -derived from the Hebrew, which means "there is a reward." In the Bible (Genesis 30:18), a son of Jacob and Leah, head of one of the twelve tribes of Israel.

Isser -A Yiddish form of Yisrael (Israel)."

Itamar -derived from the Hebrew, which means "island of palms." In the Bible (Exodus 6:23), the youngest son of Aaron and a nephew of Moses.

J

Jacob - The Anlicized form of Yaakov. -derived from the Hebrew, which means "held by the heel, supplanted, or protected." The third of the three Patriarchs and the father of the twelve sons who were founders o the tribe of Israel. The book of Genesis (32:28)

Jeremiah - derived from the Hebrew, which means "God will loosen (the bonds)" or "God will uplift." Jeremiah is one of the six Hebrew Prophets whose name is mentioned as a personal name in the Talmud. He belonged to a family of Priests living near Jerusalem, and began to prophesy in 625 B.C.E. Yirmeyahu is the exact Hebrew form.

Jesse Jesse - derived from the Hebrew, which means "wealthy" or gift." Yishai is the exact Hebrew form.

John John – The Anglicized form of Yochanan.

Jona, Jonah - derived from the Hebrew, which means "dove." Yona is the exact Hebrew form.

Jonathan - derived from the Hebrew, which means "God has given" or "gift of God." The exact Hebrew form is Yehonatan.

Joseph - derived from the Hebrew, which means "He (God) will add or increase." Yosef is the exact Hebrew form.

Joshua - derived from the Hebrew, which means "the Lord is my salvation." In the post-biblical period Joshua was one of the most commonly used biblical names.

Judah - derived from the Hebrew, which means "praise."

K

Kaduri - derived from the Hebrew, which means "my ball."

Kahana - From the Aramaic, which means "Priest."

Kalmon - A short form of Kalonymos.

Karmel - derived from the Hebrew, which means "vineyard."

Karmeli -derived from the Hebrew, which means "my vineyard."

Karmiel -derived from the Hebrew, which means "God is my vineyard" or "God is my protection."

Katan -derived from the Hebrew, which means "small." In the Bible (Ezra 8:12), one of the Babylonian Exile returnees was named Hakatan, which means "little one."

Katriel -derived from the Hebrew, which means "God is my crown.

Kehat -derived from the Hebrew, which means "faint, weak." In the Bible (Genesis 46:11), a son of Levi and a grandson of Jacob.

Kuti - A pet form of Yekutiel.

Kutiel - A short form of Yekutiel.

L

Label - A pet form of the Yiddish name Leib, which means "lion."

Lazer - A Yiddish form of Eliezer.

Leib -A Yiddish form of the German name Loeb, which means "lion."

Leibel - A pet form of Leib.

Lemech - Origin and which means uncertain. Probably a short Hebrew form of an Akkadian name. In the Bible (Genesis 4:19), a descendant of Cain.

Lemel –ajrice@yadtelajrice From the Yiddish, which means "little lamb" or "meek."

Leor -derived from the Hebrew, which means "light."

Lev Either -derived from the Hebrew, which means "heart," or from the Yiddish, meaning "lion."

Levi -derived from the Hebrew, which means "joined to" or "attendant upon." In the Bible (Genesis 29:34), the son of Jacob and Leah.

Lezer A Yiddish form of Eliezer.

Li-Or -derived from the Hebrew, which means "light is mine" or " I have light.

Leob From the German, which means "lion." Jews use it as a middle name with Judah because of the Biblical comparision of Judah to a lion (Genesis 49:9).

M

Maccabee -derived from the Hebrew, which means "hammer."

Maimon From the Arabic, which means "luck, good fortune." Moses ben Maimon (also known as Maimonides) was a Jewish philosopher who lived from 1135 to 1204.

Manasseh An Anglicized form of Menashe.

Mannes A variant form of Mann.

Manoach -derived from the Hebrew, which means "rest, resting place." In the Bible (Judges 13:2), the father of Samson.

Mashiach -derived from the Hebrew, which means "messiah, anointed one."

Matanya. -derived from the Hebrew, which means "gift of God." In the Bible (ll Kings 24:17), the earlier name of King Zedekiah.

Matanyahu A variant form of Matanya. In the Bible (l Chronicles 25:4), a son of Herman, one of King David's musicians.

Mati A pet form of Mattathias.

Matitya, Matityah - -derived from the Hebrew, which means "gift of God." In the Bible (Ezra 10:43, Nehemiah 8:4)), contemporaries of Ezra and Nehemiah.

Matityahu -derived from the Hebrew, which means "gift of God."

Matzliach -derived from the Hebrew, which means "victorious, successful."

Mazal -derived from the Hebrew, which means "star" or "luck."

Meigein -derived from the Hebrew, which means "to protect, protector."

Meir -derived from the Hebrew, which means "one who brightens or shines." In the Tamud (Yevamot 62b), a leading second-century scholar, the most brilliant of Rabbi Akiba's students.

Meiri A variant form of Meir.

Mei-Zahav Mei-Zahav - -derived from the Hebrew, which means "golden water." In the Bible (Genesis 36:39), an Edomite.

Melech Melech - -derived from the Hebrew, which means "king." In the Bible (l Chronicles 8:35), a member of the tribe of Benjamin and a descendant of King Saul.

Menachem - -derived from the Hebrew, which means "comforter." In the Bible (ll Kings 15:14), a king of Israel notorious for his cruelty.

Menashe -derived from the Hebrew, which means "causing to forget." In the Bible (Genesis 41:51), the eldest son of Joseph and the brother of Ephraim.

Mendel – From the Middle English menden, which means "to repair, to amend." Probably an occupational name for one who does general repairs. Also, a Yiddish name derived from Menachem.

Micha -derived from the Hebrew, which means "Who is like God?" A short form of Michael. In the Bible (Micah 1:1), one of the twelve Minor Prophets who prophesized in the latter part of the eight century B.C.E.

Michael -derived from the Hebrew, which means "Who is like God?" In the Bible (Numbers 13:13), a member of the tribe of Asher.

Mordechai – From the Persian and Babylonian, which means "warrior, warlike." In the Bible (Esther 2:5) Mordechai was the cousin of Queen Esther, who saved the Jews of Persia from Haman's plot to exterminate them.

Moshe -derived from the Hebrew, which means "drawn out (of the water)." In the Bible (Exodus 2:10), the leader who brought the Israelites out of bondage in Egypt and led them to the Promised Land.

N

Nachman -derived from the Hebrew, which means "comforter." In the Talmud (Betza 29b), a Babylonian scholar.

Nachmani -derived from the Hebrew, which means "comfort." In the Bible (Nehemiah 7:7), a leader of Judah who was among the Babylonian Exile returnees.

Nachmiel -derived from the Hebrew, which means "God is my comfort."

Nachson -derived from the Hebrew, which means "diviner." In the Bible (Exodus 6:23), a brother-in-law of Aaron.

Nachum -derived from the Hebrew, which means "comfort." In the Bible (Nahum 1:1), a minor Prophet of the seventh century B.C.E. who foretold the fall of Ninveh.

Naftali -derived from the Hebrew, which means "to wrestle," "to be crafty." Also, -derived from the Hebrew, which means "likeness, comparison." In the Bible (Genesis 30:8), the sixth son of Jacob; the second with his wife Bilhah.

Natan -derived from the Hebrew, which means "gift." In the Bible (ll Samuel 5:15), the Prophet who pronounced that the dynasty of King David would be perpetually established.

Nechemya -derived from the Hebrew, which means "comforted of the Lord." In the Bible (Ezra 2:2), a governor of Judah.

Nechum -derived from the Hebrew, which means "comfort." In the Bible (Nehemiah7:7), a leader of the Babylonian Exile returnees.

Netanel -derived from the Hebrew, which means "gift of God." In the Bible (l Chronicles 2:14), the fourth son of Jesse.

Netanya -derived from the Hebrew, which means "gift of God." In the Bible (ll Kings 25:23), the father of the murderer of Gedaliah.

Nissan -derived from the Hebrew, which means "banner, emblem" or "miracle." The first month of spring.

Nissim -derived from the Hebrew, which means "signs" or "miracles."

Noach -derived from the Hebrew, which means "rest, quiet, peace." In the Bible (Genesis 5:29), the main character in the story of the flood.

Noam -derived from the Hebrew, which means "sweetness" or "friendship."

O

Oded -derived from the Hebrew, which means "to restore." In the Bible (ll Chronicles 28:9), a Prophet in the name of King Ahaz.

Ofir Ofir - -derived from the Hebrew, which means "gold." In the Bible (Genesis 10:29), a son of Yaktan.

Ohed -derived from the Hebrew, which means "love" or " beloved."

Oran From the Aramaic, which means "light."

Oshiya -derived from the Hebrew, which means "salvation" or "Please, God, save!"

P

Paseachs. A variant form of Pesach. In the Bible (Nehemiah 3:6), one of Ezra's supporters.

Peretz. -derived from the Hebrew, which means "burst forth." In the Bible (Genesis 38:29), a son of Judah and Tamar.

Pesach -derived from the Hebrew, which means "to pass over" or "to limp." The Hebrew name of the Passover holiday.

Pesachya -derived from the Hebrew, which means "the pesach

Petuel From the Aramaic, which means "spacious, abundant." In the Bible (Joel 1:1), the father of the prophet Joel.

Pinchas From the Egyptian, which means "Negro, dark complexioned" or -derived from the Hebrew, which means "mouth of a snake." In the Bible (Exodus 6:25), a High Priest, the grandson of Aaron.

R

Raanan -derived from the Hebrew, which means "to restore." In the Bible (ll Chronicles 28:9), a Prophet in the name of King Ahaz.

Rachaman Rachaman - -derived from the Hebrew, which means "compassionate one (God)."

Rachamim -derived from the Hebrew, which means "compassion, mercy."

Rachmiel -derived from the Hebrew, which means "compassion for the Lord" or "God is my comforter."

Rachum -derived from the Hebrew, which means "compassionate."

Rafi Rafi – A pet form of Refael.

Rani -derived from the Hebrew, which means "my joy" or "my song."

Ranon A variant form of Ranen.

Raviv -derived from the Hebrew and Aramaic, which means "four, fourth."

Refael -derived from the Hebrew, which means "God has healed." Raphael is the archangel and divine messenger mentioned in the apocryphal books of Enoch and Tobit.

Reuel -derived from the Hebrew, which means "friend of God." In the Bible (Exodus 2:18), another name for Jethro, the father-I-law of Moses.

Reuven -derived from the Hebrew, which means "behold, a son!" In the Bible (Genesis 29:32), Jacob's firstborn son from his wife Leah.

Roni -derived from the Hebrew, which means "my song" or "my joy." Used also as a feminine name.

S

Saadya -derived from the Hebrew and Aramaic, which means "the help of God." Saadya ben Joseph (882-942) was an Egyptian born Jewish scholar and author.

Saba From the Aramaic, which means "old" or "grandfather."

Samson -derived from the Hebrew, which means "seen" or "service, ministry." In the Bible, a Judge in Israel. Shimson is the exact Hebrew form.

Samuel -derived from the Hebrew, which means "His name is God." In the Bible (1 Samuel 1:20), an eleventh century B.C.E. Prophet and Judge who anointed Saul as first of Israel. Shmuel is the exact Hebrew form.

Sanser A short form of Alexander.

Segel -derived from the Hebrew, which means "treasure." In the Bible, Israel is referred to as "a treasured people."

Sender A Yiddish form of Alexander.

Shabtai From the Aramaic, which means "rest, Sabbath." In the Bible (Ezra 10:15), a Levite in the time of Ezra.

Shachar -derived from the Hebrew, which means "dawn", or "light."

Shai -derived from the Hebrew and Aramaic, which means "gift."

Shalom -derived from the Hebrew, which means "peace."

Shammai -derived from the Hebrew and Aramaic, which means "name."

Shaul -derived from the Hebrew, which means "asked" or "borrowed." In the Bible (1 Samuel 9:2), the first king of Israel.

Shaya A short for of Yeshaya.

Shealtiel -derived from the Hebrew, which means "borrowed from EL or God." In the Bible (Haggai 1:1), the father of Zerubbabel.

Shebsel From the Yiddish, which means "sheep."

Shem -derived from the Hebrew, which means "name" and connoting "reputation." In the Bible (Genesis 5:32), the eldest of Noah's three sons.

Shemarya -derived from the Hebrew, which means "protection of the Lord." In the Bible (ll Chronicles 11:19), a son of King Rehoboam.

Shemaryahu A variant form of Shemarya.

Shemaya From the Aramaic, which means "to hear." In the Bible (1 Kings 12:22), a Prophet during the reign of King Rehoboam.

Shemayahu A variant form of Shemaya.

Shem-Tov -derived from the Hebrew, which means "good name" or "good reputation."

Shepsel From the Yiddish, which means "sheep."

Sheraga From the Aramaic, which means "light."

Shimi -derived from the Hebrew, which means "my name" or "reputation." In the Bible (ll Samuel 16:5), a member of the tribe of Benjamin.

Shimon -derived from the Hebrew, which means "to hear" or "to be heard" or "reputation." In the Bible (Genesis 29:33), the second son of Jacob and Leah.

Shimshon -derived from the Hebrew, which means "sun." In the bible (Judges 13:24), a judge from the tribe of Dan noted for his strength and courage, and success in battling the Philistines, until he was betrayed by Delilah.

Shlomi -derived from the Hebrew, which means "my peace." In the Bible (Numbers 34:27), the father of a leader of the tribe of Asher.

Shlomo -derived from the Hebrew, which means "his peace." The Hebrew form of Solomon.

Shmarya A variant spelling of Shemarya.

Shmerel A Yiddish form of Shemarya.

Shmiel A pet form of Shemuel.

Shmuel -derived from the Hebrew, which means "his name is God."

Shmulke A Yiddish pet form of Shmuel.

Shneur A Yiddish variant form of Senior.

Simcha -derived from the Hebrew, which means "joy."

Solomon -derived from the Hebrew, which means "peace." In the Bible. The king of Israel, son of King David and Bathsheba (ll Samuel 12:24).

T

Tamir -derived from the Hebrew, which means "tall, stately, like the palm tree."

Tanchum -derived from the Hebrew, which means "comfort, consolation." In the Talmud (Moed Katan 25b), a third century Babylonian scholar.

Tarfon -derived from the Hebrew, which means "torn (a torn animal)" or "predatory, cruel," hence a nonkosher animal. A name given to a prominent first-century Palestinian talmudic scholar because he erroneously ruled that an animal was nonkosher when it was actually kosher.

Tomer -derived from the Hebrew, which means "tall, stately."

Tov -derived from the Hebrew, which means "good." In the Bible (ll Chronicles 17:8), a Levite in the time of King Jehoshaphat.

Tovi A variant form of Tov. -derived from the Hebrew, which means "my good, my goodness." In the Talmud (Bava Kama 36b), a third century Babylonian scholar.

Toviel -derived from the Hebrew, which means "my God is goodness."

Toviya -derived from the Hebrew, which means "goodness of God." In the Bible (Ezra 12:60), one of the Babylonian Exile returnees.

Tuviya -derived from the Hebrew, which means "God is good" or "goodness of God." In the Bible (Zechariah 6:10), one of the Babylonian Exile returnees.

Tzachi A pet form of Yitzchak.

Tzefanya -derived from the Hebrew, which means "hidden by God" or "protected by God."

Tzemach -derived from the Hebrew, which means "plant." In the Bible (Zechariah 3:8), a man named in Zechariah's prophecy.

Tzevi -derived from the Hebrew, which means "deer, gazelle."

Tzidkiya -derived from the Hebrew, which means "righteousness of the Lord" or God is righteous." In the Bible (ll Kings 24:17), the last king of Judah.

Tzidkiyahu A variant form of Tzidkiya.

Tziyon -derived from the Hebrew, which means "excellent" or "a sign." In the Bible, Zion is used as the name of a place as well as the appellation for the Hebrew people.

U

Udi -derived from the Hebrew, which means "firebrand."

Uri A variant form of Ur. -derived from the Hebrew, which means "my flame" or "my light." In the Bible (Exodus 31:2), a leader of the tribe of Judah.

Uriel -derived from the Hebrew, which means "God is my light" or God is my flame." In the Bible (1 Chronicles 6:9), a Levite of the Kohat family.

Uzi -derived from the Hebrew, which means "my strength." In the Bible (ll Kings 15:30), a king of Judah also known as Azaeiah.

Uziel -derived from the Hebrew, which means "God is my strength." In the Bible (Exodus 6:18), a son of Kohat and a grandson of Levi.

Uziyahu A variant form of Uziya.

V

Velvol A pet form of the Yiddish Vilf (Wolf).

Volf From the Yiddish, which means "wolf."

Y

Yaakov -derived from the Hebrew, which means "supplanted" or "held by the heel." In the Bible (Genesis 25:26), a son of Isaac and Rebekah and the twin brother of Esau.

Yankel A Yiddish form of Yaakov.

Yechezkel -derived from the Hebrew, which means "God will strengthen." In the Bible (Ezekiel 1:3), one of the Prophets of the sixth century B.C.E.

Yechiel -derived from the Hebrew, which means "May God live!" In the Bible (Ezra 8:9), one of King David's chief musicians.

Yechizkiya -derived from the Hebrew, which means "May God strengthen!" In the Bible (Ezra 2:16), the head of a family of Babylonian Exile returnees.

Yechizkiyahu A variant form of Yechizkiya. In the Bible (ll Chronicles 28:12), a member of the tribe of Ephraim.

Yehochanan -derived from the Hebrew, which means "God is gracious." In the Bible (Ezra 10:6), the High Priest in the time of Ezra.

Yehonatan -derived from the Hebrew, which means "God has given; gift of God." In the Bible (1 Samuel 14:6), the son of King Saul and the very close friend of David.

Yehoshua -derived from the Hebrew, which means "God is salvation." In the Bible (Exodus 16:9), the leader of the Israelites after the death of Moses.

Yehuda -derived from the Hebrew, which means "praise." In the Bible (Genesis 29:35), the fourth son of Jacob and Leah and the founder of one the twelve tribes.

Yekutiel -derived from the Hebrew, which means "God will nourish." In the Bible (1 Chronicles 4:18), a descendant of Caleb.

Yerachmiel A variant form of Yerachm'el.

Yerucham A variant form of Yerocham.

Yesarel A variant form of Yisrael.

Yeshaya A variant form of Yeshayahu.

Yeshayahu -derived from the Hebrew, which means "God is salvation." In the Bible (Isaiah 1:1), the great eigh-century Prophet in the kingdom of Judah who was born in Jerusalem in 765 B.C.E. Isaiah in the Anglicized form.

Yeshua Yeshua - -derived from the Hebrew, which means "salvation." In the Bible (Nehemiah 8:7), another name for Joshua.

Yirmeya A variant form of Yirmeyahu. In the Bible (l Chronicles 5:24), a member of the tribe of Manasseh.

Yirmeyahu -derived from the Hebrew, which means "God will raise up." In the Bible (Jermiah 1:1), the Prophet who along with Isaiah was a giant among the Prophets of Israel.

Yisachar -derived from the Hebrew, which means "there is reward." In the Bible (Genesis 30:18), a son of Jacob.

Yisrael -derived from the Hebrew, which means "prince of God" or "to contend, fight" or "to rule." In the Bible (Genesis 32:29), a son of Isaac whose primary name is Yaakov.

Yitzchak -derived from the Hebrew, which means "he will laugh." In the Bible (Genesis 21:5), the son born to Abraham and Sara in their old age.

Yizrael A variant form of Yizr'el.

Yochanan -derived from the Hebrew, which means "God is gracious." In the Bible (ll Kings 25:23), the eldest son of Josiah, king of Judah.

Yoel -derived from the Hebrew, which means "God is willing" or "the Lord is God." In the Bible (Joel 1:1), one of the Minor Prophets.

Yona -derived from the Hebrew, which means "dove." In the Bible (Jpnah 1:1), one of the Minor Prophets, noted for swallowed by a big fish and emerging unscathed.

Yonatan A short and more commonly used form of Yehonatan. In the Talmud (Menachot 57b), a second-century Palestinian scholar.

Yoran -derived from the Hebrew, which means "to sing."

Yosef - derived from the Hebrew, which means "God will add, increase." In the Bible (Genesis 30:24), one of the twelve sons of Jacob.

Yosei A variant form of Yosi. Thirty-nine Palestinian and Babylonian scholars are named Yosei, Yosei Hagalili (Moed Katan 28) being one of the most prominent.

Z

Zalman, Zalmen, Zalmon. Yiddish short forms of Solomon.

Zecharya - derived from the Hebrew, which means "memory" or "rememberance of the Lord." One of the twelve Minor Prophets. Also one of the kings of Israel, the son of Jeroboam (ll Kings 14:29).

Zecharyahu A variant form of Zecharya. In the Bible (ll Kings 15:8), a king of Israel.

Ze'ev - derived from the Hebrew, which means "wolf." In the Bible (Genesis 49:27), when Benjamin is blessed by his father, Jacob, he is compared to a wolf.

Zeide From the Yiddish, which means "grandfather" or "old man."

Zimroni - derived from the Hebrew, which means "my son, my melody."

Zohar - derived from the Hebrew, which means "light, brilliance."

Zusa From the Yiddish, which means "sweet."

Zushe A variant form of Zusa.

Zusman, Zusmann Yiddish came from the German, which means "sweet person" or "sweet man."

NEGATIVE FEMALE AND MALE NAMES

Attention:

Your life is not doomed per se, if you own a negative name. However, one should work hard to fulfilling the prophetic call of such name. In many cases, people change their name to a meaning which a positive prophetic call. Lastly, I suggest that you always seek the presence of the Father in all things. Moreover, we all should strive for perfection and righteousness in Christ despite one's name, religion or creed.

Negative Female Names

Abda: muslim: Slave girl
Acanit (ah-chah-neet): ungandan: Hard times
Adrienne: french: Dark one
Adultera: latin: Adulteress
Alile: nigerian: She weeps; for a child born into unfortunate circumstances.
Alkas: native american: She is afraid
Alnaba: navaho indian: War passed each other
Altsoba: navaho indian: All are at war
Amaia: basque: End
Amara: esperento: Bitter
Anaba: navaho indian: She returns from war
Bacia: ungandan: Family deaths ruined the home
Basha: latin: The stranger
Bethany: arabic: House of poverty
Bian: vietnamese: Secret, hidden
Carling: old english: Hill where the old women or witches gather
Cecilia: latin: Blind
Cicuta: latin: Hemlock
Cochiti: spanish: Forgotten
Darcy: gaelic: Dark

Deirdre: celtic: Sorrow
Desdemona: greek: Ill-fated one
Discordia/Dissonantia: latin: Discord; chaotic
Duvessa: gaelic: Dark beauty
Elona: native american: Alone
Iye (ee-yeh): native american: Smoke
Jinkx/Jinx: latin?: Bad Luck; to hex; spell
Jobey/Jobina: hebrew: The Persecuted
Karayan: armenian: The dark one
Kapera: african: This child, too, will die
Leah (lee-uh): hebrew: Weary
Leiko: japanese: Arrogant
Lena: latin: Temptress
Letha: greek: Oblivion
Lorelei: teutonic: Destruction
Magara: rhodesian: Child who constantly cries
Manya/Marisha: russian: Bitter
Mara/Mary: hebrew: Bitter
Marianne/Marilyn: hebrew: Bitter
Maura: latin: Dark
Melancholia: latin: Blues; blue-devil; depression
Melinda: greek: Gentle, dark
Minna/Miren: hebrew: Bitter; bitterness
Misty: old english: Covered with a mist
Naleh: persian: Wail
Necromantia: latin: Necromancy
Nigritia: latin: Blackness
Parodia: latin: Illusion
Penthea: greek: Fifth, mourner
Perdita: latin: The lost
Phantasma: latin: Ghost; phantom
Polly: hebrew: Bitter
Sanguisuga (sahn-goo-ehs-oo-gah): latin: Blood-sucker
Sarai: hebrew: Quarrelsome
Sayeh: persian: Shade, shadow
Sezen: turkish: Feeling suspicion
Solita: latin: Alone
Tanha: persian: Alone

Tresa: german: The Reaper
Trista: latin: Sorrowful
Umbra: latin: Ghost
Ultima: latin: Aloof
Yenene (yeh-nay-neh): miwok indian: Wizard poisoning a sleeping person
Yiku: chinese: Pleasure over bitterness
Zia: hebrew: To tremble
Zila: hebrew: Shadow

Negative Male Names

Adrien/Adrian: latin: Dark one
Aitan: african: Fights for possesion
Akando: native american: Ambush
Amadi: nigerian: Seemed destined to die at birth
Arzan: persian: Cheap
Bavius: greek: Bad poet
Cash: latin: Vain
Cassius: latin: Vain
Chatha: african: An ending
Confusus/Indigestus (not kidding!): latin: Chaotic
Cruentus (croo-ehn-toos): latin: Blood-red
Daray: irish: Dark
Dard: persian: Pain
Doshman: persian: Enemy
Duglas: gaelic: Dark stranger
Duncan: irish: Dark man
Furis: latin: Thief
Furor: latin: Rage
Garrison: hebrew: Column of conquest
Gazidan: persian: Bite
Graham: anglo-saxon: Warlike
Hadrian: swedish: Dark one

Jaron: hebrew: To cry out
Kasif: persian: Dirty
Kern: gaelic: Dark
Killian: irish: War
Mahbub: persian: Drunk
Malus: latin: Bad
Maluspuer (mah-lahs-poor?): latin: Badboy
Mark: latin: Warlike
Necator: latin: Slayer
Noctivagus (nohk-tehv-ah-goos): latin: Night-walker (vampire)
Obscuratio (ohb-skew-ray-shee-oh): latin: Darkening
Patamon: native american: Raging
Sanguinarius: latin: Blood thirsty
Sanies: latin: Corrupted blood
Sard: persian: Cold
Taklishim: apache: Grey One
Talman: hebrew: To injure, to oppress
Tarik: persian: Dark
Ulysses: latin: Wrathful

The meaning of strange female and male names

Strange Female Names

A:
Abebi: yoruba: We ask for her and she came to us; She came after asking
Abida: hebrew: My father knows
Abital/Avital: hebrew: My father is dew
Abir: arabian: Scent
Abra: arabian: Example, lesson
Advena: latin: Stranger
Akanke/Amoke: nigerian: To know her is to love(pet) her
Akisatan: african: Rags are not finished (with which to bury you)
Alake: yoruban: One to be petted if she survives
Aleshanee: native american: She plays all the time
Alike: nigerian: Girl who drives out beautiful women
Alina: celtic: A distant place
Amara: greek: Unfading
Amara: kiswahili: Urgent news
Annakiya (ah-nah-key-ah): housa: Sweet face
Apara: yoruban: One who comes and goes
Arda/Ardah: hebrew: Bronzed; also the month of 'Adar'(Feb-March)
Arienh (a-reen): irish: Pledge
Audrey: english: Strength to overcome
Audun: norwegian: Deserted
Aurkene: basque: Presentation
Awenasa (ah-weh-nah-sah): native american: My home
Ayita: native american: First in the dance
Ayoka: nigerian: One who causes joy all around
Ayondela: african: "A little tree bends and bends, as we all bend toward death." Based on some philosophy.

B:
Banjoko: african: Sit down (or stay) with me
Benazir (beh-nah-zeer): persian: "The like of whom was never seen"
Bestia/Belua: latin: Beast
Bazi: persian: Play; game
Binnaz (bee-nahz): turkish: "A thousand blandishments"; charming

C:
Calliope: greek: Beautiful voice
Comoedia: latin: Comedy
Culina: latin: Kitchen

D:
Dagmar: danish: Joy of the Danes
Dagna: old german: A splendid day
Damalis: greek: One who gentles
Delilah: hebrew: 1)poor, 2)hair
Dena/Dinah: hebrew: Vindicated
Desiree: latin: So long hoped for
Dilys (dil-ees): welsh: Genuine
Durosimi: african: Wait and bury me; Don't die before me

E:
Ebru (eh-broo): turkish: Marbling(as on paper decoration)
Elita: french: Special one
Emalia: latin: Flirt
Eulalia (yoo-lay-lee-uh): greek: Fair of speech
Eve/Ive (eev-ah): kiswhili: To ripen
Ethelind: teutonic: Nobly wise

F:
Fannah: ethiopian: Fun
Fayina: russian: Free one
Fikriyyah (fihk-ree-yah): muslim: meditative

G:
Garda: teutonic: Protected
Gerda: german: Protection
Ghislaine (zhees-layn): french: Sweet pledge
Gilen (gigh-len): teutonic: Industrious pledge
Gilsa: teutonic: Pledge
Giselle (jih-zel): old german: A pledge
Grear: scottish: Watchful
Gytha/Githa (gay-thuh, gee-thah): anglo-saxon: Gift

H:
Hadara: hebrew: Bedecked in beauty
Hali: hebrew: Necklace, place name
Halimah (hah-lee-mah): muslim: Lady of patience and perseverence
Hei/Hea (heh-ah): korean: Grace
Helki: miwok indian: To touch
Hisa: japanese: Long-lasting
Hitomi: japanese: Eye
Huriye (hoo-ree-yahy): persian: "Like a Houri"; Maiden of paradise
Hwistaks: yakima indian: Dress that swishes

I:
Icimanipi-Wihopawni: apache: Travels beautiful woman
Idola: greek: Idolized
Ide (ee-duh): irish: Thirst
Imogene (ee-moh-jeen): latin: Image
Inas (igh-nahs): muslim: Well-mannered
Isidore: french: Gift of ideas
Isoke (ee-soh-keh): african: Satisfying gift
Izanami: japanese: Female who invites

J:
Jacqueline/Jamie: hebrew: Supplanter
Jael: hebrew: To ascend
Jaione (hah-oh-neh): basque: Nativity
Jarvia: old german: To flow downward
Jarvinia: german: Keen intelligence
Jendayi (jen-dah-ee): african: Give thanks
Jin: japanese: Super-excellent

K:
Kadife: turkish: Velvet
Kanene (kah-neen): african: A little thing in the eye is big
Kasa: hopi indian: Fur-robed dress
Kei (kigh): japanese: Rapture, reverence
Kendra: welsh: Knowing woman
Keturah: hebrew: Fragrance
Kiran: hindu: Ray
Kosoko: african: There is no hoe (to dig a grave with)

L:
Lakeisha: swahili: Favorite one
Lana: polynesian: To float
Leala: french: Loyal one
Ledah: hebrew: Birth
Lia: hebrew: Dependence
Liana: french: To bind
Linna: finnish: Castle
Luana: hawaiian: Enjoyment
Luli: persian: Dancing girl
Lynn: anglo-saxon: A cascade
Lysandra: greek: Emancipation

M:
Machi: japanese: Ten thousand
Machupa (mah-choo-pah): kenyan: Likes to drink
Madeline: hebrew: Woman from Magdala
Maeve: gaelic: Intoxicating one
Mai: japanese: Dance

Mallory: french: Mailed
Melanie: greek: Dark-clothed
Mia/Michaela: hebrew: "Who is like God?"
Mirit: hebrew: Sweet-wine
Minnie: teutonic: Loving memory
Molomo: african: Don't go back (to the spirit world)
Mona: greek: Solitary

N:
Nadira: muslim: Rare, choice, precious
Naia (neh-uh): greek: Flowing
Na'ilah (nah-eel-ah): muslim: One who obtains favor
Naimah (nah-ee-mah): arabic: Living a soft, enjoyable life
Naina: india: Eyes
Najida: muslim: Courageous; one who accomplishes difficult tasks
Najla (nahj-lah): muslim: "Has beautiful, wide eyes"
Nasnan: native american: Surrounded by a song
Nazli: persian: Coquettish
Nefes: turkish: Breath
Nimah: arabic: Blessing, loan
Nitara: hindu: Deeply rooted
Noella: french: Christmas
Nona: latin: Ninth
Nori: japanese: Doctrine
Novia: latin: Newcomer
Nurhan: turkish: Bright lady
Nysa: greek: The goal
Nyssa: greek: Begining

O:
Odelia: hebrew: I will praise God
Odessa: greek: A long journey
Oliana: hawaiian: Oleander
Onida: native american: The expected one

P:
Pascale (pas-cayl- ah): french: Easter
Peritia: latin: Knowledge of skill
Perfecte: latin: All-wise
Persis: greek: Woman from persia
Pogadh (poh-gah-sh? or poh-guh): scottish: Kissing
Portia: latin: Offering
Pooja: india: Prayer
Priti: india: Satisfaction

Q: (empty)

R:
Ramah: hebrew: High
Ranaa: muslim: To look
Rassia (ray-zah): old french: Thinker
Razi: arabian: My secret
Rebecca: hebrew: Tied
Reidun: norwegian: Nest-lovely
Rekha: india: Straight-line
Remy: french: From Rheims
Rishona: hebrew: First

S:
Sabirah (sah-bee-rah): arabic: Patient
Sade (shar-day): nigerian: Honor confers a crown
Salihah: african: Correct
Samirah: arabic: Entertaining companion
Sarika: india: Thrush
Scientia: latin: Knowledge
Seema: greek: Symbol
Segulah: hebrew: Treasure
Serap: turkish: Mirage
Seza: persian: Punishment; reward
Shala/Shahlaa: muslim: Having grey eyes with shade of red; species of Narcissis flower
Shandy: old english: Rambunctious
Shani: kenyan: Marvellous

Shani: kiswahili: Unusual thing; adventure
Sharman: english: A fair share
Shebari: gypsy: Gypsygirl of marriagable age; bride
Sheetal: india: Cool
Sheila: latin: Blind
Shela: celtic: Musical
Shreya: india: Auspicious
Sibongile (see-bahn-gee-lah): african: Thanks
Siddhi (seh-dee or see-dee): india: Then you must have a Riddhi
Siddiqah: muslim: "One who keeps her word"
Sikudhani (see-koo-than-ee): kenyan: A surprise
Simone: hebrew: One who hears
Skylar: welsh?: Sheltering
Skyler: norse: Projectile
Snana: native american: Jingles like little bells
Sophronia: greek: Foresighted
Stesha: russian: Crowned-one
Suravinda: india: A beautiful Yaksa
Syna: greek: Two together

T:
Tacita (tah-see-tuh): latin: To be silent
Taliah (tah-lee-ah): hebrew: Lamkin
Tamika: japanese: People
Tara: celtic: Tower, crag
Tayce (tay- see): french: Silence
Tekla/Thekla: greek: Divine fame
Tertia (ter-shuh): latin: The third
Tessera: latin: Password
Thais (thay-es): greek: The bond
Tiara: greek: Turban
Timora: hebrew: Tall(as a palm tree)
Tira: hebrew: Encampment/enclosure
Tosia (toh- shuh): latin: Inestimable
Trilby: italian: One who sings musical trills
Trishna: india: Thirst
Tryphena: latin: Dainty

U:
Uma: hebrew: Nation
Uriana: greek: The unknown

V:
Vala: old english: Chosen
Valonia: latin: Of the Vale
Vara: greek: The stranger
Velda: teutonic: Of great wisdom
Veronica: latin: True image
Vevila: gaelic: Woman with a melodious voice
Voleta: greek: Veiled one

W:
Willow: middle english: Freedom
Wilona/Willa: anglo-saxon: The desired, wished for
Winda: swahili: Hunt
Wijdan (?): arabic: Ecstacy

X:
Xenia/Ximena: greek: Hospitality to strangers
Ximena: greek: Unknown, stranger

Y:
Yemina/Yaminah: hebrew: Right hand

Z:
Zakiyah (zah-key-ah): muslim: Lady of keen perception and sharp mind
Zia: native american: Not known
Zimora: hebrew: Song of praise
Zina: african: Name
Zona: latin: A girth
Zulaikha (zoo-lay-kah): muslim: So beautiful that people gape in wonderment

Strange Male Names

A:
Achilles: greek: Without lips
Akello: ungandan: I have bought
Atman: hindu: The self

B:
Baingana: ungandan: People are equal
Baldwin: teutonic: Bald friend
Bicornis: latin: Two-horned
Bitalo: ungandan: Finger-licking
Blase: latin: Stammerer
Bud: german: To puff up
Burhan: arabic: Proof

C:
Canute: norwegian: Knot
Cameron: scottish: Crooked nose
Ceasar: latin: To cut
Cody: old german: Possessions
Clyde: welsh: Heard from afar

D:
Dallin: old welsh: Pride's people
Damen: greek: Taming
Damon: greek: Constant
Darnell: english: Hidden nook
Dasodaha: apache: He only sits there
Delsin: native american: He is so
Desmond: celtic: Man of the world
Drew: old french: Sturdy
Durand: latin: Enduring
Dutch: german: The German

E:
Eli (ee-ligh): hebrew: Elevation

F:
Faxon: teutonic: Long hair
Frasier: english: Curly-haired

G:
Gage (gayj): old french: Pledge
Gamble: norse: Old
Garridan: english gypsy: You hid
Gaspar: spanish: Master of treasure

H:
Halden: teutonic: Half Dane
Halian: zuni indian: Of Julius
Hamlin: french: Little home-lover
Hastings: german: Swift one
Henry: old german: Ruler of the home

I:
Ineptus (igh-nep-toos): latin: Awkward
Izanagi: japanese: Male who invites

J:
James/Jacobe/Jacques: hebrew-french: Supplanter
Janir: arabic: Comforter
Jarman: old english: German
Javier: french: January
Jed: arabic: The hand
Jeremiah: hebrew: Exalted of the Lord
Jiro (jee-roh): japanese: Second male
Jordan: hebrew: Descending

K:
Kasper: persian: A treasured secret
Kenan: hebrew: Possesion
Ker: english gypsy: House

L:
Lawler: gaelic: Softspoken
Leron: arabic: The song is mine
Logan: irish: From the hollow
Luscus: latin: One-eyed
Lysander: greek: Liberator

M:
Mander: english gypsy: From me
Meka: hawaiian: Eyes
Montezuma: aztec: He frowned like a lord
Mukasa: ugandan: God's chief administrator

N:
Nalren: dene indian: He is thawed out
Nelek: polish: Like a horn
Nevin: gaelic: Nephew
Nicanor: spanish: Victorious people
Nishan: armenian: Sign

O: (empty)

P: (empty)
Penn: old english: Enclosure
Platon: spanish: Broad-shouldered

R:
Roldan: teutonic: Fame of the land
Ronan: celtic: A pledge

S:
Sam: hebrew: To hear
Samien (sa-migh-an): ?: To be heard
Saul: hebrew: Longed- for
Sebastian: greek: Venerable, revered
Seth: hebrew: Appointed one
Shammara: arabic: He girded his loins
Simon: hebrew: He who hears
Sivan (see-vahn): hebrew: The ninth month

Spencer: old english: Dispenser, keeper
Stoke: english: Village
Stoyan: bulgarian: To stay

T:
Tate (tayt): native american: Windy, great talker
Tibalt: greek: People's prince
Tiro/Tironis: latin: Greenhorn
Tong (tah-om): vietnamese: Fragrant
Tremaine: english: Farm with a stone monolith

U:

V:
Van: dutch: From, of; usually used as a sort of middle name, particularly to a title.

W:
Walker: english: One who thicken cloth
Winston: english: Town of victory

X:
Ximen (zee-mehn): spanish: Obedient

Y:
Yale: german: One who pays or produces
Yarin: hebrew: To understand

Z:

Strange Names that fit in both genders

Akal: sikhism: Eternal
Bali: persian: Yes
Cassidy: irish: Clever
Chashm: persian: Eye
Dandan: persian: Tooth
Gat: sikhism: Freedom
Neshin: persian: Sit
Omnsciens (ohmn-see-ehns): latin: All-knowing
Qadim: persian: Old, ancient
Sarkash: persian: Stubborn
Shano: persian: Hear
Sheridon: irish: Wild one
Solarium: latin: Sun-dial
Zahmat: persian: Trouble

The meaning of positive female and male names

Postive Female Names

A:
Aaminah: muslim: Lady of peace and harmony
Aanisah/Anisa: muslim: Pious-hearted Lady; Good-natured
Aasta: norse: Love
Abigail: hebrew: Father of Joy; father's joy
Abira (ah-beer-ah): hebrew: Strong
Adara/Adra: arabic: Virgin
Adara: greek: Beauty
Adilah: muslim: "One who deals justly"
Adira: herbrew: Mighty; strong
Adiva: arabic: Pleasant and gentle
Adoncia (ah-dohn-chuh): spanish: Sweet
Adonia: greek: Beautiful
Adora: latin: Beloved; adored
Affrica/Afrika/Africa: irish: Pleasant
Agapi: greek: Love, affection
Agate: greek: Kind
Agatha: greek: Good
Agave: greek: Illustrious, noble
Agnes (ag-nes): greek: Chaste
Ahava (ah-hah-vah): hebrew: Beloved
Ahimsa: hindu: Nonviolent virtue
Ai: japanese: Love
Aida: arabian: Reward, pleasant
Aiko: japanese: Child of love; Little loved one
Aila: finnish: Light-bearer
Ailsa/Alyssa: teutonic: Of good cheer
Aine (an-yuh): celtic: Joy
Aintzane (ah-ee-tsah-neh): basque: Glorious
Aisha (ah-ee-sha): swahili-arabic: Life, alive
Akilah: arabic: Intelligent, logical

Akiva: hebrew: Protect
Alazne (ah-lahz-nee): basque: Miracle
Aldea: teutonic : Rich
Alethea: greek: Truth
Alicia/Alice: greek: Truthful one
Alika: egyptian-swahili: Most beautiful
Alina: polish: Bright and beautiful; Light
Aliza/Aleeza/Alisa: hebrew: Joyous; Great happiness
Aliz: hungarian: Kind
Allegra/Alegra: latin: Joyful, merry, lively
Alodie: anglo-saxon: Wealthy
Althea: greek: Wholesome
Amabel: latin: Lovable
Amadika: southern rhodesian: Beloved
Amamndine: latin: Beloved
Amara: greek: Eternally beautiful
Amata: spanish: Beloved
Amelia: latin: Industrious
Amina: muslim: Peace, security; Trustworthy; faithful, honest
Amissa: hebrew: Friend
Amity: latin: Friendship
Amy: latin: Beloved
An: chinese: Peace
Ananda: hindu: Bliss
Andreana: latin: Womanly
Aneska/Anezka (ah-nehz-kah): czech: Pure
Aneesh: muslim: Companion, affectionate friend
Anica: spanish: Graceful
Anisa: arabic: Friendly
Anke: hebrew: Grace
Anne: hebrew: Full of Grace
Annika: swedish: grace
Annora: latin: Honor
Anoush: armenian: Sweet
'Aolani: hawaiian: Heavenly cloud

Aprika: gaelic: Pleasant
Antje (ahnt-yah): german: Grace
Aquene (ah-kay-nay): native american: Peace
Aquilah: muslim: Intelligent
Ardella: latin: Wealth
Aretha: greek: Best
Aretina: greek: Virtuous
Ariadne/Ariana: greek: Very holy one
Aruna: hindu: Radiance
Asenka: hebrew: Graceful
Asha: african: Life
Ashaki (ah-shah-kee): african: Beautiful
Ashira: hebrew: Wealthy
Asma: muslim: beautiful
Audrey: old english: Noble strength

B:
Bahijah (bah-hee-yah): muslim: Joyful, delightful, happy
Basheera: muslim: Good news
Basimah: muslim: Smiling one
Bayo: nigerian: To find joy
Beatrice: latin: Bringer of joy
Betha: celtic: Life
Blanda/Blenda: teutonic: Dazzling
Bliss: english: Joy
Blythe: english: Joyful
Briana: celtic: The strong, powerful

C:
Callia: greek: Beautiful
Callista: greek: Most beautiful
Cara: gaelic: Friend
Caresse: french: Beloved
Carissa: greek: Beloved
Caron: french: Pure
Casta: greek: Purity

Catalin/Caitlin/Caitlyn/Caitrin: irish: Pure
Caterina: italian: Pure
Catherine: greek: Pure
Catriona: gaelic: Pure
Charis: greek: Grace, kindness
Charisma/Carisma: latin: Charm or charming; Charismatic
Chastity: latin: Purity
Chaya: hebrew: Life
Chiara: latin: Light
Clara: greek: Bright and clear
Corazon: fillipino: Heart
Cordelia: latin: Heart
Ciar (keer): irish: Saint's name

D:
Dalila: kenyan: Gentle
Damara: greek: Gentle
Dara: hebrew: Compassionate
Deka: somali: One who pleases
Deliciae/Delicia: latin: Sweetheart; Delightful one
Dembe: ungandan: Peace
Dena/Dinah: hebrew: Judgement
Dilber: turkish: Beautiful, attractive
Dilshad (deel-shad): persian: "Of happy heart"
Ditza: hebrew: Joy
Durriyyah (doo-ree-yah): muslim: Brilliant, glittering

E:
Electra: greek: The shining one
Elysia (e-lee-shuh): latin: Sweetly blissful
Emine: turkish: Confident
Eshe (ay-shay): swahili: Life
Etana: hebrew: Strong

F:
Farah: muslim: Joy, cheerful
Farhannah (fahr-hah-nah): muslim: Glad, joyful
Farida: persian: Incomparable beauty
Farra/Farrah: welsh: Beautiful, pleasant
Felicia: latin: Happy
Felicite: french: Fortunate
Felicity: latin: Happiness
Femi: african: Love me

G:
Gelasia (gah-lay-shuh): greek: Predisposed to laughter
Geela: hebrew: Joyful
Gleda: old english: To make happy
Grania: gaelic: Love
Guls: turkish: Laugh

H:
Hana: muslim: Happiness, peace of mind
Hanifah: muslim: True, upright
Harika: turkish: Marvelous, wonderous
Helen/Helena: greek: Light; a torch

I:
Ida: teutonic: Happy
Ihsan (igh-sahn?): muslim: Charity
Ilona: greek: Light
Ilsa (ehl-sah): teutonic: Gaitey

J:
Jamila: muslim: Beautiful, elegan
Jocosa: latin: Gleeful
Joyce: french: Joyful
Jun: japanese: Pure
Justine: latin: Just; justice

K:
Kaie (kigh-ee): celtic: Combat
Kamilah: arabic: The perfect one

Karen: english: Pure
Karima: middle eastern: Generous
Karimah: african: Generous
Kathrine/Kathryn/Katherine/Katie: greek: Pure
Kichi (kigh-chee): japanese: Fortunate
Kiyo: japanese: Pure
Kiyoko: japanese: Pure child
Kyla/Kylia: gaelic: Lovely

L:
Lacie: greek: Cheerful
Lalasa: hindu: Love
Larissa: russian: Cheerful one
Larisa/Larissa: latin: Cheerful
Lateefah: north african: Gentle, pleasant
Latifa: african: Pleasant, gentle, good humor
Laveda (lah-vee-dah): latin: Innocent one
Laurel/Laureen/Laura: latin: Honor
Leba: yiddish: Beloved
Lena: greek: Light
Lene: norwegian: Illustrious
Leora: greek: Light
Leorah: hebrew: Light to me
Limber: african: Joyfulness
Lina: middle eastern: Tender
Lisa/Lisette: hebrew/french: Concencrate to god
Litsa (leet-sah): greek: One who brings good news
Liv: norwegian: Life
Lucerna: latin: Candle-light
Lucia: italian: Light
Lucinda/Lukene: latin: Bringer of light
Lucretia: latin: Brings light
Lucy: latin: Light
Lukina: ukranian: Graceful and bright

M:
Mabel: latin: Loveable
Mahalia: hebrew: Affection
Mai: japanese: Brightness
Maisha (mah-ee-sha): kiswahili: Life
Maitane (may-tah-nee): old english: Beloved
Makoto: japanese: Truth; sincerity
Malinda: greek: Gentle one
Malu: hawaiian: Peacefulness
Manda: latin: Loveable, harmony
Mandisa: african: Sweet
Margaret: persian: Child of light
Marmara: greek: Radiant
Marnina: hebrew: Cause of joy
Meara: irish: Merry
Medicina: latin: Medicine
Megan: anglo-saxon: Strong, able
Meira: isreali: Light
Meira: hebrew: Light, connotation of sharing one's light with others
Melisanda: spanish: Honest, diligent
Melosa: spanish: Sweet
Merhamet: turkish: Mercy
Merrie: hebrew: Joyous; merry
Milena: german-jewish: Mild, peaceful
Minako: japanese: Beautiful little child
Minka: teutonic: Strong, resolute
Minna: teutonic: Resolute, strong, love
Mira: latin: short for Miranda/Miriam; "strong, wonderful"
Mirella/Mirabella: latin: Of great beauty
Miremba: ugandan: Peace
Miremba/Mireya/Mirielle: latin/spanish/french: Miraculous
Misericordia: latin: Mercy
Mochou: chinese: Sorrowfree
Moyna: celtic: Gentle, soft
Muneerah: muslim: Brilliant, shining, something that reflects light

N:
Na'imah (nah-ee-mah): muslim: Blessing, Happiness
Nadia/Nadine: russian: Hope
Nadhirrah (nahd-heer-ah): muslim: Bright face with lustre and noor; healthy and happy
Nadima: muslim: Companion, friend
Nafeesah: muslim: refined, pure, exquisite
Najiyyah (nah-jee-yah): muslim: Friendly, affectionate
Nalini: sanskrit: Lovely
Naomi: hebrew: Sweet, pleasant
Nara: celtic: Happy
Nasya: hebrew: Miracle
Nava/Navit: hebrew: Beautiful
Nayyirah (nay-yeer-ah): muslim: Luminous, shining, brilliant
Nediva: hebrew: Noble and generous
Nefsi/Nefis: turkish: Wonderful
Nehan: turkish: Happy lady
Neimah: hebrew: Pleasant
Nell: greek: Light
Nese (neh-seh or nee-seh): turkish: Joy
Neysa: greek: Pure
Nika: greek: Victory
Nina: hebrew: Grace
Nora (nohr-rah)/Nara (nah-rah): celtic: Honor
Nureen: jewish: Light
Nydia (nigh-dee-uh): latin: Refuge

O:
Obelia: greek: Pillar of strength
Olathe (oh-lah-thah): native american: Beautiful
Olayinka: yoruban: Honor surround me
Ona: lithuanian: Graceful one
Oralee: hebrew: My light
Oran/Ora: hebrew: Light
Orli: hebrew: "Light is mine"
Osran: scottish: Peace

P:
Penda: swahili-kiswahili: Beloved; "to love"
Phedra (fay- duh): greek: Bright
Phila: greek: Love
Phoebe: greek: Shining , brilliant
Pia: latin: Pious
Priya: indian: Loved one, darling

Q:
Qashang (kah-shang): persian: Beautiful
Quenby: scandinavian: Womanly

R:
Radhiyah (rahd-hee-yah): swahili: Pleased, agreeable, contented
Rafiqa (rah-fee-kah): muslim: Sweetheart, companion
Raheemah: muslim: Kind, affectionate
Rai (righ): japanese: Trust
Rajaa (rah-jay or rah-juh): muslim: Hope
Rajeeyah: muslim: Hoping, full of hope
Ramya: hindu: Beautiful, elegant
Rana: kiswahili: Happiness, rest
Rashida: african: Righteous
Raziya: swahili: Sweet, agreeable
Rayna: hebrew: Pure, clean
Rena: greek: Peace
Renana: hebrew: Joy, song
Risa: latin: Laughter
Robin: old english: One who shines with fame
Roni: hebrew: My joy
Roshni: indian: Light
Ruth: hebrew: Companion, friend

S:
Saar-rah (sahr-rah not 'sarah'): muslim: Lady who's charming manner brings joy
Sachi: japanese: Bliss
Sachiko: japanese: Bliss child
Sada: japanese: The chaste
Sadiyah: arabian: Lucky, good fortune
Sadiqah: muslim: Truthful, sincere
Safi/Saffiyah/Safiya: kiswahili: Clean, pure
Saidah (sah-ee-dah): african: Happy, fortunate
Sakari: native american: Sweet
Sakinah: muslim: Tranquility, calmness
Sakti: hindu: Energy, goodness
Salimah: arabic: Safe, healthy
Salome (sahl-oh- mee): hebrew: Peace
Saraid: celtic: Excellent
Sefa: turkish: Pleasure
Selima: hebrew/arabic: Hope/Peace
Serenity: latin: Tranquility; peace
Shahla: afghani: Beautiful eyes
Shaine: hebrew: Beautiful
Shakira: arabic: Grateful
Shana: hebrew: Beautiful
Shani: swahili: Marvellous
Shayna: yiddish: Beautiful
Shayndel: yiddish: Beautiful
Shobi: hebrew: Glorious
Sukutai (soo-koo-tay-ee): african: Hug
Sarisha: hindu: Charming
Shanata: hindu: Peaceful
Shanti: indian: Peace
Shina: japanese: Virtue, good
Shu: chinese: Good
Sinead (sin- ayd): irish: Gracious
Siobhan (shuh- vahn): irish: Gracious

Siran: armenian: Lovely
Siroun (see-roon): armenian: Lovely
Sitembile (see-tem-bee-leh): african: Trust
Sive (see- vuh): irish: Sweet
Soo: korean: Excellence, long life
Suad: muslim: Good fortune
Subhaga: india: A fortunate person
Suki: japanese: Beloved
Sun: korean: Goodness
Surrayyah: muslim: Free of worry; happy

T:
Tahira: muslim: Pure, chaste, clean
Tahirah: arabic: Chaste, pure
Taite (tayt): anglo- saxon: Cheerful
Taka: japanese: Tall, honorable
Takiyah: north african: Pious, righteous
Takoda: native american: Friend to all
Tam (tham): vietnamese: Heart
Tamma: hebrew: Perfect
Tao: chinese: Peach, symbol of long life
Taslimah (tahs-leem-ah): muslim: Salutations, peace
Tateeyopa: native american: Happy hostess; her door
Temina: hebrew: Honest
Thadea: greek: Courageous
Thalia: greek: Joyful
Than (tan): vietnamese: Brilliant
Thana: arabic: Gratitude
Thirza: hebrew: Pleasant
Tirza: hebrew: Pleasant; Delightful, delight
Tracy/Tracey: latin: Bold and courageous
Treasa: irish: Strong
Trina: greek: Pure
Trind/Tryne (treend or treen): swedish-dutch: Pure

U:
Ulani: polysnesian: Cheerful

V:
Valora/Valoria: latin: The Valorous
Valene/Valora: latin: Strong
Valentina/Valerie: latin: Strong
Vashti: persian: Beautiful
Velika: old slavic: Great
Vera/Verity: latin-english: True, truth
Vevina: gaelic: Gaelic sweet lady
Vinaya: india: Good behavior
Vivien: english: Full of life
Vrinda (vreen- dah): hindu: Divine virtue and strength

W:
Wan: chinese: Beautiful

X:
Xaviera (zah-veer-ah): arabic: Brilliant

Y:
Yegane (yeh-gah-nee): persian: Incomparable beauty
Yeira(yehr-ah): hebrew: Light
Yesmina: hebrew: Right hand, strength
Yeva: russian: Life- giving
Yoko: japanese: Positive child, female

Z:
Zada (zay-dah): syrian: Lucky one
Zahira: arabic: Shining, luminous
Zakia: hebrew: Bright, pure
Zarifah: muslim: Graceful
Zayn: muslim: Beautiful, graceful
Zelenka: czech: Little innocent one

Zelia: greek: Zeal
Zemirah: hebrew: Song of joy; hospitable
Ziva: hebrew: Bright, radiant, aglow, splendor
Zoe (zoh- ee): greek: Life
Zohar (zoh-har): hebrew: Shining, brilliant
Zuhairah: muslim: Blossom, radiant, shining
Zulema: arabic: Peace

Postive Male Names

Adley: hebrew: Just
Alacer: latin: Light-hearted
Alan: gaelic: Handsome, cheerful
Alano: spanish: Handsome
Alcander: greek: Strong
Anders: swedish: Strong, manly
Andrew: latin: Manly
Andrey: russian: Strong, manly
Andries: greek: Manly
Anker: greek: Manly
Aron/Aaron: hebrew: Enlightened
Arsen: greek: Strong
Arsenio: greek: Manly, virile
Asher: hebrew: Lucky, blessed, happy
Austin: latin: Majestic Dignity
Avis: welsh: Refuge in battle

B:
Benen: irish: Blessed
Benett: latin: Blessed
Bem: nigerian: Peace
Bent: latin: Blessing
Bert: old english: Bright
Boone: french: Good
Brian: celtic: Strong, powerful

C:
Cadan: turkish: Sincerely
Cavan: gaelic: Handsome
Cemal: arabic: Beauty
Chaim (kigh-eem): hebrew: Life
Chance: french: Luck

Clement: french: Merciful
Cody: irish: Helpful
Cole: greek: People of victory

D:
Darren: gaelic: Great
David: hebrew: Beloved
Dugan: english: To be worthy
Dust (doost): persian: Friend

E:
Emlyn: latin: Charming

F:
Felix: hebrew: Happy
Fergus: celtic: Of manly strength

G:
Galen: gaelic: Calm

I:
Isaac: hebrew: Laughing one
Itzak: hebrew: Laughter

J:
Jeffery/Jeff: old german: Peace
Jerolin: latin: Holy name
Jivin: hindu: To give life

K:
Kurt: old german: Courageous Advice

L:
Leif: swedish: Beloved, descendant
Li (lee): chinese: Strength
Lucas: latin: Bringer of light
Lukyan (loo-ke-yan): russian: Bringer of light

M:
Magnus/Myer: latin: Great
Max: latin: The greatest

N:
Naeem: north african: Benevolent
Neron: spanish: Strong, stem
Noe (noh-eh): spanish: Peace, rest

P:
Pax: latin: Peace

R:
Radman: slavic: Joy
Ranen: hebrew: Joyous
Reese: welsh: Ardent one
Renny: gaelic: Small but mighty
Rhett: welsh: Enthusiastic
Riley: irish: Valiant
Runako: african: Handsome

S:
Salim: arabic: Peace
Seung (sung): korean: Successor, winning
Shing: chinese: Victory
Shunnar: arabic: Pleasant
Soloman/Solomon: hebrew: Peaceful
Soterios: greek: Savior

Stasio (stah-shyoh): polish: Stand of Glory
Sterling: english: Genuine, valued
Sulaiman (soo-lah-e-mahn): north african: Peaceful

T:
Terence: latin: Tender, gracious, good
Torin: latin: Tender
Tovi: hebrew: Good

V:
Valor: latin: Strong, brave
Vito: latin: Conqueror
Vincent: latin: Conquering

W:
Walden: teutonic: Mighty

X:
Xavier (zay-vyer): arabic: Bright

Z:
Zenon (seh-nohn): spanish: Living
Zion (zigh-un): hebrew: A sign, excellent
Ziven: slavic: Vigorous and alive

Positive names for both genders
Aaron: hebrew: Enlightened
Kou: japanese: Light, ray
Yasu: japanese: Peaceful or tranquil
You: japanese: Sunshine; Positive

THE HEBREW ALEPHBET

PSALM 119

The 22 Letters of God the Father

God created the universe by speaking. His will was made manifest by using the twenty two Hebrew letters to form his words. God said "let there be light and there was light'. Each letter is a way of life.

LETTER	VALUE
ALEPH	1
BETH	2
GIMMEL	3
DALET	4
HEH	5
VAU	6
ZAYIN	7
CHET	8
TET	9
YOD	10
KAF	20
LAMED	30
MEM	40
NUN	50
SAMECH	60
AYIN	70
PE	80
TZADDAI	90
KUF	100
RESH	200
SHIN	300
TAU	400

THE NEW TESTAMENT

GREEK NUMBERING SYSTEM

The New Testament was written in Greek. Calculating information or names in the New Testament will require an underdstanding of these values.

LETTERS	VALUE
AJS	1
BKT	2
CLU	3
DMV	4
ENV	5
FOX	6
GPY	7
HQZ	8
IR	9

EXAMPLE

The numbers of Paul:

Paul or 7133 = 14 and 1 + 4 = 5

PAUL was an organizer of people. His name means small. Five represents change, favor, grace and the organization of people. Paul lived as a true five as he traveled town to town teaching and preaching Christ Jesus.

THE OLD TESTAMENT

HEBREW NUMBERING SYSTEM

The Old Testament was written in Hebrew. Calculating information or names in the Old Testament will require an underdstanding of these values.

LETTERS   **VALUE**

Letters	Value
AIQJY	1
BKR	2
CLGS	3
DMT	4
EHNX	5
UVW	6
OZ	7
FP	8

EXAMPLE

The numbers of Moses

Moses or 47353 = 22 and 2 + 2 = 4. Twenty Two is a number foundation. This number is known for carrying the errors of other people. Moses did not have to murder the Egyptian attacking his fellow Hebrew. He had options. As a result, Moses was not allowed to enter the promise land. The first letter of Moses is the letter 'M'. God the Father chose Moses to build the tabernacle because Moses was methodic, detailed and understood the need for structure. Moses was called to change the religious foundation of the Israelites from polytheism to monotheism.

THE HEBREW MONTHS

Month	Equivalant	Meaning	Tribe	Letter
Tishrei	Sept-Oct	Newness	Ephraim	Lamed
Cheshwan	Oct-Nov	Inner Change	Menashah	Nun
Kislev	Nov-Dec	Expectations Dreams	Benjamin	Samech
Tevet	Dec-Jan	Purification	Dan	Ayin
Shevat	Jan-Feb	Inner Renewal	Asher	Asher
Adar	Feb-Mar	Joy	Naftali	Kuf
Nissan	Mar-Apr	Moving Forward	Judah	Heh
Iyar	Apr-May	Healing	Issachar	Vau
Sivan	May-June	Reception	Zevulum	Zayin
Tammuz	June-July	Reality	Reuben	Chet
Av	July-Aug	Deliverance Wholeness	Shimon	Tet
Elul	Aug-Sept	Inner Reflection	Gad	Yud

Christainity cannot exist without Judaism. The Old Testament was known as the Hebrew Bible and still among Jews. Every Chrsitain would benefit from understanding Jewish culture, literature and History. Jews are the chosen people of God the Father because they were charged with ushering in the practice of monotheistic worship of the true and living God. In adiition, they are good stewards of their land. Judeo-Christain studies are vital for personal growth and understanding. The ancient Hebrews had a deep appreaciation for time, letters, words and names. The list on this is an excellent reference point for your study of numbers, letters, words and Jewish culture.